HISTORY OF

WITH

SKETCHES OF ITS LEADING WORTHIES.

BY

R. N. WORTH, F.G.S., Etc.,
AUTHOR OF
'*THE HISTORIES OF PLYMOUTH AND DEVONPORT*,' '*TOURIST'S GUIDE TO DEVONSHIRE*,' '*WEST-COUNTRY GARLAND*,' ETC.

CHEAP EDITION.

1895.

CONTENTS.

CHAPTER		PAGE
	INTRODUCTORY NOTE	vii
I.	EARLY HISTORY	1
II.	EXETER	12
III.	EXMOUTH AND THE EXE ESTUARY	47
IV.	AXMINSTER AND THE AXE	59
V.	SIDMOUTH	74
VI.	HONITON	79
VII.	OTTERY ST. MARY	84
VIII.	COLLOMPTON AND BRADNINCH	87
IX.	TIVERTON	91
X.	BAMPTON	98
XI.	SOUTH MOLTON	101
XII.	CREDITON	105
XIII.	CHULMLEIGH	112
XIV.	BARNSTAPLE	115
XV.	ILFRACOMBE AND LYNTON	128
XVI.	LUNDY ISLAND	136
XVII.	BIDEFORD	141
XVIII.	GREAT TORRINGTON	154
XIX.	HOLSWORTHY AND HATHERLEIGH	162

Contents.

CHAPTER		PAGE
XX.	OKEHAMPTON	167
XXI.	LYDFORD	173
XXII.	TAVISTOCK	179
XXIII.	BUCKLAND MONACHORUM	194
XXIV.	PLYMOUTH, DEVONPORT, AND STONEHOUSE	201
XXV.	PLYMPTON	230
XXVI.	MODBURY	240
XXVII.	KINGSBRIDGE AND SALCOMBE	245
XXVIII.	TOTNES	254
XXIX.	DARTMOUTH	267
XXX.	ASHBURTON AND BUCKFASTLEIGH	277
XXXI.	TORQUAY, PAIGNTON, AND BRIXHAM	291
XXXII.	NEWTON	305
XXXIII.	TEIGNMOUTH AND DAWLISH	311
XXXIV.	CHUDLEIGH AND BOVEY TRACEY	316
XXXV.	MORETONHAMPSTEAD AND CHAGFORD	320
XXXVI.	DARTMOOR	326
XXXVII.	DIALECT AND FOLK-LORE	335

INTRODUCTORY NOTE.

SIXTY years have passed since the last successful attempt was made to produce a complete History of Devonshire; and the volume of the brothers Lysons has remained from that day to the present the most valuable contribution to the general historical literature of the county. Of late, however, many revisions have been made in local history: and though Devon has not again been treated as a whole, there are few of its corners which have not been made the subject of independent and painstaking research; while immense masses of original materials have been collected which were either unknown or inaccessible when the Lysonses were engaged on their great work. With what has been done at the State Paper Office, all who are interested in these topics are familiar. The local inquiries of the Historical Manuscripts Commission have thrown great light upon many obscure places of the Devonian record. Much attention has been paid to the archives of public bodies. The muniments of the Corporation of Exeter, and of the Dean and Chapter of Exeter Cathedral, have been arranged and calendared by Mr. Stuart Moore, who has also investigated those of the

Corporation of Dartmouth. The records of the Corporation of Plymouth have in like manner been brought together and indexed by the author; while Mr. J. R. Chanter has carefully examined the muniments of Barnstaple; and Mr. E. Windeatt those of Totnes.

This acquisition of new material, together with the adoption of stricter methods of inquiry and the more careful investigation of authorities, has led, in the course of the last thirty years more especially, to the re-writing in detail of much Devonian history. Among those who have taken a prominent part in this work, and to whom this volume is most largely indebted, are the late Sir John Bowring, the late Dr. Oliver, the late Rev. S. Rowe, the late Mr. R. J. King, the late Mr. J. B. Davidson, Messrs. P. F. and J. S. Amery, Mr. C. Spence Bate, F.R.S., Mr. J. R. Chanter, Messrs. W. Cotton, F.S.A., and R. W. Cotton, Mr. F. T. Elworthy, Mr. P. O. Hutchinson, Mr. R. Dymond, F.S.A., Mr. T. Kerslake, F.S.A., Mr. P. Q. Karkeek, Mr. G. W. Ormerod, F.G.S., Mr. W. Pengelly, F.R.S., F.G.S., Mr. G. Pycroft, Mr. J. Brooking Rowe, F.S.A., F.L.S. (whose presidential address at Crediton to the Devonshire Association contains a full list of printed books and MSS. dealing with local topography and history), Mr. E. Windeatt, and Mr. J. T. White. So many points of interest, however, still continue unsettled, and the history of so many places and families, after all that has been done, still remains to be explored, that the work of the Devonshire historian must yet be largely tentative. While presenting, therefore, what it is hoped will be found an accurate statement of the present position of historical inquiry in Devon, the need of further investigation is fully recognised by the writer, with the certainty that much still accepted as historical must, sooner or later, be set aside by a better informed and more searching criticism.

More than a sketch of the great history of Devon and of its famous muster-roll of worthies this work cannot pretend to be. A county which is all but the largest in the kingdom; which has afforded the earliest traces of the existence of man in these islands; which has never from the dawn of recorded history occupied a secondary place in the national life; which again and again in the hour of England's need has found the man; whose worthies, century by century, claim the first rank in every class—soldiers, sailors, lawyers, divines, inventors, poets, artists, explorers, statesmen, men of science; which, by the staunchness of its common folk no less than the courage and skill of their leaders, has more than once proved the pivot whereon the destinies of the State have hung;—the history of such a county is the history of England, and must be rather hinted at than expressed in the compass of these pages. But they will not be altogether unworthy of the noble Devon whose record they set forth, if their readers judge of what is wanting by what is said; and are led for themselves to fill in an outline which it is hoped may at least claim the merit of being inclusive, definite, and clear.

One word as to the arrangement. Neither of the existing units of county organization supplied exactly what was needed for the purpose in hand. It was therefore decided to treat the places of chief historical interest in their respective localities as centres, and to group around them their more immediate territorial associations. The order is mainly topographical. Beginning with Exeter, under which head—as subsequently under Plymouth—general points of county history are treated, a circuit is taken through East, North, West, and South Devon, and the survey ends in the great central waste of Dartmoor.

HISTORY OF DEVONSHIRE.

CHAPTER I.

EARLY HISTORY.

DEVONSHIRE stands alone among the counties of England in its peculiar relation to the question of the antiquity of the human race. Traces of Palæolithic man are indeed scattered throughout the kingdom, but in Devon only is there fairly consecutive evidence. The contemporaneity of man with the extinct quaternary mammalia was lifted from the level of argument to that of demonstration by the discoveries at the Windmill Hill Cave, at Brixham, in 1858. The retrospect of Devon is thus inferior in antiquity to that of no part of the British Isles, if we assign due proportion and weight to the inferential and material narrative which commonly passes under the name of prehistoric; and, moreover, it is a record of singular completeness.

That the men of Palæolithic times inhabited, or at least visited, the whole county of Devon, is proved by the manner in which their traces have been found on every hand. The caves at Brixham and Torquay; the submerged forests in Barnstaple Bay, and at other points of the Devon coast; the beds of the rivers; the depths of the peat-bogs; the wild wastes of the moors; the cliffs, as at

Croyde and Bovisand; the low-lying gravels of the Axe Valley—these teem with the flint-chips, arrow-heads, axes, and scrapers of the earliest Devonians who have left a trace behind. Mr. Pengelly, F.R.S., has advanced cogent reasons for the belief that the earliest men of the most famous of the Devon caves, Kent's Hole, Torquay, were 'inter-glacial, if not pre-glacial.' The 'earliest men '— for it is a remarkable fact that the investigations in Kent's Cavern have yielded evidence of the existence of man in Devon from the Palæolithic, in the Neolithic, the Bronze, and the Iron Ages.

Next to the Palæolithic men of Devon came the Barrow-builders; but the gap between the two is so wide that, while the cave-men of Palæolithic date were of the period of the extinct cave mammalia, no barrow has yielded even fragmentary traces of these animals.

Of the two great classes of barrows, the long and the round, the latter only occur in Devon. This is a curious fact; for long-barrows are peculiarly abundant in the adjoining counties of Dorset and of Wilts, and round-barrows yet exist in Devon by hundreds, almost thousands. The inference seems either that the long-barrow builders did not dwell farther west than Dorset, or that all vestiges of them have been destroyed on the western side of the Dorsetshire border. In all probability the Devonians of the long-barrow period were of a different race to the long-barrow people—possibly the direct descendants of the later Palæolithic men, supplanted and driven into the corners of the country by the long-headed long-barrow builders, as these were supplanted and driven by the round-headed builders of the round-barrows, and as in historic times Kelt and Saxon were in turn hunters and hunted. The long-barrow period seems to be represented in the West by chambered round-barrows, and by interments which have received the trivial name of 'giants' graves.' The most remarkable examples of these were discovered at Lundy Island, where two stone kists were found to contain two gigantic skeletons, the larger covered with limpet-shells. Like the long-barrows, with which they are presumably contemporaneous, these 'giants' graves' and chambered-barrows belong to the Age of Stone.

The round-barrows are the most important factor in the earlier history of Devon. Abounding in every part of the county, either continuously or by record, they illustrate almost every variety of barrow interment associated with the Bronze Age, thus indicating the occupation of the West by a bronze-using people over a very long time. How far back this may extend we cannot say. The Barrow Period was undoubtedly of great duration; but there is good reason to believe that barrow interment continued down even to post-Roman days. It is important to note, as indicating variations in race, in time, or in custom, of a very important character, that interment by cremation is all but universal in the barrows of Devon and of Cornwall; while in Wilts and Dorset the proportion of unburnt bodies is as high as a third and a fourth. Moreover, while in Devon the few unburnt interments are in the contracted form, as usual, in Dorset the extended position prevails.

One of the most difficult questions of Western Archæology is that of the age and origin of the Bronze Period, to which these round-barrows in the main belong. It is seen almost from the first in somewhat settled form, and it is traceable downwards until it merges in historic civilization; but its connection with the Stone Period is to all appearance hopelessly obscured. There is, however, evidence of vast antiquity. The Western Peninsula was the chief, if not the only, source of tin for the bronze-users of Europe, save, perchance, upon Asiatic confines. The tin-mining of the West, therefore, dates back to the introduction of the use of metals on the Continent; and when we attempt to give to this great epoch in the history of man a definite chronological position, 'Cornwall proves that tin-streaming was carried on at Carnon and Pentuan at a time when the mammoth either still existed in the West of England, or had not long disappeared; and when the general level of Devon and Cornwall was at least thirty feet higher than it is now.' Within the historic period no such change has taken place. Considerations of this kind led Dr. Wibel to conclude that the civilization of the Bronze Age originated in the West of England; while M. Furnet has suggested a European civilization contemporary with that of the East, dealing with minerals before the arrival of the Kelts and their intervention in metallurgy. The fact that the early bronze weapons were evidently made for a small-limbed people gives marked support to the latter theory.

That there was a distinct and well-marked civilization in the West in pre-Roman times is indeed shown, not only by the references of Greek and Roman writers to the ancient tin trade of the Cassiterides with the Mediterranean ports, but by the relics of the later Bronze Age which Devon has yielded. Coins of the type which Dr. Evans, F.R.S., assigns to about 150 B.C. have been found in the county at Cotley, near Axminster, Exeter, and Mount Batten, near Plymouth; while an ancient cemetery in the last locality has yielded mirrors, and various implements, ornaments, and weapons of bronze (now preserved in the Museum of the Plymouth Institution), all the characters of which are Keltic, and not Roman. In some localities such remains would undoubtedly suggest a post-Roman origin. Here they are evidently the final types of the older pre-Roman civilization; not necessarily of any great antiquity, nor free from foreign characters, but influenced alike in origin and progress by an earlier intercourse with the civilized world than that of Roman date.

This superior civilization of the West was probably the

leading cause of the peculiar form taken by the Roman occupation in the ancient Keltic Kingdom of the Dunmonii, which included both Devon and Cornwall. Attempts have been made to prove the existence of Roman roads and Roman stations throughout the extreme West of England, but without success. The so-called Roman roads of the older antiquaries are really the British trackways, which here as elsewhere the Romans adapted to their purpose. The British Fosseway ran from Exeter over Dartmoor, crossed the Tamar near Tavistock, and continued along the central highlands of Cornwall by Cenion (Truro) to Giano (Marazion) in Mount's Bay. There was only one Roman station of any note within Devonian confines — the *Isca Dunmoniorum* of the 'Itinerary' of Antonine. This undoubtedly is Exeter. Moridunum, which in the 'Itinerary' intervenes beween Isca and Durnovaria (Dorchester), was in Devon, but the site has not been clearly identified.

The long-accepted story of Roman conquest and sway in Devon rests solely upon a mistaken identification and a forgery. The false identification is the gloss of Geoffrey of Monmouth, or one of his editors, that the Caer Pensaulcoit which Vespasian besieged was Exeter, instead of Penselwood, on the Wilts and Somerset borderland. The forgery is the 'Chronicle' attributed to Richard of Cirencester. There is thus no evidence that the Dunmonii were ever conquered by the Romans; and the conclusion of Mr. Beale Poste appears irresistible—that 'they retained their nationality under their own native princes.' The same long-continued foreign intercourse which had given the Western Peninsula its superiority in civilization prompted its residents rather to welcome than oppose the people with whom they were on such friendly terms, and from whom they derived so much advantage.

Exeter, indeed, was both a Roman station of importance and the head of the Roman power in the district.

The only other points in Devon that appear by their names to indicate the presence of Roman soldiery are on the same parallel, near North Lew—Chester Moor, Scobchester, and Wickchester. West of Exeter no proofs of Roman occupation, beyond an individual settlement here and there, have ever been found, though traces of Roman intercourse are by no means wanting. North and east of Exeter there are only remains of Roman villas, as at Hannaditches, near Seaton, while another is said to have occupied the crest of a cliff near Hartland. The full significance of these facts, in considering the character of the Roman Period in Devon, is best seen when we compare non-Roman Devon with thoroughly Romanized Somerset, in which Roman structural and other relics of importance—temples, potteries, villas, mines—have been found in over one hundred places.

The later Dunmonii were a numerous as well as a fairly civilized race. In every part of the county there are to be found earthworks, some of very considerable magnitude, which have commonly been classed by antiquaries as hill-forts, camps, or castles. By far the greater majority of these are, however, simply the enclosures of ancient villages or towns—the evidence, not of long-continued or desperate warfare, but of a settled and comparatively dense population.

Whether, when the Romans left Britain, and the Britons had to rely upon their own efforts for protection against northern and sea-borne marauders, Devon shared to the full extent in the general despair is doubtful. The preservation of an independent, or quasi-independent, status would tell in its favour. It is impossible to credit the assertion that Picts and Scots carried their raids so far west. Probably Dunmonia, continuing its trade in metals with the East, enjoyed for a while comparative quiet, and was one of the last places visited by Saxon or by Dane. The Saxons were familiar with the Channel coast, 'the Saxon shore,' long ere they reached Devon and Cornwall; and the Danes make their first historical appearance in the West as the allies of the Cornish race against their own Teutonic kin in the reign of Ecgberht, when they were defeated by the Saxons in a great battle just over the Tamar at Hingston Down.

Obscurity shrouds the advent of the Saxons in Devon. The only important contemporary record is the 'Anglo-Saxon Chronicle;' and that does not carry us further back than the eighth century in its Devonian references. Saxon intercourse with Devon began in an individual form, and by colonization rather than by conquest. When the Saxons of Wessex reached the county they had become Christians, and had begun, as Mr. J. B. Davidson says, 'to make progress by colonization as well as by the sword.' And the late Mr. R. J. King showed how in all probability settlements were pushed beyond the border 'by small bodies of men, either by force or peaceably, but on the whole establishing themselves in more peaceful fashion than would be the case when an entire district lay at the mercy of the conqueror after a great battle.' The peculiar character and distribution of the place-names of Devon lends great support to this view; and as immigrant peoples usually accepted the place-names they found until further distinctions became necessary, and as the Keltic names of Devon can only have been retained where there was continuity of occupation, or association, it follows that wherever in Devon such names are most plentiful, there we have the best proof of extended intercourse and early Saxon colonization.

This would not have been the case, however, had not the Saxon completed by war what he had begun in peace. Colonization in the end did give place to conquest. Mr. J. B. Davidson has shown conclusively that the Saxon annexation of Devon must be placed somewhere between 710—in which year Ine fought the Welsh king Gereint, and shortly after which he made Taunton the chief defence of his new frontier—and 823, in which the Weala and the Defena—that is, the men of Cornwall and the men of Devon—fought a battle at Gafulford, probably an ancient passage on the Tamar. In 710 the whole force of Devon and Cornwall was wielded by Gereint; in 823 the men of Devon and the men of Cornwall were marshalled as two opposing hosts. But, inasmuch as there is no reason to suppose that Ine pushed his conquests further, and as the 'Chronicles' expressly state that in 813 Ecgberht harried the West Wealas, while William of Malmesbury defines that monarch's first great military act as the conquest of Cornwall, the possible limit of the subjugation of Devon is narrowed between the years 728 and 800. Of the kings of Wessex who fill this interval, the only one to whom the conquest can be assigned is Cynewulf—755-784—who is recorded to have fought many battles against the Brit-Wealas. It is possible that William of Malmesbury may have used the word Cornwall to include part of Devon, in which case the work begun by Cynewulf was completed by Ecgberht. If he employed that term with modern limitations, Cynewulf brought all Devon under his sway.

A theory that there was a partial conquest of Devon by the Saxons, and that the Exe became a frontier between the Welsh and English, has been held by several distinguished authorities, including the late Sir Francis Palgrave. But the data are insufficient. Sir F. Palgrave based his hypothesis upon an agreement ascribed to the reign of Æðelred, between certain Dunsæta. Reading this Devnsæta, or Defena, Sir Francis interpreted it to be an agreement 'between the Wylisc Devonshire men and the Englisc Devonshire men.' The reference, however, is not to Devonshire men at all, but to certain 'dwellers on the downs,' probably inhabitants of Wales proper.

True, William of Malmesbury states that in 926 Æðelstan drove the Britons out of Exeter, which they had inhabited sharing equal rights with the English, and fixed the boundary of his province along the Tamar. Mr. T. Kerslake has also shown that Exeter is really divisible by the dedications of the ancient parishes into British and Saxon quarters. A certain joint occupancy of that city must therefore be held proven. It is further probable that, at the time of Cynewulf's invasion, Exeter was more Saxon than Keltic; and there is reason to believe that then, and long after, it enjoyed a kind of independence. But however this may be, it is manifest that under Æðelstan the county at large was cleared of the Keltic race—save, perhaps, in a few isolated spots—and that whatever Keltic blood there is now in Devon must date from before the Saxon Conquest, or have been acquired mainly from Cornwall, since directly it is tested this 'ingenious theory of a bisected Devonshire, half Saxon, half British, with Exeter as a border fortress, and the river Exe as a boundary, vanishes into thin air.'

One of the most cogent arguments against the theory is the fact that we find no trace in the place-names of Devon of a graduated Keltic element westward, which must be apparent if the county had been so parcelled, or the Saxon expulsion of the Britons had not been complete and final. The Saxon element in the local topographical nomenclature is quite as decided on the eastern bank of the Tamar as it is upon the north coast; and the Keltic names in the former locality are not a whit more plentiful than in some other parts. It has been thought that the recesses of Dartmoor may have retained their Keltic population long after the rest of Devon had fallen under Saxon rule; but this cannot have been so, for Dartmoor has hardly a Keltic name left, save upon the borders, with which Saxon dwellers in the lowlands must have been more or less familiar.

We may call in aid, too, the Saxon place-names to supply the great gaps in the recorded history of the county which the 'Saxon Chronicle' fails to cover. They show that the early Saxon occupation of Devon must have been mainly of the individual and peaceful kind already suggested. The ordinary enclosure of the 'tun' is scattered throughout the county, and is not predominant anywhere, though somewhat less frequent in the north-west than the south. The more defensible 'stocks' are commonly associated with the navigable rivers, then the great highways of piratical marauders, and needing rallying-points and strongholds, especially when Danish inroads became periodical. The frequent 'burys' are in many cases not of direct Saxon origin, but mark the site of some old earthwork. The three most distinctive and notable marks of Saxon occupation are to be found in the affixes 'worthy,' 'cot,' and 'hay,' which have a very peculiar and suggestive distribution. 'Worthy'—probably in the main a farm-place, with enclosures to protect the cattle from the ravages of wild beasts—is most common on the borders of Dartmoor, and particularly to the south and west, where not only the name but the thing still exists in the traces of the original walls and banks. 'Cot,' which shows the fullest evidence of individual action, and on the smallest scale, is almost peculiar to the west and north-west. 'Hay,' which represents an enclosure of a field character, has its chief centre in the east.

There has, so far, only been found in Devon one definite trace of the Teutonic mark—the existence of a certain tenure of 'landscore' in the neighbourhood of Plymouth. But the mark would only survive in a modified form when Devon was absorbed into Wessex. The existence of the family group is not much clearer. Personal and individual settlements abound, and there are some few traces of associative effort; but we do not find, nor can we expect to find, precisely the same polity as is presented by the shires and kingdoms first settled by the Saxons, which was complete of its kind. The constitution of Devon, however, is purely Saxon from village to shire: each of its hundreds has a Saxon name, each of its ancient municipalities originated in a Saxon community; and in some of its towns, as Tavistock and Ashburton, the elder form of government is still easily distinguishable in the continued existence of the portreeve, or *portgerefa*, of the original free township, elected by the freeholders as representatives of the estates of the original settlers.

As far as we may judge from the hundred lists, as given in 'Domesday,' the original hundreds of Devon numbered twenty-six, which would give a Saxon population of the county when Saxon government was first completely established of about 15,000. The population enumerated in 'Domesday' is 17,434; and the free dwellers would not make the total exceed some 25,000.

But the purport of this chapter is mainly to summarize the prehistoric times of Devon—those antecedent to the Saxon Conquest. That end served, the further details of the county history will be found under the various heads.

CHAPTER II.

EXETER.

THOSE who believe that this island derives its name from Brutus, the Trojan, will have no difficulty in accepting the allied legend that before Brute built London he founded Exeter. But as these once popular articles of faith are sadly at a discount, we may dismiss them without further concern. The origin of the city is really unknown. The hill round which the Exe flowed long ages since, as it flows still, was chosen by the Kelts for the site of one of their towns, and it may have had a yet earlier appropriation. When the Romans made the castrum of the Exe the headquarters of a legion and the chief seat of their power in the extreme West of England, Exeter was already a place of importance and antiquity; and that is all we really know. It may have been one of the marts where the ancient Briton trafficked with the merchants of Phœnicia, but the authority for saying so is very small. Palgrave held that the city was a free republic before the reduction of the inhabitants of West Britain, and that it enjoyed franchises and liberties 'before any Anglo-Saxon king had a crown upon his head or a sceptre in his hand.' At whatever date, then, the first hut was built in the forest on the 'red hill' above the marshes of the Exe, Exeter flashes into history already a great town. Each race dominant in England has made it a stronghold—Kelt, Roman, Saxon, Dane, and Norman. Hardly a great party in the State, though its proud motto is *Semper fidelis*, but has ruled therein in turn.

A few feet beneath the modern city lie remains which show that Exeter was no Roman station in name only. Its claims to be the *Isca Dunmoniorum* have been seriously, but fruitlessly, questioned. Roman coins by the thousand, with pottery and other articles of kindred origin, have been found in almost every excavation within the circuit of the ancient walls, and are still discovered.

When the Romans left Exeter it retained a large proportion of the specialized civilization they had imported. Moreover, its trading status, by keeping up a connection with the exterior world, would have the effect of continuing its more polished characteristics. Exeter did not rise, therefore, to note under the Saxons when it was chosen as the meeting-place of a Witenagemot, and when Æðelstan replaced its rude earthworks by massive walls and towers. It simply maintained the position which had belonged to it for ages. So when Eadweard the Confessor transferred thither the See of Devon and Cornwall from Crediton, Exeter was merely asserting its position, not only as the chief town of Devon, but as the most important city of all the West. Never was this shown more completely than when the Conqueror appeared before its walls; and when, in the eloquent words of Dr. Freeman, Exeter 'stood forth for one moment to claim the rank of a free imperial city, the chief of a confederation of the lesser towns of the West—when she, or at least her rulers, professed themselves willing to receive William as an external lord, to pay him the tribute which had been paid to the old kings, but refused to admit him within her walls as her immediate sovereign.' And though the city had to yield, it yielded on such terms as fairly secured its ancient liberties, and left it still one of the four chief cities of the realm, holding equal rank with London, York, and Winchester.

There has never been a time of intestine strife, from the dawn of history down to the Wars of the Commonwealth, in which Exeter has not been regarded as the key of the West. Well indeed might the quaint city chronicler, Izaacke, tell us:

> 'In midst of Devon, Exeter city, seated
> Hath with ten sieges grievously been straitned.'

In the wars between Charles and the Parliament, indeed, Plymouth, by its obstinate and unbroken adhesion to the popular side, led the fortunes of the Western Peninsula; and the possession of Exeter was, for the first time, of secondary importance. The prestige was recovered, however, when William of Orange made it the focus of his operations, and within the walls of Exeter won the adhesion of Devon, Somerset, and Dorset, and thence a kingdom.

Forty royal charters are said to have been conferred upon the ancient city; and royalty has been a frequent guest within its walls. Edward IV. gave the Corporation one of their swords of state; Henry VII. another sword and a cap of maintenance; Henry VIII. made it a county; Edward VI. rewarded its stubborn resistance to the Western Rebels by the gift of a manor; Elizabeth conferred the proud motto '*Semper fidelis*,' which candour compels the admission has been chiefly shown in a staunch adherence to the ruling powers; the second Charles, as his mark of favour, gave the citizens the portrait of his Exonian sister; the third William re-established the ancient mint.

Setting aside the story of the capture of Exeter by Vespasian as something more than mythical, the first siege of the city recorded in history, if Matthew of Westminster is to be accepted as sufficient authority, was in 633, when Penda was the leader of the besiegers and

Cadwalinus (whose nephew Brian held the city) the chief of the relieving host. There is nothing intrinsically improbable in this; and it is certain that Saxon influence had made itself felt in the vicinity at quite as early a date. There are grounds, however, for believing, as already shown, that the Saxon made his way in Devon to a large degree by the more peaceful methods of immigration, and that it was not until the time of Æðelstan that Exeter became a thoroughly Saxon town. But long before Æðelstan Exeter had been harried by a foreign foe, more savage even than the early Saxon. The Danes took up their winter quarters there in 877; and in 894 their siege of the city was raised by Ælfred, who committed the spiritual oversight of the city, and in effect the ecclesiastical headship of the Saxons in Devon, to his favourite Asser.

The first great historical disaster recorded of Exeter is its capture by Swegen in 1003. Two years previously the Danes in large numbers had landed at Exmouth and marched on Exeter, which was stoutly defended. The forces of Devon and Somerset gathered with all speed under their reeves, Eadsige and Kola, and were utterly defeated at what is now the suburb of Pinhoe. Then the Danes burnt the 'hams' at Pinhoe and Clyst, 'and rode over the land; and their "after" was ever worse than their "former,"' and they returned with great booty to their ships. There is a curious tradition that a small annuity received by the vicar of Pinhoe represents a reward bestowed upon the mass priest of that place for his skill and daring in procuring a supply of arrows on this occasion, when the ammunition of the English was falling short.

When the terrible massacre of the Danes by Æðelred in 1002 brought Swegen upon the fated land once more, no place felt his revenge in more deadly fashion than Exeter. The city was then in the height of prosperity.

Its religious establishments were so notable that in after-days they were said to have conferred upon it the name of Monkton—a statement for which there is not the least historical authority. It was populous, and the inhabitants held out bravely; but they had a traitor within their walls. The Norman Hugh, favourite of Queen Emma, and her reeve of the city, on the 19th of August, 1003, admitted the Danes within the walls, and Exeter was so ravaged with fire and sword that for the while ruin seemed complete and recovery hopeless. But Cnut favoured it, and the Confessor raised its chief monastery to cathedral rank; and half a century from the Danish sack Exeter was prosperous once more, with nearly 500 houses.

Nothing indicates more clearly the renewed importance and independent spirit of Exeter than the answer returned by the citizens to the Conqueror when he demanded submission. 'We will neither take any oath to the king nor allow him to enter our city; but the tribute which, following ancient custom, we were wont to give formerly, the same we will give to him.' But William would have 'no subjects after this fashion.' Marching upon Exeter, he was met by the civic chiefs, who promised all that he required, but when they returned were persuaded to forego their pledges and trust rather to their skill in war and the strength of their defences. Then, 'filled with rage and wonder,' William assaulted the stubborn town. For eighteen days he unavailingly assailed it by all the methods known to the warriors of those times. What would have been the result had the siege continued it is hard to say; but the citizens found that whether William could break down their active resistance or not, he could starve them. So they asked for pardon and peace, and found him clement.

Exeter did not stand quite alone in its opposition to William. The citizens were stimulated to the course they took by the presence of Gytha, the mother of

Harold, who had taken refuge within their walls (she escaped before the surrender), and they are said to have roused the sister burghs of Devon to join in their resistance. That Lydford and Barnstaple did so seems proven by the waste recorded to have been made there since the Conquest, in 'Domesday.' Totnes, to all appearance, made quiet submission. Had all the West been united under one head, and that a capable one, the tide of victory might have been rolled back, even upon the great Norman chief. But this was not to be.

The most important result, in one respect, of the surrender of Exeter to the Normans was the erection of Rougemont Castle on the 'red hill' dominating the city —a site which had been occupied by older defensive works, but which had never seen anything so elaborate as this first Norman fortalice of the West of England. Scanty as the remains now are, they suffice to show that it was once a citadel of prime importance. Building commenced in 1068, and could hardly have been finished when, in the following year, a band of brave Saxons who had taken up the cause of the sons of Harold assailed the city. They were easily beaten off, however, with heavy loss by the Norman garrison, probably helped by the citizens in their new-found loyalty. The invading host of Godwin and Edmund were annihilated in a fierce battle on the banks of the Tavy; and there was an end once and for ever of all organized attempts to throw off the hated Norman yoke. After three years of nearly incessant conflict the West gave up the struggle. The last Devonshire man of note to continue such resistance as might yet be offered was Sithric the Saxon Abbot of Tavistock, and he at length joined the famous Hereward in the Camp of Refuge at Ely.

Such peace as could be enjoyed by a Saxon city held by a Norman garrison, Exeter had for just seventy years. Then Baldwin de Redvers, grandson of its first Norman

Governor, made Rougemont a stronghold for Matilda, and proceeded to oppress the citizens, who, according to Exonian wont, continued faithful to the ruling powers. They sent to Stephen for help. Baldwin determined to destroy the city ere aid could come, and fire and sword had begun their work, when they were happily stayed by the appearance of 200 horsemen, Stephen's advanced guard. Ere long the whole army arrived; Baldwin's troops were driven within the castle, and a siege commenced, which continued for three months. Force appeared unavailing, but when the supply of water failed the castle was surrendered. With it fell the last hopes of Matilda in the West. The whole strength of her party in Devon had been concentrated at Exeter. Baldwin's castle at Plympton had been given up by its garrison without striking a blow; and all Baldwin's friends had submitted to the King with the exception of Alured, son of Judhel of Totnes, who, abandoning his own indefensible 'strength,' by a clever stratagem joined Baldwin in Rougemont. And once more, in the twelfth century as in the eleventh, the fate of Exeter was the doom of Devon.

Exeter was one of the many towns upon which John conferred the right of mayoralty, which here indeed meant rather a change of name for the chief magistrate than the grant of new civic powers. The city had formed part of the dowry of Berengaria; but it was granted in 1231 to Richard, Earl of Cornwall and King of the Romans; and in 1265 its first parliamentary representatives were elected. Twenty years later Edward I. held a Parliament at Exeter itself, at which a statute was passed to remedy the abuses of coroners. Edward on this occasion kept Christmastide within the ancient city. If the Black Prince, as some authorities assert, landed at Plymouth on his return from the battle of Poictiers, he passed through Exeter with his royal captive; and though this is very doubtful, it is quite certain that he did visit Exeter on more than one occasion, on his way to and from Plymouth, which was his favourite port. In 1388 Exeter gave the title of Duke to John de Holland, who suffered attainder in 1399. Restored to his son John in 1443, after it had been held by Thomas Beaufort, the title was finally lost by the disinheritance of the third Holland Duke, Henry, who was reduced to beg his bread in exile.

The city pronounced emphatically on the Lancastrian side, that generally taken in the West of England. Henry VI. was entertained for eight days in 1452 with the best the 'church and city' could afford, clergy and citizens sharing the cost. In 1469 it sustained a twelve-days' siege from Sir William Courtenay of Powderham, on behalf of Edward IV., which was raised by the mediation of the clergy; and in April, 1470, Clarence and Warwick made Exeter their refuge, on the failure of their efforts, before they went to Dartmouth and embarked for Calais. Margaret was at Exeter after Barnet, arranging for the final effort which for the time quenched the hopes of the Lancastrians in blood at Tewkesbury; and Exeter was the place where the Lancastrians of the West mustered under Sir John Arundel and Sir Hugh Courtenay. Clarence paid several visits to Devon in the Lancastrian interest. However, Exeter was able to suit itself to the times, for when Edward IV. came hither with his wife and infant son, he was received so loyally that he gave the Corporation the sword which is still carried in state before the chief magistrate. But Edward was well able to enforce his will, and that the citizens knew.

Their loyalty to the ruling powers was even more plainly manifested when, in 1483, Richard III. came into the West. Edward had been content with a purse of 100 nobles; Richard was offered, and 'graciously accepted,' 200. Much need there was to keep him in good humour, for Thomas Grey, Marquis of Dorset, had pro-

claimed the Earl of Richmond in the city; and it was
during this visit to Exeter that Richard had his own
brother-in-law, Sir Thomas St. Leger, beheaded in the
castle-yard. It was there, too, that the incident happened
recorded by Shakespeare in the well-known lines :

> 'When last I was at **Exeter,**
> The mayor in courtesy showed me the castle,
> And called it Rougemont : at which name I started,
> Because a bard of Ireland told me once
> I should not live long after I saw Richmond.'

In common speech the two words would have been almost
identical in sound.

It was only to be expected that Perkin Warbeck
should make Exeter the first object of his ambition.
Landing at Whitsand Bay, near the Land's End, in
September, 1497, ten days later he appeared with his
motley host before the city walls. The citizens, as usual,
held with the King *de facto ;* and the Courtenays (**Edward**
Earl of Devon, and William his son) drove Warbeck off,
after he had made desperate attacks upon the city gates,
which he succeeded in setting on fire. Then Henry, on
his march into the West, made Exeter his headquarters.
Hither Warbeck was brought a prisoner; and it was in
the Cathedral Close that the King had the captured
rebels brought before him 'bareheaded, in their shirts,
and halters about their necks,' and 'graciously pardoned
them, choosing rather to wash his hands in milk by forgiving, than in blood by destroying them.'

The next stage in Exonian history is supplied by the
Western Rebellion, the most formidable popular opposition
to the Reformation that England saw. It was almost
wholly a rural movement, and had little support from the
towns. The uprisings of town populations are commonly
associated with the idea of progress, however subversively
it may be urged ; when the country rebels, its action is
commonly retrogressive. This movement was undoubtedly,

in one sense, economical. Twenty-four religious houses, some of great wealth and extensive charities, had been suppressed in Devon. The poorer dwellers in their neighbourhoods felt the loss severely. Not only did alms cease, but the new holders of the Church estates proved harder landlords than the monks. The progress of enclosure, and the substitution of pasturage for tillage, increased this disadvantage. Little was required to fan the vast amount of smouldering discontent thus created into flame.

The occasion for the outbreak in Devon was the abolition of the mass, and the substitution of the Prayer-Book service; and the rebellion commenced in the parish of Sampford Courtenay, far away from any town on the northern skirts of the great waste of Dartmoor. The new service was used there on the 9th of June, 1549; but on the following day the parish priest was compelled to resume his vestments and say mass as usual, by a body of the inhabitants, headed by William Underhill, a tailor, and Segar, a labourer. This popular element was evidently directed from without. From Sampford Courtenay the rising soon spread into the adjoining parishes. The efforts made by the justices to suppress it were very feeble and very vain. William Hellions, a Fleming settled at Sampford, was killed: probably, being a Fleming, he was also a Protestant. Presently Somerset and Cornwall joined in the movement.

Crediton was then adopted as the place of rendezvous. Hither flocked the disaffected from all parts of the West of England; and ere long a strong force assembled, led by men of repute and family—Sir Thomas Pomeroy, of Berry-Pomeroy; Sir Humphry Arundel, of the great Cornish family of that name; Coffin, Winslade, and others. Sir Peter and Sir Gawain Carew, marching on Crediton, found the roads barricaded, and met with a strong resistance. The rebels had garrisoned a row of barns with matchlock-men, and these were dislodged by setting the barns on fire. Thenceforward the 'Barns of Crediton' became a rallying-cry. The Carews were unable to make head against the storm. Marching upon Exeter 10,000 strong, the rebels called the city to surrender. The summons was refused, and, assault being unavailing, siege commenced.

Lord Russell, then Lord Lieutenant of the county, hastened to the aid of the Carews; but his force was small, and until he could gather strength he resorted to negotiation. The rebels were willing to make peace, but it must be upon their own terms—and these terms show clearly enough that the rising by this time was no longer a popular outburst, if it had ever really been so. The proposals were not such as would come from a body of country folk, however eager for their old faith. Dictated in a professional sense so far as the religious articles were concerned, in their economical relations they were prompted by an aversion to new blood.

It was demanded that the Six Articles should be observed, as in the reign of Henry VIII.; that Catholic worship should be restored in all its details; that they who would not worship the Sacrament hung over the high altar should die like heretics; that the Bible and all books of Scripture in English should be called in, 'for we are informed that otherwise the clergy shall not of long time confound the heretics;' that Dr. Moreman and Dr. Crispin should be sent them, and have livings given to preach the Catholic faith; that Cardinal Pole should be pardoned and promoted to the King's Council; that no gentleman should have more servants than one, 'except he may dispense one hundred mark land, and for every hundred mark we think it reasonable that he may have a man;' that the half part of all abbey and chantry lands in each county should be appropriated to establish therein, in the place of two of the chief abbeys, 'a place for devout persons, which shall pray for the King and the Commonwealth.'

Such demands were of course inadmissible; but Russell continued in his headquarters at Honiton until he was strengthened by the arrival of sundry German and Italian mercenaries. The first skirmish with the insurgents was at Feniton Bridge, whence he returned to Honiton. Then he met and beat them at Woodbury, and followed them up through the Clyst Valley, inflicting such loss upon them on the 5th of August at St. Mary Clyst, though they fought desperately, that the siege was raised. Most of the rebels who escaped retreated to Sampford, and there, in its cradle, the rebellion as an organized movement was finally crushed. The leaders were sent to London, and with the exception of Sir Thomas Pomeroy, tried and executed. He saved his life, but lost his estates. Of the common sort 4,000 were slain. For miles round Exeter the country was so harried and spoiled that for years the marks of desolation remained. Welch, the stalwart vicar of St. Thomas by Exeter, who had been very active in the siege, was hanged in full canonicals on his own church tower; and there his body remained until the accession of Mary turned the rebel into a martyr.

This siege of Exeter lasted from the 2nd of July to the 6th August. During the last ten days the citizens suffered severely from famine, and were reduced to live on horse-flesh and 'horse-bread.' Nor were they free from other difficulties, for the Catholic party in the city outnumbered the Protestant, and treachery was threatened. Fortunately, whatever their faith, the Mayor and his brethren were loyal. They were rewarded by the renewal of their charter, and the grant of the valuable manor of Exe Island.

In 1555 Exeter had some share in the effort made by the Carews before mentioned, with Sir Thomas Dennis and others, to arouse popular feeling against the reception of King Philip in England. But this hardly reached beyond a demonstration; and Peter escaped to the Continent in a vessel belonging to Walter Ralegh, Sir Walter's father.

At the commencement of the war between Charles I. and his Parliament Exeter was seized by the Earl of Bedford, Lord Lieutenant of the county, and garrisoned by him in the Roundhead interest. The Earl of Stamford, defeated at Stratton in May, 1643, was the Governor. He was at first besieged by Sir John Berkeley, and afterwards by Prince Maurice, and surrendered in the September following his defeat. There is little doubt that the bulk of the inhabitants were Royalists, for the appointment of Sir John Berkeley as Governor was received with great joy. Exeter thenceforth was regarded as one of the most secure Cavalier strongholds in the kingdom.

In May, 1644, having bid her husband farewell for the last time at Abingdon, Henrietta Maria took up her abode in Exeter; and on Sunday, the 16th of June following, the Princess Henrietta Anne, afterwards Duchess of Orleans, was born. The Earl of Essex was then coming into the West, and the Queen asked him to refrain from assaulting the city, and subsequently to give her a safe-conduct to Bath. Essex would give a pass to London, but in no other way would help her. Ill and suffering as she was, she had therefore to escape. The river was blockaded, and she fled by land, leaving her child behind. Passing through Okehampton, Launceston, and Truro, she reached Falmouth, set sail on the 14th July, and on the 15th landed at Brest. Some wonderful stories are told of the difficulties and privations of her escape; but there is excellent evidence that she was escorted by Prince Maurice to Launceston, if not beyond, where she was among friends, and that she was never in any real danger.

The Exonian Princess, who had been left in charge of Lady Moreton and Sir John Berkeley, was baptized in the font yet remaining in the cathedral. Her portrait in the Exeter Guildhall, by Sir Peter Lely, was presented to the city, as a recognition of the kindness of the citizens, by Charles II. in 1671. She had then been dead a year, and there were grave suspicions that her death was caused by poison. She was first seen by her father in July, 1644, when he visited the city in company with Prince Charles, and was welcomed by the Corporation with the acceptable gift of £500.

Exeter, which had several important outposts in the neighbouring parishes, was blockaded by Fairfax in the spring of 1646, and was surrendered to him in April of that year. The Princess, who had been duly cared for in the articles of surrender, was taken to Paris by Lady Moreton.

The city saw the closing scenes of the fruitless rising for the restoration of Charles II., under Penruddock and Groves, in 1655. They proclaimed Charles II. King of England at South Molton, but before they could gather their forces to a head, were captured and conveyed to Exeter, where they were afterwards tried. Penruddock and Groves, both Wiltshire men, were beheaded in the castle, others of their associates hung at Heavitree, and the bulk banished and sold into slavery. The Restoration was, however, hailed at Exeter even more heartily than at the other boroughs in the West, whose loyalty was, for the most part, somewhat effusive. The temper of the citizens, indeed, changed as time went on; and Jeffries at Exeter enacted some of the direst cruelties of his Bloody Assize. But he left popular feeling only dormant, not extinct.

'William the Deliverer' made his entry into the city by the West Gate on the 9th November, 1688, four days after his landing at Brixham. Lord Mordaunt and Dr.

Burnet on the previous day had found the West Gate closed, but without barricade or fastening, so that it was speedily opened. The civic authorities were then on the side of the Stuarts. The Bishop and the Dean fled, but the Mayor contented himself with ordering the gate to be closed, and with excusing himself for receiving William on the score that he had taken an oath to his lawful King James, by whom he had recently been knighted. The inhabitants generally welcomed William gladly, and though the day was very wet and rainy, he made his entrance with considerable state. The Deanery had been chosen as his residence; and thence he crossed the yard to the cathedral, where *Te Deum* was sung for his safe arrival in England. The Prince occupied the Bishop's throne, and the cathedral was crowded. When Burnet read the Declaration, setting forth the reasons of the invasion, such of the cathedral clergy as were present left the place, while the majority of the congregation responded to Burnet's 'God save the Prince of Orange' with a hearty 'Amen.'

At Exeter William remained several days, holding his Court at the Deanery, recruiting his army, and gradually receiving the accession of men of influence in Devon and the adjoining counties of Somerset and Dorset. It was at the suggestion of Sir Edward Seymour that the 'gentlemen of Devon' formed a 'general association,' and formally pledged themselves to the Prince's cause by signing a Declaration drawn up by Burnet. By this time the Mayor and Aldermen thought it wise to pay William all respect; and the Dean not only found his way back, but enrolled himself as one of William's followers. Before the Prince left Exeter the conflict was practically over, and the fate of James was sealed. The welcome of the people of the ancient city, and the general, if somewhat tardy, adhesion of the men of greatest weight in the West of England, had won the battle before a blow was struck.

This visit of William of Orange is the last great link that connects Exeter with the vital national history. Thenceforward its record is that of a more local life.

The ecclesiastical history of Exeter is to a large extent that of Devon likewise. We have dismissed as altogether idle the idea that in Saxon times it was called Monktown from the number of its religious edifices. Still, the outlying parish of St. Sidwells takes name from Sativola, or Sidwella, a virgin martyr said to have been beheaded with a scythe, and buried here in 740; and it was to Exeter that Winfrith, the future apostle of Germany, came to be taught some half century earlier. But the definite ecclesiastical history of the city begins with the transference thither by Leofric of the seat of the See of Devon and Cornwall, and the setting up of his bishopstool in the monastery of St. Mary and St. Peter.

Mr. Davidson holds there is good evidence to show that this monastery was founded by Æðelstan, probably in the year 926; and that it was at the great gemot held at Exeter, April 16, 928, that Æðelstan's laws were promulgated, and the Church consecrated. This minster is believed to have occupied the site of the east part of the present Lady Chapel of the cathedral. It was restored under Eadgar in 965, and almost entirely rebuilt by Cnut in 1019. To this already ancient Saxon foundation, then, Leofric came in 1050. The occasion was one of singular pomp, for the Bishop was personally installed in his new chair by Eadweard the Confessor himself and Eadgytha, his Queen, the one taking him by the right hand and the other by the left, praying blessings upon all that should increase the see, and denouncing 'a fearful and execrable curse' upon all who should diminish or take aught therefrom!

There was need of this execration if it could have been made effective, especially if its retrospective action could have been assured. Æðelstan is said to have endowed the monastery with twenty-six manors, and with one-third of the relics which he collected. Other gifts had undoubtedly been made. Yet when Leofric took to the minster, all its lands in possession consisted of two hides at Ide, near Exeter, with seven head of cattle! When he died in 1073 he left it again wealthy. He had recovered lands at Culmstock, Branscombe, Salcombe, St. Mary Church, Staverton, Sparkwell, Morchard, Sidwell, Huish, Brixton, Topsham (taken away again by Harold), Stoke Canon, Sidbury, Newton St. Cyres, Norton, and Traysbeare; and he added to the estates of the see of his own gift lands at Bampton, Aston, Chimney, Dawlish, Holcombe, and Southwood. In a very real and practical sense, therefore, and not by title merely, Leofric was the founder of the See of Exeter. Moreover, he entirely reformed the foundation upon which his bishopric had been grafted. Originally there were three religious houses within the Close—a nunnery, a monastery, presumably founded by Æðelred about 868, and the minster of St. Mary and St. Peter. The ravages of the Danes made the monks and nuns fly in terror, the buildings being destroyed and the charters burnt, and but for the religious zeal of Cnut there would in all probability have been an end of Æðelstan's minster altogether. What Leofric did was to remove the monks and nuns, adding both the nunnery and Æðelred's monastery to the minster, and establishing in the latter canons under the Lotharingian rule.

No part of the present cathedral saw the stately enthronement of Leofric, though it has been suggested that the little chapel of the Holy Ghost, next the Chapter House, may be a portion of the Saxon fane. The Norman cathedral was begun by William Warelwast, nephew of the Conqueror, and Bishop of Exeter (1107-1136). By him were built the great transeptal towers, with the choir and its apse, and the eastern bay of the nave; but this work was not completed until the episcopate of Henry Marshall (1194-1206), who added the Lady Chapel. The north and south towers were thus transeptal from the first, and not, as formerly thought, the western towers of the Norman building adapted as transepts some century and a half after they were erected.

Less than a century elapsed from the completion of the Norman cathedral ere it began to be replaced by the present structure, one of the finest examples of symmetrical Decorated Gothic in existence. Bishop Quivil (1280-1291) was the founder of the new structure, and the beginner, in the Lady Chapel and transepts, of the work of transformation, which was continued in the choir by Bishop Bitton (1292-1307), and not completed—though Quivil's plans were evidently followed—until Bishop Grandisson (1327-1369) carried out the nave. The noble west front, with its 'statues of prophets and apostles, martyrs, saints, and kings'—a screen of great interest and of singular beauty, even in decay—originated with Bishop Brantyngham (1370-1394). The Chapter House was built by Bishop Bruere (1224-1244), but took its present form in the episcopates of Bishops Lacy, Neville, and Bothe (1420-1478). The two chief accessory features of the interior—the choir screen, which now bears the organ, originally *la pulpytte*, and the magnificent episcopal throne, with its towering canopy of carved oak—are the work of Bishop Stapledon (1308-1327), who also erected the elaborate sedilia. The misereres are the earliest extant in this country, and are assigned to Bishop Bruere. Such are the chief master builders of this noble fane; but for four centuries from the date of the accession of Warelwast there was hardly a bishop to whom the cathedral was not indebted for some addition in structure or detail. We see it now, however, almost fresh, so far as the interior is concerned, from the restoration of Sir Gilbert Scott, which gave rise to an amount of controversy on points of technicality and taste unusual even in such relations. But there has never been any difference of opinion respecting the beauty of the modern carved work which he designed, and which Messrs. Farmer and Brindley executed.

Several of the Bishops are buried in the cathedral, Leofric first of the number. Among the holders of the see who won more than local repute and fame were Leofric, who was Lord Chancellor; Walter Stapledon, Lord High Treasurer, founder of Stapledon's Inn at Oxford, now Exeter College; Bishop Brantyngham, who held the same office; Bishop Stafford, Lord Privy Seal, who completed the foundation of Exeter College; Bishop Neville, Lord Chancellor; Bishops Fox and Oldham, founders of Corpus Christi College; Bishop Coverdale, translator of the Bible; Bishop Hall, afterwards of Norwich; and Bishop Trelawny, one of the seven Bishops sent to the Tower by James II., and the hero of the famous burden (modernized):

> 'And shall they scorn Tre, Pol, and Pen,
> And shall Trelawny die?
> There's twenty thousand Cornishmen
> Will know the reason why.'

Among the religious houses of Exeter and its immediate vicinity which fell at the Dissolution were the Benedictine priory of St. Nicholas, originally with the church of St. Olave an appendage of Battle Abbey, and founded by the Conqueror; the Cluniac priory of St. James; Franciscan and Dominican convents; and the Benedictine priories of Cowick and Polsloe (nuns). The priory of St. Nicholas became independent under Rufus, and, like the houses of the Carmelites at Plymouth, and the Benedictines at Buckfast, portions of the site have been recently purchased by the Roman Catholics, and in part restored to the olden uses.

Most notable among the Exeter parishes is that of St. Petrock, which lies in the very heart of the ancient city,

and is less than two acres and three quarters in extent.
It has given Exeter a long array of distinguished citizens;
indeed, as Mr. R. Dymond says, 'The fortunes of more
than one distinguished English family were founded on
shrewd bargains driven by some mercantile ancestor
within that small area.' The dedication to a British saint
appears to define the parish as part of that division of
Exeter in which for a time the Briton dwelt side by side
with the Saxon. There is little doubt, moreover, that it
was one of the twenty-nine city churches to which the
Conqueror directed the payment by the city provost of a
silver penny yearly out of the city taxes. Its most notable
antiquarian feature is the fact that it has an all but
complete series of churchwarden accounts from the year
1425, presumed to be unrivalled for antiquity and continuity.

Exeter, indeed, is rich in the matter of local records.
At the fine old Guildhall in the High Street, which dates
from 1466, though its front is late Elizabethan (1593), are
the municipal archives, extending back to the thirteenth
century, arranged and calendared by Mr. Stuart Moore,
who did the same for the muniments of the Dean and
Chapter. Among the chief treasures of the latter the
chiefest is the volume known as the 'Exon Domesday;'
but there are still several relics of the library given by
Leofric to his minster, though his Missal and several
other works have found their way to the Bodleian. The
most important volume of Anglo-Saxon date remaining at
Exeter is the unique collection of Anglo-Saxon poetry
known as the 'Codex Exoniensis;' and the miscellaneous
documents include some authentic and important Anglo-
Saxon charters.

By the death of Henry VIII. Devonshire had become
largely Puritan, though the majority of the inhabitants
were probably still Catholic. One martyr was burnt under
Henry, Thomas Benet, who suffered at Exeter. Only

one perished under Mary, a poor woman of Launceston, called Agnes Prest. But Cardmaker, *alias* Taylor, Chancellor of Wells, burnt at Smithfield in 1555, was an Exonian. The absence of religious activity in this reign seems to prove that the Protestantism of Devon was not very pronounced. The fact that under Elizabeth the Visitation Commissioners left so much untouched in the churches, and that so many magnificent rood screens remained down to the day of churchwardenism, and even yet continue, clearly points also to the existence in the county of a Catholic element of some strength and importance. Under Elizabeth Puritanism took deep root in the West; and the establishment of 'Prophesyings of the Clergy' paved the way for the formal introduction of Presbyterianism. The seed then sown sprang into active life in the ensuing reigns, and was fostered with vigorous growth by the proceedings of the Court of High Commission. The records of that tribunal contain the names of Devonshire men and women of all ranks of society—members of the oldest and most respected families side by side with those of poor husbandmen and handicraft folk, recorded only in these dismal annals of the time. The most remarkable point is the fact that they are almost wholly from the rural districts and the smaller towns. Was it the recognition of the growing strength of popular feeling that caused the larger communities to be passed by? Assuredly it was not because they were wanting in Puritanism, for they were its very heart and life. Thus when Thomas Ford, born at Brixton, nigh Plymouth, preached against the altar set up by Dr. Fewens at Magdalen College, Oxford, and was expelled the University, the Corporation of Plymouth chose him as their lecturer. It took a letter under the royal signmanual and one from Laud to make them change their minds. That they had purely submitted to circumstances was abundantly evident not many years later, when Plymouth proved the one unconquerable centre of Western Puritanism.

In a county which saw so much sharp 'controversy' during the struggle between Charles and the Parliament, it was inevitable that religious institutions should be largely affected. Nowhere were the changes so great as in Exeter, because in no place was the Church of England so strongly or so influentially represented. The cathedral was denuded of its clergy and divided into 'East and West Peters' by a 'Babylonish wall,' while sundry of the parish churches were dismantled and sold, being recovered and put to their former uses, however, after the Restoration.

Walker (himself an Exonian), in his 'Sufferings of the Clergy,' estimates the total number of deprivations under the Commonwealth in Devon at a third of the whole body of clergy. The county then contained 394 parish churches. He gives the names himself of just 200 as deprived; but when the doubtfuls are weeded out, errors corrected, and allowance made for pluralities, 128 remain, which agrees very closely with Walker's own calculation. Most of the ejections were from rural parishes; but while Episcopacy was represented in almost all the large towns, Presbyterianism had gained so great a hold in many localities that the abolition of Episcopacy made no change in them; and subsequent events proved that there must have been left in the livings of the county a considerable body of clergy who were either Episcopalian at heart, or who knew how to trim their course to suit the favour of the party in power.

When the Act of Uniformity was passed, in 1662, 132 Presbyterian and Independent ministers were ejected. The Episcopalians sequestrated and the Puritans ejected were thus about equal in number; but the areas of deprivation were by no means identical. In 44 towns and parishes, including nearly all the chief centres of population, both parties suffered in turn. In about 70,

Episcopalians only were turned out; in about 50, only Presbyterians and Independents; but at one time or another, more than half the parishes in the county were affected. Of the sequestrated Episcopalians, some 50 regained their livings. Of those who had replaced them, still more conformed and retained under the Bishop what they had received under the Presbytery. Most of the ejected Puritans endeavoured to keep their people together; and about one-half availed themselves of the provisions of the short-lived Declaration of Indulgence of 1672. When William of Orange landed at Torbay, among the heartiest in their welcome were those of the ejected who remained, and their faithful followers. They were in the main of the middle ranks of society, but included many members of the leading families.

It is rather a remarkable fact that the old Presbyterian organization of the county still survives. On the 18th October, 1655, there was founded the Exeter Assembly, an association of Presbyterian ministers (to which Independents were afterwards admitted), intended to deal with matters of doctrine and discipline. The original articles, signed by 131 ministers, and the original minutes, are still preserved; and the Assembly, which in process of time became first Arian and then Unitarian, still holds an annual meeting for worship and business. The last survivor in Devon of the ejected of 1662 was John Knight of Littlehempston, who died in 1715. The minutes of the Assembly show that there were then in existence 59 congregations which had been founded by his brethren and himself, with a total attendance of 21,750. Of these, 30 continue to this day unbroken and with many offshoots. In more than half the parishes or places for which licenses were granted in 1672, the elder Nonconformity still remains.

There is the fullest evidence that for more than 400

years Exeter was the seat first of a Saxon and then of a Norman mint. The earliest coin extant is a silver penny of Ælfred, who began his reign in 872; and the latest is a penny of Edward I., 1272-1307. During this period at least 254 varieties are known to have been struck, in the reigns of Ælfred, Eðelstan, Eadmund, Eadred, Eadwig, Eadgar, Eadweard the Martyr, Æðelred II., Cnut, Harold I., Harthacnut, Eadweard the Confessor, Harold II., William I., William II., Henry I., Stephen, Henry II., John, Henry III., Edward I. The coins are all pennies; and the most numerous are those of Æðelred, Cnut, and the Confessor, which comprise more than five-sixths of those known to have been struck before the Conquest. More than 100 types and varieties exist of Æðelred alone; and the largest collection is that in the Royal Cabinet at Stockholm, relics of the ancient Danegeld which Æðelred was the first to impose.

After the lapse of some three and a half centuries, the Exeter mint was again worked by Charles I. during his struggle with the Parliament. Most of his coins are dated 1644; but many of the 37 varieties known to exist were struck in the following year. They were all of silver, and include 'half-pounds,' crowns, half-crowns, shillings, sixpences, groats, threepennies, and pennies.

William III. was the last to employ the Exeter mint. His coins were half-crowns, shillings, and sixpences; dated 1696 and 1697.

Of the seventeenth-century tradesmen's tokens, Exeter issued a far larger proportion—just 90—of the 360 known to have been struck in Devon than any other town; and there could hardly be a better index to its relative importance. Norwich alone, in all the provinces, had so many issuers. Plymouth struck barely half the number.

The trade of Exeter forms a feature in its history almost comparable in importance with its ecclesiastical record. The commerce of the ancient city in Saxon times led to the settlement therein of so large a number of foreigners, that they were compelled by the inhabitants to take part in the resistance offered to William. Woollen manufacture became the staple industry, and so continued until the decay of the cloth trade of Devon, in the latter half of the eighteenth century. In 1458 the Tuckers and the Cordwainers had a fierce dispute anent precedency in the civic processions. The Cordwainers and Curriers had been incorporated in 1387; and the Tuckers must have had something like the same antiquity, for the decision was that they were of equal dignity, and that they were to walk abreast, one of each trade. The Weavers and Fullers, however, into whose hands the chief business of the city eventually fell, were not incorporated until 1490; and it was only in 1540 that the Exeter folk successfully established their right against the inhabitants of Crediton to maintain the weekly woollen market which they had founded ten years earlier. To such dimensions did the woollen trade of Exeter grow that goods to the value of half a million were annually exported to foreign marts—to Spain, Portugal, Italy, Germany, and Holland. Moreover, the Exeter merchants were travelled men, speaking many languages fluently; and Sir John Bowring, the greatest linguist of the West of England, and one of the most distinguished of Exonians, records his early indebtedness to their instructions. Sir John's father was himself a woollen manufacturer; and though Sir John died so recently as 1872, he remembered well when a 'large proportion of the working classes of Exeter wore a bright green apron of serge, fastened with a girdle of the richest scarlet. These were the tuckers of the privileged guild of fullers, weavers, and shearmen,' whose hall still stands on Fore Street Hill, now the meeting-place of the oldest lodge of Masonry in the county. This great and flourishing fraternity Sir John lived to see 'reduced to a few score of ancient people . . still the recipients of the bounties, and many of them the occupants of the almshouses built or endowed by those who had prospered in the woollen trade.' Decay seems to have arisen from various causes. For one thing, masters and men were thoroughly bound up in the trammels of a restrictive policy, which prevented the adaptation of the trade to the changed conditions of the markets. The hour of trial came, but not the men to lead. The introduction of machinery, discountenanced in every way by the members of the old guilds, but fostered elsewhere, also played its part. But even yet the manufacture flourishes in a few Devonshire towns, which had the advantage of enterprise and skill; and the Devon serges retain in Eastern countries the reputation they have enjoyed for centuries, and win their way to wider appreciation at home.

The external trade of the city was so considerable seven centuries since that Isabella de Fortibus, Countess of Devon, a lady of great force of character, having quarrelled with the citizens, as the readiest means of injuring them threw what has since been called Countess Weir across the Exe. The citizens appealed to the law, which was clearly on their side; and at length an opening was made in the weir through which ships could pass. A quarrel with an Earl of Devon a century later led in process of time to the construction of the finest commercial undertaking of which England in its day could boast. Izacke gives a gossiping narrative of what he alleges to be the cause of the whole affair. While Exeter market, as a rule, was noted for its supply of fish, one unlucky day there happened to be but three 'pots' on sale, when the caterers of the Earl and of the Bishop both came to buy. Each wanted the whole; neither would give way. So Mayor Beynion was appealed to, and settled the matter by giving one pot to each of the disputants, and keeping the third for the general public.

'Whereupon the Earl, in his high displeasure, maliciously destroyed the haven.' Of a truth, 'a mighty matter about a pott of ffish.' This was in 1311. In 1316, Hugh Courtenay neither forgetting nor forgiving, matters became even worse. ' His displeasure grew into anger, and from thence to an extreme hatred and revenge, and he devised all possible means to destroy the city!' Be all this as it may—and even important communities like Exeter had often difficulty in holding their own against such powerful neighbours as the Courtenays—the damage done to the Exe led in process of time to the formation of the Exeter Canal, by which vessels reach the city quays from the sea—one of the earliest works of the kind in the kingdom. It was opened in 1566, one Trew being the engineer.

The enterprise of the citizens had been developed by a great mercantile brotherhood. The Guild of Merchant Adventurers of the City of Exeter originated in troublous times. In July, 1549, while Lord Russell lay at Honiton, unable to advance against the Western rebels for want of men and means, three men of the old city—John Bodlie, Thomas Prestwood, and John Periam—raised the funds which enabled him to resume his march, and crush the rising. This, and the loyalty of which it was but an illustration, led, ten years later, to the charter, by Elizabeth, of the Merchant Adventurers, who commenced operations in August, 1560. It was high time that something should be done to encourage commerce, even if after the fashion of these days by way of monopoly. In 1557 it was reported to the Queen that no man in the city or county of Exeter had any ship of his own, neither means to take up vessels. Too much of their money had been disbursed ' to the Quene's mat^{ie} by way of lone.' One of the first important acts of the guild was to grapple with this point; and we find the brethren, in 1566, taking up certain vessels on freight on behalf of the Corporation, and thus establishing a foreign carrying-trade with ships that are noted as belonging to the city, as well as to other ports in the county. The ventures were for Spain and Portugal, and the goods sought wines and raisins. Subsequently this special branch of trade was conducted by a Spanish Guild. As years rolled on the ideas of the Merchant Adventurers enlarged, and their business ramifications extended to the New World. They would have nothing to do with Ralegh's attempts in Virginia; but they adventured with Adrian Gilbert and John Davis in their voyages for the 'discovery of China,' the special object being to open up a trade in woollens. They contributed also to the last expedition of Sir Humphry Gilbert, though they thought the 'tyme of the yeare to be far spente.' They did not respond to the invitation to join with Drake and Norris, on behalf of Don Antonio. They were traders, and apparently kept strictly within commercial limits, so far as the fashion of the times allowed. Nothing is known of the circumstances under which this once important corporation came to an end. It is believed to have flourished most under the first James, and to have collapsed during the troublous times of the Civil Wars. Practically nothing whatever was known of its internal affairs until its early minutes were discovered among the archives of the Weavers' Guild, and made the text a few years since of an admirable narrative by Mr. William Cotton.

Notwithstanding all efforts at rivalship, Exeter has maintained its position as the chief town in Devon worthily. Its manufactures and special industries have one by one died out. In general commerce it has been long distanced by communities more favourably placed with regard to the sea; but it still enjoys the advantages conferred by the neighbourhood of more notable families than are to be found so thickly planted in any other part of Devon. It remains the capital of the shire. The courthouse, which has replaced its ancient castle, continues the seat of county government. Its citizens have never been found wanting in public spirit. Witness to this latter point a host of institutions and charities, and the Museum, Free Library, and Art Gallery, the finest building devoted to the promotion of science, literature, and art, west of Bristol. An historic past has been worthily succeeded by an active present.

Exeter has a marvellous muster-roll of worthies. Archbishop Langton, the framer of Magna Charta, is reputedly of Exonian birth. Archbishop Baldwin, who died at Tyre in 1191, while engaged on a crusade, was certainly a native of the city; and so was his contemporary Josephus Iscanus, 'the Swan of Isca,' the most distinguished of our mediæval Latinists. Then we have Cardinal Robert Pullein, who came from Exeter to Oxford in the reign of Henry I., the reviver of learning in that university. John Hoker, *alias* Vowell, the first historian of the county, was born at Exeter about 1524, and died in 1601; and his far more famous nephew, Richard Hooker the 'judicious,' saw the light at Heavitree in 1553, and died in 1600. It is worthy of note that while Exeter thus produced the chief defender of the Established Church, it gave Puritanism also one of its most prominent leaders in John Reynolds—born at Pinhoe 1549, died 1607—the chief representative of Puritanism at the Hampton Court Conference, and one of the translators of the Authorized Version of the Bible. John Reynolds was originally a Catholic, his brother William a Protestant. Each sought to convert the other, and succeeded! Contemporary with these were the Bodleys—Thomas, Jonas, and Laurence; the first and most famous being the founder of the Bodleian Library.

The farmhouse of Dunscombe, near Crediton, which still shows traces of its former importance, is the ancient

seat of this family. Sir Thomas Bodley was born at
Exeter in 1544, and left England at the early age of
twelve with his father, John Bodley, who was a staunch
Protestant, and lived an exile at Geneva until the accession
of Elizabeth. His studies, begun in the university of
Geneva, were then continued at Oxford. His chief public
work was done in connection with the Court, the Queen
employing him in many embassies and negotiations of the
first importance. His public career lasted from 1583, when
he was made gentleman usher to the Queen, until 1597,
when he retired from pursuits found both toilsome and
vexatious, and entered upon the great work which will
make his name ever memorable—the refounding of the
library which had originated with the 'good Duke'
Humphry of Gloucester. He died in 1612.

Lord Chief Baron Peryam (1534-1604) was another
worthy of Elizabethan Exeter, and so in part was the
famous Nicholas Hilliard (1547-1619), the most distinguished English portrait and miniature painter of his
day. Son of a leading citizen named Robert Hilliard, he
was brought up to the trade of a goldsmith and jeweller,
and acquired such fame by his portraits of royalty and
members of distinguished families, that Donne said of him:

'A hand or eye
By Hilliard drawn, is worth a history
By a worse painter made.'

Hilliard's only recorded predecessor in Devonian art was
John Shute, of Cullompton, who also worked in miniature,
and who died in 1563. Contemporary with the later
years of Hilliard was the first sculptor of note produced
by the county, Nicholas Stone (1586-1647), and almost an
Exonian, seeing that he was born at Woodbury.

The seventeenth century yields such names as Sir
William Morice (1602-1676), Secretary of State to Charles
II.; James Gandy (1619-1689), an admirable portrait-
painter and colourist; Sir Bartholomew Shower, lawyer

and reporter, and his brother John, an eminent Dissenting divine; Tom D'Urfey (1628-1723), wit and songwriter, the descendant of one of the colony of Huguenot families settled at Exeter, to whom the church of St. Olave was assigned as a place of worship; the Princess Henrietta (1644-1670); Simon Ockley (1678-1720), orientalist and historian; and Lord Chancellor King, Baron Oakham, the son of a grocer, and nephew of Locke (1669-1743).

Then of the eighteenth century we have Thomas Hudson (1701-1779), the fashionable portrait-painter of his day, and 'master' of Reynolds; Francis Hayman (1708-1776), the chief historical painter of his time, and the first Librarian of the Royal Academy; William Jackson (1730-1803), the composer; Sir Vicary Gibbs (1752-1820), Chief Justice of the Common Pleas and Chief Baron of the Exchequer; Lord Gifford (1779-1826), Chief Justice of the Common Pleas and Master of the Rolls; John Herman Merivale (1779-1844), the accomplished author and reviewer; Sir W. Follett, born at Topsham (1798-1845), Attorney-General; and Sir John Bowring (1792-1872), the most many-sided of literary Exonians, familiar with every European language, and the leading Oriental tongues; a political economist of the school of Bentham, his mentor and friend; a traveller and a diplomatist; the investigator of the commercial relations of England with the Continent; the negotiator of several important treaties; and sometime Governor of Hong Kong.

The heaviest loss Exeter has had of late is that of Edward Bowring Stephens, A.R.A. (1815-1882), the most distinguished sculptor the West of England has produced, of whose skill Exeter boasts the possession of some of the finest examples.

Many of the local notables were connected with the woollen trade, and the little erewhile suburban parish of St. Leonards can claim at least five peerages, with a score of baronetages and knightages, for the descendants of its quondam inhabitants. The great mercantile house of Baring and its peerages date back to Matthew Baring, son of a Lutheran pastor at Bremen, who came to Exeter about 1717, and, after learning the serge manufacture with Edmund Cock, married the daughter of a rich grocer named Vowler, and founded a flourishing factory. His son John was member for Exeter (1776-1803). Another son, Francis, became a baronet in 1793. His daughter Elizabeth married John Dunning, Lord Ashburton; and the title was revived in 1835—after the death in 1823, without issue, of Richard Barrè, the second lord—in Alexander, Sir Francis's second son, while his grandson Francis was created Baron Northbrook in 1866. The founder of the family of Duntze, since represented in the baronetage, was also a native of Bremen, who settled in Exeter, and engaged in the woollen trade. Sir John Kennaway, again, is descended from a family largely engaged in the same manufacture. John Cranch, the zoologist, who perished in the Congo expedition, was the son of a working fuller of the city.

Alike in their historical and personal associations, the suburban and surrounding parishes of Exeter have exceptional interest and importance. Heavitree, which forms part of the parliamentary area of Exeter, but not of the 'city,' under the title of Wonford was the head of the hundred in which Exeter is situated, and which still retains its ancient name. As Wenford it appears in 'Domesday,' part of the Royal demesnes which had been held by Eadgytha; and Heavitree, or Hevetrove ('hive-tree'), was then an insignificant manor, belonging to Ralph de Pomeroy. How the lesser name supplanted the greater is not very apparent. There is an absurd legend that names Heavitree from 'heavy-tree,' *i.e.* the gallows, because it was the common place of execution. The

Cluniac Priory of St. James, here founded in 1146 as a cell to St. Martin in the Fields, near Paris, passed to King's College, Cambridge. Polsloe Priory for Benedictine nuns, founded by William Lord Briwere, temp. Richard I., continued until 1538, when its revenues were worth £164 8s. 11d.

The parish of St. Thomas, lying west of the Exe, does not form part either of the ancient city of Exeter or its county, though included within its modern parliamentary limits. It has been a place of some little note, though overshadowed by its great neighbour. At Cowick was a cell of Benedictine monks, from the Abbey of Bec Harlewin, to which the estate had been given by William Fitz-Baldwin. Here Hugh Lord Courtenay was buried in 1340. Seized with the rest of the possessions of the alien priories by Henry V., it was eventually restored, and was granted, about 1462, to the Abbey of Tavistock. Another religious foundation here was the cell of St. Mary de Marisco, an appendage of Plympton Priory. This was at Marsh Barton. Floyer Hayes, for many centuries the seat of the Floyers, was held under the Earl of Devon, by the service of waiting upon the lord paramount whenever he should come into Exe Island, the tenant being seemingly apparelled with a napkin about his neck or on his shoulders, and having a pitcher of wine and a silver cup in his hand, whereof to offer his lord to drink.

Stoke Canon is claimed as having been given to his minster in Exeter by Æðelstan, and subsequently by Cnut to his thegn Hunuwine, from whom presumably it passed to the minster. Cnut's grant at least is certain, and he was traditionally regarded as the donor. In 'Domesday' it appears simply as Stoche. Brampford Speke is also entitled to regard, from its connection with the ancient family of Speke, now settled in Somerset, but once holding a distinguished position in Devon. Of this family was descended Captain Speke, the associate of Captain Grant in the discovery of the source of the Nile, in 1863, and himself a Devonshire man, born at Orleigh Court, near Bideford. One of his ancestors is said to have been hung by Jeffries, after that brutal judge had breakfasted with him at his house at White Lackington. There is a tradition that certain paths in Devon were appropriated to the sole use of the Spekes, and hence called 'Speke-paths.' Thorverton manor was given to the Abbey of Marmoustier in Tours, by Henry II., but was bought of the monks by Sir John Wiger, and given by him in 1276 to the Dean and Chapter of Exeter, in support of three chantry priests celebrating specially for the souls of Henry de Bracton (from whose estate a part of the purchase-money had come) and of Sir John Wiger and his benefactors.

Pynes, in Upton Pyne, the present seat of the Northcote family (who were at Northcote in East Downe as early as the year 1103), came to them by the marriage of Sir Henry Northcote, the fifth baronet, with the heiress of Stafford. Hence the additional name of Stafford, so familiar in the title of the Earl of Iddesleigh when he was Sir Stafford Northcote. Prior to acquiring Pynes, the Northcotes were at Hayne, in the parish of Newton St. Cyres. Here lived Sir John Northcote, the first baronet of the family, a member of the Long Parliament, who left behind him a volume of notes on the proceedings of that body, and served as colonel for the Parliament in the earlier part of the Civil War. The Northcotes were allied with some of the most distinguished houses of the West, and with the Plantagenets. By marrying heiresses they extended their own importance and possessions; and among the families they thus represent are Helion, Meoles, Mamhede, Drew, Haswell, and Stafford.

The Bampfyldes have been settled at Poltimore since the reign of Edward I., and entered the ranks of the baronetage in 1641. Sir John Bampfylde became for a time Governor on behalf of the Parliament of the town of Plymouth, and his son, Sir Copleston Bampfylde, took a leading part in the restoration of Charles II. The family were raised to the peerage as Barons Poltimore in 1831. Among the houses with which the Bampfyldes are allied, or whom they represent, are Pederton, St. Maure, Copleston, Codrington, and Gorges.

Settled at Akland, in the parish of Landkey, for sixteen descents before the Visitation of 1620, the ancient family of Acland for nearly three centuries have made their home in the vicinity of Exeter. Sir John Acland was the builder of the house at Columbjohn, which gave title to the baronetcy at its creation in 1644, and which was garrisoned by its owner for the King. At one time it contained the only Royalist garrison in the county; but in March, 1646, it was the headquarters of Sir Thomas Fairfax. This mansion has been destroyed, and the present seat of the Aclands is at Killerton, in the same parish of Broad Clyst. Originally built in the year 1788, Killerton was greatly enlarged and improved by its late owner, Sir Thomas Dyke Acland, to whom the distinguished honour was paid of the erection of a statue on Northernhay, Exeter, in his lifetime, 'as a tribute for private worth and public integrity, and in testimony of admiration of a generous heart and open hand, which have been ever ready to protect the weak, to relieve the needy, and to succour the oppressed of whatever party, race, or creed.' The Aclands take their second name of Dyke as representatives of the old Somersetshire family of that name.

CHAPTER III.

EXMOUTH AND THE EXE ESTUARY.

EXMOUTH is one of the comparatively few places in Devon that finds mention before the Conquest, though the earlier references to Exanmutha in all likelihood really refer to the river, or estuary, and not to any town. Thus it was clearly at the 'mouth of the Exe' that the Danes landed in 1001, when they defeated the men of Somerset and Devon at Pinhoe. Evidence exists, however, that Exmouth was a local habitation, as well as a name, some forty years later. There is extant a grant of half a mansa of land by Eadweard the Confessor to a thane named Ordgar in 1042; and this half-mansa Mr. J. B. Davidson has shown is practically identical with the present parish of Littleham, in which the older part of modern Exmouth stands. Among the boundaries mentioned in the charter is Lydewic næsse, and this Lydewic seems equivalent to 'Shipwick,' the shipping or sailors' village. Another boundary-mark pointing to ancient settlement, is the 'plegin stowe' or 'playing-place.' Ordgar gave Littleham to the Abbey of Horton, which was annexed in 1122 to Sherborne, and to Sherborne the manor continued to belong until the Dissolution. One of the rights of the Abbey was the ferry over the Exe, from Prattshide —which apparently supplanted Lydewic as the name for ancient Exmouth—to Starcross, so named because the landing was at a flight of stone stairs, adjoining a cross set up by the abbot. This ferry, it has been thought highly probable, was rented by the Drakes of Prattshide, who were certainly the ancestors of the Drakes of Ash, and possibly of those of Tavistock, thence of Buckland and Nutwell.

The name Exmouth long continued to be applied to the port rather than the infant town. The word is so used under King John; and in 1347 it must have been Exeter under the title of Exmue, and not any Exmouth ville, that furnished ten ships and 193 men for the expedition against Calais. Exmouth was, indeed, only a 'Fisschar Tounlet' when Leland saw it about 1540; and therefore it must again be the port that is intended when it is recorded that the Earl of March, afterwards Duke of York and Edward IV., sailed thence in 1459 for Calais, after the first battle of St. Albans. But Exmouth itself was of sufficient note, a few years later, to give Devon one of its stoutest Elizabethan seamen, Richard Whitbourne, who was present when Sir Humphry Gilbert took possession of Newfoundland in 1583; who served, in 1588, in a ship of his own as a volunteer against the Armada; and who was the chief agent in the colonization of 'Avalon in the New-found-land,' under James I. In the narrative of his voyages he describes amusingly what he had taken for a 'Maremaid,' but wisely adds, 'Whether it were a Maremaid or no, I know not; I leaue for others to judge.'

Exmouth was made a Royal garrison in the wars of the Commonwealth. A fort was erected on the sand-bar at the entrance of the river, and held out for forty-six days under Colonel Arundell before he surrendered, March 16, 1646, to Sir Hardress Waller. And here comes in a curious point of topography.

The ancient harbour not only had a bar, but a rock in the channel, called the 'Chickstone,' so much in the way, according to Westcote, that it grew to be proverbial that, 'if we desire to be rid of anything we forthwith wish it to be on Chickstone.' The bar, or Warren, in the seventeenth century was connected, not with the Dawlish side of the river as now, but with the Exmouth shore, and here stood the fort. The entrance into the river from the sea was by the western bank and not the eastern; and it was possible to cross from Exmouth to the Warren by stepping-stones as late as 1730. There is a story told, too, of a captain who, by trusting to an old chart, ran his vessel high and dry one night on the track of the ancient channel.

Littleham, after the Dissolution, came to Sir Thomas Dinnis; and, by descent, eventually to the Rolles, its present lords.

The northern portion of Exmouth lies in the parish of Withycombe Ralegh. This passed to the Raleghs from the Clavells, and hence became one of several parishes that took and have retained the name of Ralegh as a distinctive title. It seems an almost hopeless task to attempt to connect the different branches of this widespread and distinguished race with the original stock of the Raleghs of Ralegh in Pilton, or to reconcile the discordant pedigrees. Yet there is no doubt the connection exists. Wymond Ralegh, grandfather of the famous Sir Walter Ralegh, whose seat was at Fardell, near Plymouth, held estate in Withycombe Ralegh; and this may have been one of the causes that induced his son Walter to remove to this neighbourhood, and thus give to Hayes Barton in East Budleigh the honour of being the birthplace of the most accomplished Devonian of Devon's greatest age. According to Westcote, Withycombe Ralegh was held by the service of finding the King two good arrows stuck in an oaten cake whenever he should hunt on Dartmoor.

The Drakes were large owners of property in Withy-

combe Ralegh, and the first wife of Walter Ralegh, the
father, was a Joan Drake. For his third he married
Katherine Champernowne, widow of Otho Gilbert, and
mother of Sir Humphry and Sir Adrian Gilbert. To no
other Devonshire woman has it been given to have three
such famous sons to represent her in the list of worthies.
Hayes Barton, where Sir Walter was born in 1552, still
stands, and there are several interesting memorials of the
family in the church. To attempt to trace the life of
Ralegh, even in bare outline, is impossible here. More
than any other man of his time, he was the epitome of
the restless, many-sided spirit of the age—courtier, statesman, philosopher, sailor, soldier—accomplished in all
manner of honourable professions, and a leader in each
one. His apprenticeship to arms being passed with the
Huguenots in France, his first sea voyage was taken
with Humphry Gilbert's disastrous colonizing expedition
in 1578. Next he served in stern fashion against the
Irish insurgents, and thus acquired the lands upon which
he afterwards introduced the cultivation of the potato.
Upon his return from Ireland he began his career as a
courtier; and he rose so rapidly that in 1587 he succeeded
Hatton as Captain of the Guard. Four years before this,
however, he had contributed the *Ralegh* to the expedition
in which Sir Humphry Gilbert took possession of Newfoundland, although her crew deserted their companions.
In 1584 he sent out the vessels, under Amadas and
Barlowe, which proved the abounding fertility of Virginia;
and in the following year planted a colony at Roanoake,
under Ralph Lane. Though his designs were doomed to
final failure, and no plantation made by him survived,
Ralegh persevered in the effort, at the cost of much
treasure and pains, for years; and in the event it was
under his patent, though in other hands, that the first
English colony of Jamestown was founded. As Lord
Warden of the Stannaries, Ralegh was chiefly concerned

Exmouth and the Exe Estuary. 51

in the land preparations for the reception of the Armada in Devon and Cornwall; but he joined the fleet and had his share in the great victory when his work on shore was done. With the rise of Essex at Court the influence of Ralegh waned; while his secret marriage with Bessie Throgmorton threw him into deep disgrace, and Elizabeth in her anger sent him to the Tower. Released from durance, he retired to his manor of Sherborne, and there planned his expeditions to Guiana, the second of which, in 1595, he himself conducted. Next we have him, by his wise advice, securing the success of the expedition to Cadiz in 1596, and winning all the honours of the 'Island Voyage' in 1598. When Elizabeth died, Ralegh had regained his old position at Court; but the accession of James was the prelude to his downfall. Falsely accused of conspiracy, he was imprisoned in the Tower from 1603 to 1616. Then came his last voyage to Guiana, in search of the golden city of Manoa, in which his 'braines were broken' by the loss of his son; and in October, 1618, at the dictation of Spain, the cowardly pedant James struck off the head of the noblest Englishman of the day, who died with 'the grace of a courtier, the dignity of a philosopher, the courage of a soldier, and the faith of a Christian.'

East Budleigh was originally a market town, and, according to Pole, had a Sunday market. It seems to have been a little port, vessels frequenting the estuary of the Otter, up to the fifteenth century; but Leland says that in his time the haven was 'clene barred,' and that the shipping had left for a hundred years. Budleigh Salterton, upon the coast here, has developed of late years considerably as a bathing-place. Here is the best exposure of the Budleigh Salterton pebbles, a large proportion of which contain Silurian fossils, and which seem to have been derived from pre-Triassic extensions of Silurian and Devonian rocks into the area now occupied

4—2

by the Channel. In the distinctive name of the contiguous parish of Newton Poppleford, popple = pebble, and is still a current form of speech.

Topsham ranks next to Exmouth of the towns of the Exe estuary. Though in modern days little more than a riverside suburb of Exeter, it was anciently a port of considerable importance. It was a market-town so far back as the reign of Edward I.; and it was for a long period the chief seat of Exeter commerce, large vessels coming no further than its quay. Topsham seamen had a good deal to do also with the development of the fishing-trade with Newfoundland; and as one result of this it is recorded that in the reign of William III. it had more trade with Newfoundland than any other port in the kingdom, London alone excepted. Unjustly taken from the see of Exeter, as Leofric notes, by Harold, the manor was for several generations in the Courtenays, who used their connection with it to the disadvantage of Exeter, when differences arose between the citizens and their powerful neighbours. On their attainder it passed to the Crown, afterwards vesting in the De Courcys. It is now the property of the Hamiltons. Topsham had its share in the troubles of the seventeenth century. When Exeter was held by the Royalists, they built a fort here, which was battered down by the Earl of Warwick, the Parliamentary Admiral, who killed therein some seventy or eighty men. For a short time in October, 1645, Topsham was the headquarters of Sir Thomas Fairfax.

Weare, once the seat of a younger branch of the Hollands, Dukes of Exeter, has been the residence of the Duckworths since 1804, in which year it was purchased by Admiral Sir Thomas Duckworth, the hero of the passage of the Dardanelles in 1807, when for the first time Constantinople saw the fleet of an enemy.

Topsham in all probability affords an instance of the

preservation of a personal name from Saxon days, and is equivalent to ' Topa's ham.' In the sixteenth and seventeenth centuries it was frequently called Apsom. It is Topeshant in ' Domesday.'

The little stream of the Clyst, which falls into the Exe at Topsham, has given name not only to the hundred of Clyston, but to more manors and parishes than any other river in the county save the Teign—a fact which indicates the comparative populousness of this rich valley in Anglo-Saxon times. There are Clysthydon, named from its ancient lords the Hydons, now long in the Huyshes; St. Lawrence Clyst, of old time in the Valletorts, one of the estates which Elize Hele bequeathed to charitable purposes; Broad Clyst, already noted; Honiton Clyst; St. Mary Clyst, in the church of which Walter Ralegh, father of Sir Walter, took refuge from a band of the Western Rebels for the restoration of Roman Catholicism, and was rescued by a party of Exmouth seamen; and Clyst St. George, a small estate in which, held by the annual tender of an ivory bow, was reputed to have been in the family of Sokespitch from Saxon times, but was really granted to them by Henry de Pomeroy, temp. Henry II. Of other Clysts which have not survived as parishes, Clyst Fomison is now the parish of Sowton; while Bishops Clyst, in Farringdon and Sowton, once in the Sackvilles, was an ancient episcopal manor and residence, and a little market town.

Nutwell, in the adjoining parish of Woodbury (which takes name from ancient earthworks upon the high range of moorland called Woodbury Common, and gave title in the eleventh century to a fraternity known as the Woodbury Guild), is the chief seat of the Drakes of Tavistock, the descendants of Thomas Drake, brother of the renowned Sir Francis. It was long held by the Dinhams, then passing successively to the Prideauxes, Fords, and Pollexfens. These Drakes were on the Parliamentary side during the wars of the Commonwealth, and Nutwell was garrisoned in that behalf. The first house of importance here seems to have been built by Lord Dinham, in the reign of Henry VII. The present Drakes of Nutwell represent the old family through double female descent. The first baronet of the line was Francis, nephew of the circumnavigator, created in 1622; and this title became extinct in 1794, when the last baronet bequeathed his estates to his nephew, Lord Heathfield. On his dying without issue, they passed in like manner to his nephew, Thomas Trayton Fuller. The name of Drake was resumed and a new baronetcy created in 1821.

Opposite Topsham, on the western shore of the estuary, lies Exminster, indicated by its name as a place of ecclesiastical importance in Saxon times, but to which little that is noteworthy appears to attach. At the present day it has rather an unpleasant reputation as the location of the County Lunatic Asylum. The manor was bequeathed by Ælfred to his younger son, and at the Domesday Survey was held by William Chievre, in succession to Wichin, but was not of any note. Several distinguished families have been connected with Exminster. The Courtenays, who are still lords of the manor, are said to have had a magnificent mansion here. Peamore, now the seat of the Kekewich family, was formerly in the Cobhams and Bonviles, Tothills and Northleighs. Shillingford, given to Torre Abbey by its founder, William Lord Briwere, was purchased by the Southcotes after the Dissolution, and, with other property in the parish, has long been held by the Palks. The vicarage is appendant to Crediton.

Next to Exminster comes Kenn, with its chief village of Kennford, described in old records as a borough, and having a market granted to its ancient owners, the Courtenays, about 1299. The manor is now the property of Lord Haldon, whose principal residence, Haldon House, is in this parish. Haldon House was originally built by Sir George Chudleigh, the last baronet of that family, but the mansion and grounds owe their present aspect to the improvements effected since they were purchased by Sir Robert Palk. The Palks are an old Devonshire race, who were seated at Ambrook, in Ipplepen, as early as the fifteenth century. Sir Robert Palk, the first baronet, the son of Henry Palk, sometime member for Ashburton, became Governor of Madras, and in India acquired both title and fortune. In India, too, he formed a very close friendship with Major-General Lawrence, to whom he erected a monument at Haldon, and whose name has been continued in the family ever since. Sir Lawrence Palk, M.P. for South Devon (as his grandfather had been for the undivided county), was raised to the peerage in 1880.

Powderham Castle holds the first place among the ancient mansions of the county. No other great house continues so fully its olden glories. Nearly six centuries have passed since the Courtenays first seated themselves by the Exe, at Powderham, and there, amidst many vicissitudes, they have continued. At the compilation of 'Domesday,' Powderham was one of the two Devonshire manors of William de Ow, and on his forfeiture came to a family who thence took name. The attainder of John de Powderham led to the manor becoming the property of Humphrey de Bohun, Earl of Hereford; and his daughter Margaret, in 1325, brought it to her husband Hugh, the second Courtenay Earl of Devon. Earl Hugh gave it to his younger son Philip, by whom the castle was built, and in his descendants it has remained. When the earldom of Devon, newly revived by Queen Mary, was thought to have failed, through the death, without issue, of Lord Edward Courtenay, in 1556, the Courtenays of

Powderham continued simple knights, and subsequently baronets, until Sir William, the third holder of the baronetcy, was created Viscount Courtenay of Powderham in 1762. William, the third viscount, in 1831, however, established his claim to the earldom created by Queen Mary in 1553 (the title having been merely dormant, and not extinct, for 265 years); becoming, in fact, the tenth earl, though only the second who had borne, the title under Mary's patent. The present Earl of Devon is the eighteenth Courtenay lord of Powderham.

Powderham Castle saw service during the struggle between Charles and the Parliament, when it was strongly garrisoned for the King. An attack made by Fairfax in December, 1645, proved a failure, and the Roundheads in their turn garrisoned the church. The castle was, however, taken early in the following year by Colonel Hammond.

The House of Courtenay is the most distinguished family of Devon. They have been called 'the ubiquitous Courtenays,' for there is hardly a parish in the county which is not linked with their history by some traces of lordship or alliance. The history of the English branch of this great house, whose famous coat of three torteaux 'at once waved over the towers of Edessa, and was reflected by the waters of the Seine,' has been set forth most graphically by Gibbon. Ranked among the chief barons of the realm, it was not 'till after a strenuous dispute that they yielded to the fief of Arundel the first place in Parliament. Their alliances were contracted with the noblest families—the Veres, De Spencers, Bonviles, St. Johns, Talbots, Bohuns, and even the Plantagenets themselves; and in a contest with John of Lancaster, a Courtenay, Bishop of London and afterwards Archbishop of Canterbury, might be accused of profane confidence in the strength and numbers of his kindred. In peace the Earls of Devon resided in their numerous castles and manors of the West, and their ample revenue was appropriated to devotion and hospitality. In war they fulfilled the duties and deserved the honours of chivalry. They were often entrusted to levy and command the militia of Devon and Cornwall. They often attended their supreme lord to the borders of Scotland and Wales, and in foreign service they sometimes maintained four-score men-at-arms and as many archers. By sea and land they fought under the standard of the Edwards and Henrys. Their names are conspicuous in battles, tournaments, and in the original lists of the Order of the Garter. Three brothers shared the Spanish victory of the Black Prince, and in the lapse of six generations the English Courtenays learned to despise the nation and country from which they derived their origin. In the quarrels of the Roses the Earls of Devon adhered to the House of Lancaster, and three brothers successively died either in the field or on the scaffold. A daughter of Edward IV. was not disgraced by the nuptials of a Courtenay. Their son, created Marquis of Exeter, enjoyed the capricious favour of his cousin Henry VIII.; and in the camp of the Cloth of Gold broke a lance against the monarch of France. Among the victims of the jealous and tyrannical Henry, the Marquis of Exeter was one of the most noble and guiltless. His son Edward lived a prisoner and died in exile; and the secret love of Queen Mary, whom he slighted for the Princess Elizabeth, has shed a romantic colour on the story of this beautiful youth. The relics of his patrimony were conveyed into strange families by the marriage of his four great-aunts, and his personal honours, as if they had been legally extinct, were revived by the patents of succeeding princes. But there still survived a lineal descendant of Hugh, the first Earl of Devon, a younger branch of the Courtenays, who have been seated at Powderham Castle above 500 years, from the reign of Edward III. to the present hour. Their estates have been increased by the grant and improvement of lands in Ireland, and they have been restored to the honours of the peerage. Yet the Courtenays long retained the plaintive motto which asserts their innocence and deplores the fall of their ancient house—'*Ubi lapsus, quid feci?*'

The little town, or rather village, of Starcross, which lies on the western side of the Exe Bight, is the most important centre in the parish of Kenton; and since the construction of the South Devon Railway, efforts have unavailingly been made to give it a commercial character. It is best known now for its large philanthropic establishment, the Western Counties Idiot Asylum. In Saxon and early Norman days it was a royal demesne, and subsequently held by the Courtenays until their attainder. Kenton then reverted to the Crown; and after its grant by Elizabeth to Lord Clifton, passed in rapid succession through Exeter, Hungerford, Monk (Duke of Albemarle), and Grenville, until, early in the last century, it was once more acquired by the House of Courtenay. Kenton lies beneath the long Greensand ridge of Haldon; and the local proverb runs:

> 'When Haldon wears a hat,
> Kenton beware a scat;'

a cap of clouds on Haldon being an almost certain sign of rainy weather.

CHAPTER IV.

AXMINSTER AND THE AXE.

EAST DEVON has all the marks of a populous and troubled border-land of vast antiquity. Nowhere in all Devon are there so many remains of the so-called 'camps' or fortified towns of the early Kelts within so narrow an area. Taking Broaddown near Honiton as a centre, and excluding earthworks of minor importance, we have, for example, Blackbury Castle, Bilbury Castle, Dumdun Castle, Farway Castle, Hocksdown Castle, Hembury Fort, Musbury Castle, Membury Castle, Stockland Great and Little Castles, Sidbury Castle, Widworthy Castle, Woodbury Castle—all entrenchments, without masonry, notwithstanding their 'castle' name. Within a radius of six miles from Sidmouth, there are yet existing ninety-three tumuli, many of notable size and considerable antiquarian interest. The boundary-line between Devon and Dorset, moreover, instead of following the natural features of the country, is of so intricate and peculiar a character as to render it evident that it was the result of hard and continual fighting, in which the possession on either side of strong positions played an important part. And so, in later times, though still in what are really prehistoric days, as far as the absence of written record goes, we have the important fact indicated by the character and relations of the hundreds of East Devon that it was the first district of the county which the Saxons occupied in force, and in which, in the earlier years of Saxon domination, most frequent changes took place.

Axminster and the valley of the Axe, clustered with ancient towns and villages, first claim attention. One of a group of 'minsters,' the like of which is not to be found elsewhere, Axminster was in all likelihood founded by King Ine, to commemorate and consolidate his conquests, after the great battle in 710, in which he defeated Gereint, the king of the West Welsh. The town itself was doubtless of far older date, and may even have had being in some form in pre-Keltic times. The valley of the Axe has of late years yielded from its gravels such large numbers of chipped chert implements as to show the existence of a considerable population in Palæolithic days. It certainly was in some sense a Roman settlement, for it lies on their direct route between Dorchester and Exeter.

This, however, is, and must remain, largely tinged with speculation. The first direct mention of Axminster in history is as the burial-place, in 785, of Cyneheard the Ætheling, who killed Cynewulf. We must dismiss, as unhistoric, a tradition that the minster was founded by Æðelstan, and priests placed therein to pray for the souls of seven earls and five kings who fell here in a great battle at Calesdown, the fight raging to Colecroft by Axminster. That the tradition, which is of very great antiquity, refers to actual fighting, may be granted; but the minster is much older than the date thus assigned, and there appears to have been grafted upon the original legend some memories of Brunanburgh, with which, indeed, this fight has been mistakenly identified. But Brunanburgh, the description of which in the 'Saxon Chronicle' is such a fine example of Anglo-Saxon poetry, was certainly not waged in the West, and Devon cannot claim 'that battle so fierce and so bloody, that never was there bloodier seen from the days when the Saxons and the Angles, famous smiters in war, came over the broad seas to put the Britons to rout.'

Two Alseminstres are mentioned in 'Domesday.' One held by the King had four serfs, thirty villeins, and twenty bordars, with a couple of mills, and was worth twenty-six pounds a year. The other held by Eddulf, under William Chievre, had four serfs and twelve bordars, and was worth twenty pounds annually. Probably both manors were included in the present parish, the first representing the modern town, which would seem to have continued with the Crown, possibly until John granted it to his trusty noble, William Lord Briwere, from whose family it passed to the Mohuns. John confirmed the market to Briwere in 1204, to be held on Sundays as accustomed ; and a few years later made the town a free borough. Briwere built a castle, of which every vestige has disappeared, though walls have been found in excavating which apparently belonged to such a structure.

For some centuries the history of Axminster is that of the famous and dominant Abbey of Newenham, planted in the pleasant meadows by the winding Axe by Reginald and William de Mohun in 1246 ; Reginald, however, being the accepted founder. The first Cistercian colony consisted of twelve monks and four lay brethren, under John Goddard as abbot, from the monastery of Beaulieu. The permanent buildings were begun in 1250, and were of great magnificence and beauty, for the Abbey had many friends, and Bishop Bronescombe and Bishop Grandisson were among its most liberal benefactors. Reginald de Mohun chose Newenham as his burial-place, and there his body was deposited in January, 1257-8, the first of a long line of illustrious personages, Bonviles and Mohuns and others, whose bones are now washed out by the encroachments of the river from the long-desecrated site. The church took thirty years in building, and was 280 feet long; breadth across the transepts, 152. At the surrender the estates were valued at £227 7s. 8d. A fragmentary wall is all that remains to mark the site. At the Dissolution the manor of Axminster passed to the Marquis of Dorset, then to the Duke of Norfolk, and was sold in the reign of James I. to Lord Petre, in whose family it remained until 1824.

Axminster was a good deal worried during the Civil Wars of the seventeenth century, through being utilized by the Royalist troops in their approaches to Lyme; and though the sympathies of the town leant rather to the Cavaliers, it must have had a peculiarly unpleasant time. Prince Maurice made it his headquarters for a while in April, May, and June, 1644, but retired on the approach of Essex. Subsequently, on the petition of the wealthier residents, a royal garrison was placed at Axminster under the command of Sir Richard Cholmondeley. This only made matters worse, for the Roundheads of Lyme, under the command of Colonel Ceeley (October 25th), assaulted the town, routed the Royalists, and killed their captain. And when, in the ensuing month (November 15th), Major Walker, who had succeeded Sir Richard, attacked Lyme, not only was he killed, with many of his followers, but the remnant of the Cavaliers were chased into Axminster Church, whence they could not be dislodged.

Axminster became Fairfax's headquarters in October, 1645; and it was at the village of Membury that he received 'the only affront' put upon him in the West of England: a party of Royalist cavalry, led by Goring and Wentworth, making a night attack, getting within the guards, and capturing some sixty prisoners. Sir Shilston Calmady had been killed in a skirmish at Membury in the previous February.

The town was the rendezvous of the Duke of Monmouth on his first day's march from Lyme, where he had landed June 11, 1685; and here it was thought his first battle would have been fought. The Devonshire and Somerset militia, and the forces of Monmouth, were all marching upon Axminster from different points within view of the insurgents; but the latter, doubling their speed, gained the town first; and Monk, who was in command of the train-bands, deemed it expedient to retire. Had Monmouth then taken Exeter, which he could easily have done, the fortune of the campaign might have been wholly different. That he had many staunch followers in Axminster is recorded in the pages of the 'Axminster Ecclesiastica,' a singular contemporary record of the Independent Church there, which notes also many of the local horrors of the Bloody Assize.

It was at Axminster that Lord Cornbury deserted from James II. to William of Orange. He had brought three regiments of cavalry from Salisbury westward, under pretence of making a night-attack upon some Dutch troops at Honiton. Suspicion being excited, and his orders not being forthcoming when demanded, he then made the best of his way to William with a few followers only, instead of the important contingent he had hoped to secure.

Apart from the miserable vestige of Newenham, Axminster has only one antiquity, its church, originally a fine fabric, still retaining a Norman doorway, and with a couple of early effigies: Alice de Mohun, daughter and heiress of Lord Briwere, and Gervase de Prestaller, her father's chaplain.

Axminster gave name to a kind of carpet, which was first manufactured there, in 1755, by Mr. Thomas Whitty, a clothier, who developed the idea from an attempt to imitate the Turkey fabrics. Eventually he produced the finest carpets ever made in England; and the manufacture was carried on by the Whitty family until 1835, when the looms were removed to Wilton. Among those who attempted to retain the business in the town was Dr.

Buckland, Dean of Westminster, the celebrated geologist, and author of 'Reliquæ Diluvianæ,' who was born at Axminster (1784-1856), and acquired his taste for science in the Lias quarries of the locality.

As Newenham Abbey is the one Cistercian house of Devon which has the least to show for its former greatness, so its neighbour-house of Ford is that which retains the most. Ford lies seven miles from Axminster, and is now in Dorset; but as the site, up to the year 1842, formed a detached portion of Devon, it falls into place in the history of this county. A Cistercian house had been founded at Brightley, near Okehampton, under the patronage of the De Redvers family, in 1135. The patron died in 1137, before the establishment was permanently founded; and finding it impossible to make good their position for themselves, the monks resolved to return to the mother-house of Waverley. They were on the road, and had reached Thorncombe, when they were met by Adelicia, sister of their former benefactor, Richard the Viscount. She gave them the manor of Thorncombe, on which they stood; and thus, instead of returning to Waverley, they founded the Abbey of Ford. This was in 1141. In September, 1142, Adelicia died also; and her remains, with those of Richard de Redvers, which were removed from Brightley, were buried within the church. At the same time, the monks translated the remains of their first abbot, another Richard, who had died at Brightley.

The Abbey flourished under the care of a series of abbots, who contributed some prominent names to the general history of the kingdom. The third abbot, Baldwin of Exeter, originally a monk at Ford, became Archbishop of Canterbury, after filling the See of Worcester. John, the confessor of King John, a great theologian, made Ford famous for its learning. The church was completed in 1239. The last abbot was

Thomas Charde, suffragan to Bishop Oldham, an eminent scholar and divine, and, as the buildings of his time show, an able architect. At the surrender, in 1539, the revenue amounted to £374 10s. 6¼d.

The Abbey passed in the first place by lease to Richard Pollard, but was afterwards bought by him. Sir John Pollard, his son, sold it to his cousin, Sir Amias Poulett; and he to William Rosewall, Elizabeth's attorney-general. Sir Henry Rosewall sold it to Edmund Prideaux, under whom Inigo Jones converted the domestic buildings into a stately mansion. The Abbey continued in the Prideaux, Gwyn, and Fraunceis families until 1847, when it was once more sold; and after being for a short time the property of Mr. G. F. Miles, became that of Mr. Evans. It was for some time the residence of Jeremy Bentham.

Although not a vestige remains of the monastic church, the so-called chapel being really the chapter-house, ' no Cistercian building in England, perhaps none in the world, is in so perfect a state as that of Ford.' Thus Mr. J. Brooking Rowe, who points out also that, ' in spite of the interference with his architecture, and the incongruities of Inigo Jones's additions, Charde's [Perpendicular] work remains pre-eminently beautiful, and renders Ford Abbey perhaps the most interesting building architecturally, as it is archæologically, in the West Country.'

Returning to Axminster, and commencing our survey of the lower portions of the Axe Valley, we find the first point of interest in the remnant farmhouse of Ashe, a couple of miles from Axminster towards Seaton, and just over the borders of Musbury parish. Ashe is connected with more than one distinguished personage, but is specially identified with one of the greatest of English generals. Given by the Courtenays to a family which thence took name, it passed by marriage to the Drakes, then of Exmouth. The most distinguished member of the Drakes of Ashe was that Sir Bernard Drake whom Prince, in his 'Worthies,' records to have boxed Sir Francis Drake's ears for assuming the wyvern in his coat. Be the story true or false (and Prince is not always trustworthy, while in this case his own connection with the Drakes of Ashe may count for something) Sir Bernard was a brave sailor, and did good service against the Spaniards and Portuguese. He died in 1586, stricken at the Exeter Assizes by gaol-fever, which killed the judge—Serjeant Flowerby—five magistrates, and eleven jurymen.

Elizabeth, daughter of John Drake, grandson of Sir Bernard, married Sir William Churchill, of Minthorne, Dorset, who, as a staunch Royalist, was greatly harassed during the Commonwealth. This led to his living for some time with his wife at her father's house. Hence it was that at Ashe there was born in June, 1650, John Churchill, afterwards Duke of Marlborough; and hence the name of that famous warrior is registered among the Axminster baptisms.

The life of the Duke of Marlborough belongs to national history rather than local, like that of so many more of Devon's famous worthies. It was among his own native hills, indeed, that he bore a part in subduing the insurrection of Monmouth; but he seems in later life to have had little if anything to do with the county, of which the victor of Blenheim, with all his failings, must be ranked as one of the most distinguished ornaments. He died in 1722, after having won the highest honours the nation could bestow.

John Drake, uncle of Churchill, was created a baronet in 1660, and his son re-edified Ashe, which had been greatly damaged during the Civil Wars, utilizing Newenham Abbey, of which one of his ancestors had been steward, as a quarry! The baronetcy came to an end with its sixth holder in 1733, and the estate passed to his widow. Her daughter by a second husband, Colonel Speke, married Lord North, at Ashe chapel; and during a visit in 1765, that statesman was so scared by the cries of a body of reapers, who were ' crying the neck ' at the close of harvest, with upraised hooks and the traditional shout, ' We have un !' that he thought his life was threatened. His friend Sir Robert Hamilton, seizing a sword, rushed out to repulse the ' enemy,' when the time-honoured custom was explained and all fears allayed.

Another notable house in the vicinity of Axminster is Shute, for a long time the chief residence of the Bonviles, and as such the centre of the Yorkist interest in the West. William Lord Bonvile was the chief adherent of the party of the White Rose in Devon, and played a prominent part in the local controversies of the day. His daughter Margaret married Sir William Courtenay, whose family were almost to a man Lancastrian, but the feuds of the Bonviles and the Courtenays were none the less severe on that account. What has been termed a duel, in all probability a set-fight, between Lord Bonvile and Thomas Courtenay, Earl of Devon, came off upon Clyst Heath. In October, 1455, Nicholas Radford, ' who was of counseil with my Lord Bonvyle,' and who lived at Upcott Manor, near Crediton, was murdered by a party of men headed by the Earl of Devon's eldest son ; and when Parliament met complaint was made of the ' grete and grevous riotes done in the West Countrey betwene th' Erle of Devonshire and the Lord Bonvile, by the which som men have been murdred, some robbed, and children and wymen taken.' Bonvile was not, however, the only staunch friend of the House of York in these parts. There still remain at Olditch, in Thorncombe, a few walls of the mansion of Lord Cobham, which was attacked by a party of some 200 men ' with force and armes arayd in man'r of werre ' under James Butler, Earl of Ormond—Cobham being as hearty a partizan of the White Rose as Wiltshire was of the Red.

The Bonviles were one of the families extinguished by these wars. Lord Bonvile was beheaded after the second battle of St. Albans, and his son and grandson being killed at Wakefield, Shute passed to his daughter Cicely, who, by her marriage with Sir Thomas Grey, Marquis of Dorset, became ancestress of Lady Jane Grey. Shute, which retains its fine old Tudor gatehouse, has for some three centuries belonged to the Poles.

The intricacies of its ground-plan have been assumed to indicate a British origin for the little town of Colyton; and it is clearly one of those ancient places that have grown up by slow degrees around an original hamlet, and along the lines of the trackways connecting the houses of the first settlers. Though never a place of any great importance, it has been associated with not a few notable families—the De Dunstanvilles and Bassets, Yonges, Courtenays, Poles, Petres, and Drakes among the number. The hamlet of Colyford, midway between Colyton and Seaton, is probably of older date, was chartered by the Bassets and the Courtenays, and had its fair and its mayor, to whom the profits of the fair belonged. Colyton, held by Harold before the Conquest, became a royal demesne. It had a fair, granted by King John; and for some centuries was the chief market of the district.

The most notable manor in the parish is Colcombe, an ancient seat of the Courtenays, who built a castellated mansion there about the year 1280. They held it until the attainder of the Marquis of Exeter in 1538. Then the house fell into decay, but was rebuilt early in the seventeenth century by Sir William Pole, the Devonshire historian and antiquary. Since his postcrity preferred to live at Shute, Colcombe Castle, as it is popularly called, was again deserted. Colyton, however, made its first mark in history in connection with this quondam dwelling of the Courtenays; for Colcombe became the headquarters of a detachment of Royalists, and as the neighbouring town of Lyme was devoted to the Parliamentary interest, there was more than one sharp encounter, which did not materially help the integrity of the building. All that remains of this ancient mansion now forms part of a farmhouse; and the most interesting memorial, alike of Colcombe and the Courtenays, yet to be found in Colyton, is the 'Little Choky Bone' monument in the fine old church of St. Andrew. A noble altar tomb, with canopy, contains the recumbent figure of a girl wearing a coronet, with the royal and Courtenay arms. 'Margaret, daughter of William Courtenay, Earl of Devon, and the Princess Katherine, youngest daughter of Edward IV., King of England, died at Colcombe, choked by a fishbone, A.D. MDXII.' So runs the inscription; but there are doubters, both as to the assignment of the memorial and the cause of death. Many of the Poles are buried in the church, and among them the antiquary, whose 'Collections' have formed such a rich storehouse for the modern historian and genealogist. The Poles have been settled in Devon from the reign of Richard II.

In the town of Colyton are yet portions of the 'Great House,' long the residence of the Yonges. Here Sir Walter Yonge, in 1680, entertained the Duke of Monmouth in his progress in the West of England. The Puritanic sympathies of the townsfolk generally were plainly manifested, not only when Colcombe was held by the troops of Prince Maurice, but when the duke landed at Lyme. Many Colyton men joined his standard; not a few were present at Sedgmoor; and history, as well as tradition, has sad tales to tell of the fate of those who fell into the hands of 'Kirke's lambs,' or came before Jeffries. One of these stories is that a wool-trader named Speed was boiled in his own furnace; and in any case Colyton had its full share of hangings and quarterings. Several men employed by Sir William Yonge in building his mansion at Escot, now the seat of Sir John Kennaway, and who joined the insurgents, were hung within a mile of his gates, though he himself escaped.

The most notable worthy of Colyton parish is Sir Thomas Gates, born at Colyford; who, with his neighbour and friend Sir George Somers, a native of the little Dorset port of Lyme, sailed for Virginia, with a fleet of nine vessels, in 1609. The vessel in which were Gates and Somers was separated from the rest of the fleet by a storm, and driven on the 'still vext Bermoothes.' No lives were lost, and the stout-hearted adventurers took possession of the little archipelago for the King, under the name of the Somers Islands. At length they built vessels to transport themselves to Virginia; and on their arrival Gates took up his office as Governor, and held it until his death in 1620.

Axmouth is only the shadow of its ancient self; but its antiquity is well attested by the fact that, although some distance from the sea, it bears this name instead of Seaton, which is really at the river's 'mouth.' Another reason, alike for its age and ancient importance, is that it gave name to one of the original hundreds of the county, and this the smallest, so that the population here in the early days of Saxon rule must have been comparatively dense. Moreover, it was a member as Axanmuða of the Woodbury Guild. The hill above is crowned with earthworks; and traces have frequently been found which prove Axmouth to have once been something more even than the 'olde and bigge fischar toune' of Leland. The church apart, it is a very unimportant place now.

Axmouth appears in 'Domesday' as part of the royal demesne; but it passed to the Redverses, and was given by Richard de Redvers to the Abbey of Monteburgh in Normandy. Loders Priory, near Bridport, was a cell to this abbey; and Axmouth eventually became an appendage rather of Loders than of the mother house. When

Henry V. seized the possessions of the alien monasteries,
Loders was dissolved, and Axmouth given to the Abbey
of Sion. That in its turn suppressed, Axmouth became
part of the jointure of Queen Catharine Parr, and
Edward VI. gave it to Walter Erle. For some two
centuries it has been the property of the Hallets. Sted-
combe House, a seat of the Erles, was garrisoned by Sir
Walter for the Parliament, but taken and burned in March,
1644, by a party of Prince Maurice's troops. The Erles
then resided at Bindon, now a farmhouse, but retaining
many traces of its ancient state, particularly its domestic
chapel. Sir Walter Erle had been imprisoned for refusing
to lend money to the King, and in revenge seized Lyme
for the Parliament in 1642. At Rousdon, which is a
member of the manor of Axmouth, Sir H. W. Peek has
erected the most magnificent modern mansion in Devon.

Probably no greater divergence of opinion concerning
any matter of Devonian topography has arisen than
touching the site of Moridunum, the lost Roman station
between Durnovaria and Isca Dunmoniorum. The early
writers generally, from Camden onwards, including
Stukeley, Musgrave, Gale, Hoare, and Borlase, place it
at Seaton, regarding *sea* and *mor* as equivalents. Horseley
locates it at Eggardun, eight miles from Dorchester;
Baxter at Topsham, four miles from Exeter; Mr. J.
Davidson and Mr. P. O. Hutchinson at Hembury Fort;
Mr. J. B. Davidson at Honiton; Mr. Heineken at Dump-
don. In truth, the whole district is singularly barren
of traces of Roman presence and intercourse, though
abounding in 'camps' and relics of ancient life. Moreover, while one interpretation of Moridunum is Mòr-
y-dun, 'sea-town,' another is Mawr-y-dun, the 'great hill
fortress.' Probably Hembury is the true site. There are
remains of a 'camp' at High Peak, Sidmouth, that meet
the requirements of the Itinerary as to distance.

Whether Seaton be the lost Roman station or not, a few years ago it was a mere village; now it is a 'watering-place.' In time of yore, like other towns along this line of coast, where the sea has made great inroads, it was a port of some importance. But even when Leland wrote, he had to say, 'Ther hath beene a very notable haven.' That the Romans did something more than visit the neighbourhood, the foundations of a Roman villa, excavated at Hannaditches in 1859, amply testify. The older antiquaries have much to say of the discovery of the remains of vessels and of the original harbour-works; but of late little has been found, though enough to show that the Axe was navigable in the Middle Ages to a considerable distance from the sea; and to justify the conclusion therefore that in Roman times the harbour, whatever the precise situation of the town, was one of very considerable importance. Probably this is as far as we can now get. The first definite authority here is 'Domesday.' Beer and Flveta, which included Seaton, are set forth as belonging to the Priory of Horton, in Dorsetshire, and as having an enumerated population of fifty-five. The Earl of Moreton had taken from Beer a ferling of land and four salt-works, but at Flveta the Priory had twenty salt-works, and this was Seaton proper. When under Henry I. (1122), the possessions of Horton went to the Abbey of Sherborne, Beer and Seaton passed with them, and so continued until the Dissolution. The growth of Seaton as a port was fostered by its monastic lords; and in the fourteenth century it had attained such importance that it furnished two ships and twenty-five men as its contingent to the Calais expedition. A century later new harbour-works were needed, and we find Bishop Lacy granting forty days' indulgence to true penitents who should contribute to the works '*in nova portu in litterore maris apud Seton.*' These works were the basis upon which at various times efforts were made to restore to Seaton something of its old mercantile importance. The Erles of Bindon took the matter in hand, and the late Mr. J. H. Hallet spent considerable sums. Nay, in the early part of the present century a novel effort was made by the farmers of the neighbourhood, who sent so many men each, according to the sizes of their farms, to dig out the ancient harbour, and actually made considerable progress before their efforts were defeated by a flood.

At the Dissolution, Seaton, like Axmouth, became part of the jointure of Queen Catharine Parr, the reversion being granted by Henry to John Frye of Yarty. He sold it to the Willoughbys, and the heiress of Willoughby brought it to the Trevelyans, its present lords.

The fishing village of Beer is about a mile from Seaton, and the property of the Rolles. There is a local tradition that it was resettled in the time of Elizabeth by the crew of a wrecked Spanish vessel, who found the place almost depopulated by the plague. Beer was the chief smuggling haunt of the East-Devon coast in the past century; and here lived the prince of Western smugglers, 'Jack Rattenbury,' the pluckiest and luckiest of them all, whose memory has already passed into the heroic, not to say the mythical stage. Beer is a seat of the Honiton lace manufacture. In the Middle Ages the chalk hills behind supplied the most famous local 'freestone' of the county —the 'Beer stone' used for much of the older work in Exeter Cathedral, and in the churches of Eastern Devon, and finding its way much farther afield. The original quarries are subterranean workings of great extent.

CHAPTER V.

SIDMOUTH.

No town in Devonshire has yielded a more concise and complete numismatological record than Sidmouth; for it dates back to the time of the Romans, and has representatives of almost every reign since the **Conquest**, with illustrations of foreign intercourse in the **coins of French** and other nations. Probably other ancient **seaports might** prove equally rich, but none have been worked so vigorously **by** competent local antiquaries. The most interesting find of Roman times is the fragment of a bronze centaur, supposed to have adorned one of the standards. Sidmouth in Roman days had an open harbour, but this has been long destroyed by the recession of the red sandstone cliffs; and the little river now percolates to the sea through the pebbles of the beach—so that Sid*mouth* is now altogether a misnomer. It is probable, however, that in addition to the outer harbour the channel of the Sid itself formerly afforded access to shipping.

The recorded history of Sidmouth begins with the possession of the manor by Gytha, mother of Harold. It was then an appendage to Otterton, and after the Conquest was given to the Norman St. Michael's Mount. The Prior of Otterton acted as the deputy of the abbot of the superior house. The Otterton cartulary is yet in existence, and contains a list of the inhabitants of Sidmouth in **1260** with the service of each. The whole sum raised for the lord was about £18 a year, and Mr. P. O. Hutchinson has calculated that the 160 tenants represent a population at that date of some 600. Even then Sidmouth must have been of some little importance, and it evidently retained its harbour. The 'port' is mentioned in the early part of the fourteenth century; and the bailiff of the ville of Sidmouth, as a seaport town, sent a representative to a shipping council of Edward III.

St. Michael's Mount, as an alien house, lost the rich manor of Sidmouth in 1414, and it was given to the Convent of Sion. The year before the Dissolution it was leased by Agnes Jordan, the last abbess, for ninety-nine years, to Richard Gosnell. The manor, however, reverted to the Crown, and was granted by Elizabeth to Sir William Peryam. James sold it to Christopher Mainwaring, and he disposed of the great tithes to Dorothy Wadham (who gave them to Wadham College), and the manor to Sir Edmund Prideaux of Netherton, in whose family it continued for nearly two centuries.

One of the proofs of the antiquity of Sidmouth is the occurrence of remains of Norman work in the walls of the church, rebuilt, with the exception of the tower, in 1859-60, and dating historically from the dedication in 1259. The west window of this church is a memorial to the Duke of Kent, father of Queen Victoria, who died at Sidmouth in 1820. The window is a very fine one by Ward and Hughes, and was presented by her Majesty.

Sidmouth may now seem an unlikely place to have attracted the attention of the Duke and Duchess of Kent as a pleasant residence for themselves and their infant daughter; but it had sprung into considerable notoriety as a fashionable resort some twenty years before, and retained its reputation as the Torquay of the period for a score of years afterwards. George IV., when Prince of Wales, lived here for a short time with Lord Gwyder;

and the fame of Sidmouth spread so far that in 1831 it attracted for three months the Grand Duchess Hélène of Russia. These were the golden days of the little watering-place, to which the old inhabitants still look fondly back, although their town now enjoys all the advantages of railway communication, and is keeping fairly abreast of the times.

Concerning Otterton there is not much to say. The Priory to which Otterton itself, Sidmouth, and other manors in the neighbourhood belonged, as a cell of St. Michael's Mount in Normandy, was a small foundation for four monks only. It is said to have originated with King John, but it is quite as likely that he simply confirmed an arrangement previously existing. Its connection with the Mount lasted until the fall of the alien houses. The remains of the Priory are very scanty—a few fragments of crumbling wall adjoining the church, and the venerable 'fayre house' built by Richard Duke, purchaser after the Dissolution, and the ancestor of the Duke family, now represented in name and blood by the Yonges of Puslinch, near Plymouth, and the Coleridges of Ottery, the two coheiresses of Duke marrying into the families of Yonge and Taylor, and the heiress of Taylor marrying Coleridge.

Bicton is associated with a very peculiar tenure, and with an amusing series of historical blunders. Soon after the Conquest, Bicton manor was granted to one of the Norman followers of William—a certain William the Porter, whose duty it was to keep the door of the gaol, and who held Bicton by this service. This tenure continued for some 700 years, down to the year 1787; and the early owners of the manor-house at different periods took the names Portitor, De Porta, De la Porte, and Janitor. From the Janitors it came to the La Arbalisters, the Sackvilles, and the Coplestones, and by sale to Robert Denis, whose heiress Anne carried it to Sir

Henry Rolle, of Stevenstone, from whom it descended to the late Lord Rolle. It is now held by trustees during Lady Rolle's life for the Hon. Mark Rolle, brother of Lord Clinton. It was under the present family that the ancient tenure came to an end. It had lasted long enough to float a marvellous series of traditions, over which nearly every historical writer in the county has tripped—based upon the idea that where the tenure was there the gaol must have been also! Thus it is gravely said that the county gaol was first at Harpford, and then at Bicton, before it was removed to Exeter. Westcote states that Henry I., who simply confirmed to John Janitor the keeping of the gate of Exeter Castle and gaol, moved the gaol to the city; and the Lysonses aver that it was moved from Bicton to Exeter for greater security in 1518. Proof, however, is quite clear to the contrary. Mr. P. O. Hutchinson discovered in the 'Hundred Rolls' of Edward I. the statement that Bicton was held in serjeantry by the service of keeping 'Exeter Gaol;' and another entry to the same purport in the 'Testa de Neville.'

The village of Branscombe, with its partially Norman church, claims a niche not merely in county but in general history, from its personal connections. Soon after the Conquest the property of a family named after the place, it passed to the Wadhams, by whom it was held for eight generations. Nicholas and Dorothy Wadham, the last owners of that name, founding Wadham College, appropriated thereto great portion of their wealth. When Nicholas Wadham died, in 1609, he left his estate to the families of Wyndham and Strangways. A monument in the church is appropriated to Dorothy Wadham. The Wadhams lived in an old house still standing, called Edge, or Egge.

Sidbury, like many other villages and hamlets of the district, is a seat of the lace-manufacture. At Sand is the old Elizabethan mansion of the Huyshe family; and in the church, originally Norman, but rebuilt, is an inscription recording the death of one Henry Parson, 'in the second-first climacteric year of his age;' and what that might have been in Arabic figures, no one has been able to decide.

A stone at the 'Hunter's Lodge,' five miles from Sidmouth on the Honiton road, is the subject of very diverse traditions. According to one, it is the slaughter-stone of a band of witches; according to another, it covers a heap of treasure. Like some other huge stones in the neighbourhood, it is said to go down into the valley to drink when it hears the clock strike midnight; though a neighbour varies the performance by turning round three times when twelve is heard. The latter piece of folk-lore wit closely resembles the story told of Roborough Rock, near Plymouth—a craggy mass which from one point presents a singularly exact profile of George III. This rock turns round whenever it hears the cock crow; and, if report speaks true, the performance has been eagerly watched for by credulous rustics.

CHAPTER VI.

HONITON.

UNLESS we are to assume that in Honiton we have the lost Moridunum, its history begins with 'Domesday,' when it was held by Drogo under the Earl of Moreton, who had succeeded Elmer the Saxon. It was even then, however, a place of no little importance, gelding for five hides, and having land for eighteen ploughs, with a recorded population of twenty-four villeins and ten serfs and bordars. Moreover, it had a mill worth 6s. 6d., and two salt-workers, rendering 5s. The manor, however, did not reach the sea or a tidal estuary, for the salt-works were those referred to as having been appropriated by the Earl of Moreton at Beer, so that each 'salinarius' had charge of two 'salinæ.'

In the reign of Henry I. we find Honiton in the Redvers family, and in that line it continued mainly until it came to the Courtenays. These held it until 1807, when the third viscount sold it because—so current gossip averred—his nephew had twice been defeated in contesting the representation. From that time until the borough was disfranchised it changed hands several times, its chief value lying in the political influence conferred.

Although situated on the main road into the county from the south-east, Honiton makes a poor figure in the national history; and, save as a Parliamentary borough, its importance has always been very slight. It sent representatives so far back as the thirteenth century; but intermitted for some hundreds of years, and did not resume until 1640. For a long period it was very much of a family borough. Members of the Yonge family sat almost continuously from 1640 to 1796; and the Courtenays and Dukes were frequent representatives. The most notable member of modern days was the famous Lord Dundonald, when Lord Cochrane. Contesting the borough in 1806, and losing the election, he paid all who voted for him ten guineas. Shortly afterwards there was another election, and the result of this liberality was that he went in with flying colours. Then he declined to pay any more, and denounced the venality of his constituents. The borough was finally disfranchised in 1868. It was only made a municipality in 1846.

There is a curious nut for antiquaries to crack in the seal of the Honiton Corporation. So far as the device goes, it is a copy of one presented to the town by Sir W. J. Pole in 1640; but what this original device meant no two writers seem to agree. The engraver of the modern seal interpreted it thus: A pregnant female figure to knees—whether kneeling is not clear—before a demi-figure erased, with long hair, but apparently a male. Above, a huge hand, fingers as in benediction; below, a spray of honeysuckle in bloom. One of the old antiquaries calls the demi-figure an idol, and the hand obstetric, and connects the device with an old legend that barren women in Honiton, in old time, were directed to pass a whole day and night in prayer in St. Margaret's Chapel, when they would become pregnant by a vision. It has also been thought to have some connection with the fanciful etymology which interprets *Honi* as 'shame.'

Honiton many years flourished exceedingly by the wool trade; and for some two or three centuries has been a seat of the manufacture of the lace to which it has given name, though less Honiton lace is now made in Honiton itself than in several of the other towns and villages in the district. The art is said to have been originally introduced by Flemish refugees, of whom many settled in the neighbourhood, their descendants being yet traceable by their names, though in many cases these are anglicised. But the art may be of older date and have extended over a much wider area, for it is to this manufacture that Shakespeare alludes in 'Twelfth Night,' in language as apt now as if written but yesterday in East Devon itself:

> 'The spinsters and the knitters in the sun,
> And the free maids that weave their thread with bones,
> Do use to chant it.'

Like other East and North Devon towns, where thatch has abounded, Honiton has had its fires; and in 1765, 115 houses and the Chapel of Allhallows were burnt. This will account for the general absence of traces of antiquity. There was an ancient chapel of Thomas à Becket.

The worthies of Honiton are few and far between. The Pole family, now of Shute, appear to have sprung from the little town; but the most important individual notable of old time is Thomas Marwood, physician to Queen Elizabeth, who died—according to the epitaph on his tomb in the old parish church — at the age of 105. Honiton was also the birthplace of Ozias Humphry, R.A. (1742-1810), an artist of great merit; and of William Salter (1804-75), the painter of the 'Waterloo Banquet.' One of his finest works, 'The Entombment of Christ,' was given by Salter to the church of his native town.

In the parish of Gittisham, but close to the Honiton boundary, Johanna Southcott was born, about the year 1750. She was a woman of enthusiastic spirit, and, though illiterate, of much natural ability. She founded a sect which at one time had over 100,000 members, and which lingered on with a few earnest adherents—the men distinguished, in shaving-days, by unfashionable beards—until the last few years. Her special claim was to prophetic power, and to being the woman of the Revelation; and in that capacity, deceived apparently by disease, she in her old age avowed that she was about to become the mother of Shiloh; nor were the hopes of her followers finally abandoned with her death in 1814.

An amusing legend attaches to a spot called 'Ring-in-the-Mire,' where the parishes of Honiton, Farway, Gittisham, and Sidbury meet. Ring-in-the-Mire is a small swamp, whence a stream issues; and the story is that Isabella de Fortibus, Countess of Devon, having been annoyed by disputes between these parishes concerning their boundaries at this point, ordered a party from each to attend her, rode to the place, took a ring from her finger, and threw it into the marsh, declaring that where the ring fell these parishes should meet, and that she would never more be pestered by their disputes. The name is undoubtedly of great antiquity; but the tradition seems made to order; and, in all probability, 'Ring-in-the-Mire' is a corruption of a far older and possibly Keltic name. 'Mire' is suspiciously like *mawr*.

Netherton, in the parish of Farway, was given by Walter de Clavill to the Monastery of Canonleigh, and became the seat of the Prideaux family in the reign of Queen Elizabeth, its first owner of that name being Sir Edmund Prideaux. Between Buckerell and Broad Hembury rises the high ground which is crowned by the fine earthwork now known as Hembury Fort, with 'its adjunct or outwork, the long promontory occupied by Bushy Knap and Buckerell Knap.' Hembury is the finest 'camp' in East Devon, and is the best claimant to be regarded as Moridunum. Broad Hembury was parcel of the barony of Torrington, and was given by William Lord Briwere to Dunkeswell, the abbot of which, about 1290, obtained the grant of a weekly market. At Carswell was a small Cluniac Priory or cell to Montacute. Toplady, author of the 'Rock of Ages,' was vicar here.

Mohuns Ottery, in Luppitt, was long the seat of the famous baronial family of Carew, who claim the honour of a traceable descent from Anglo-Saxon times. Several members of this house acquired great renown in arms. The Carews obtained Mohuns Ottery by the marriage of Eleanor, elder co-heiress of Sir William Mohun, who died in 1280, to John Baron Carew. Her son, another John, who died in 1363, was one of the heroes of Cressy, and held the distinguished post of Lord Deputy of Ireland, losing his second son in the Irish wars. Thomas Carew, grandson of the Lord Deputy, was likewise famed for his military prowess, and took part in the victory of Agincourt, when he kept the passage of the Somme. Several of the family came to untimely ends. Sir Edmund Carew, who was knighted on Bosworth Field, was killed in France in 1513; and three of his grandsons fell in kindred ways. Sir John Carew, soldier and sailor, was blown up in his vessel, the *Mary Rose*, while engaging a French carrack. Philip Carew, Knight of Malta, was slain by the Turks. Sir Peter Carew was killed in Ireland. The last of the Carews of Mohuns Ottery was Sir Peter, uncle of the last mentioned, and he settled the manor on Thomas Southcott, who had married his niece. Sir George Carew, Master of the Ordnance to Elizabeth, created Earl of Totnes in 1626, was a younger son of this house, now represented by the Carews of Haccombe.

CHAPTER VII.

OTTERY ST. MARY.

THE earliest feature in the history of Ottery is ecclesiastical. Undistinguished then from other Otreis that took name from the river along which they lay, it was granted by the Confessor, in 1061, to the Abbey of St. Mary at Rouen, and thus acquired an association which in later times gave it the title of St. Mary Ottery, or Ottery St. Mary. 'Domesday' records it the wealthiest manor in the district. Taxed at 25 hides in the time of the Confessor, there were 46 carucates in 1086. Moreover it had 17 serfs, 55 villeins, 24 bordars, and 5 swineherds, by way of population. There were three mills, and a saltwork at Sidmouth, in the land of St. Michael; and the latter fact will help to explain the association of saltworks with Honiton.

Bishop Grandisson, however, is the real founder of Ottery, as we have it now. He seems to have had differences with the monks of Rouen, finally settled by his purchase of the manor from them in 1335. Two years later he founded the College at Ottery, dedicated to Our Lady and St. Edward the Confessor, of which the noble church is now almost the only structural relic. This College, which he endowed most liberally, consisted of forty members with a warden, and one of its earliest prebendaries was that Alexander Barclay to whom we owe the English 'Ship of Foolis.'

Ottery has the finest parish church in Devon, remarkable in its transeptal arrangements as being a reduced copy of Exeter Cathedral. Local tradition will have it that the cathedral is the copy, an assertion which a glance at the two buildings is sufficient to controvert. The church was originally built by Bishop Bronescombe, possibly on the site of an older edifice of which no traces remain, but was largely added to and in part rebuilt by Grandisson, who erected therein some family monuments. To the Early English work of Bronescombe, and the Decorated of Grandisson, the Perpendicular Dorset aisle was added by Cicely, daughter and heiress of Lord Bonvile (lord of the manor of Knighteston in Ottery parish), who married, first, the Marquis of Dorset, and, secondly, the Earl of Stafford. The farmhouse of Bishops Court takes its name as being reputedly a residence of Bishop Grandisson.

When the College was dissolved a corporation was created, to whom Henry VIII. granted the church and its appurtenances, with the collegiate buildings, tithes, and other properties (saving the tithe of corn), the duty of the corporation being to pay certain annuities to the vicar and schoolmaster, and to maintain the church and school; the latter apparently a free grammar school, which took the place of the ancient school of the College.

It is to this fact that Ottery owes its most famous personal associations, for it was while his father, the Rev. John Coleridge, was both vicar of Ottery and master of the school that Devon's foremost poet, Samuel Taylor Coleridge, was born here in 1772 (d. 1834). Since then the names of Coleridge and of Ottery have been inseparably associated; and the fame won by the author of 'Christabel' and the 'Rime of the Ancient Mariner' has been continued in succeeding generations of his family. Among the Coleridge memorials in Ottery churchyard is a magnificent granite cross of Irish character, erected in

1877, to commemorate the late Sir John Taylor Coleridge (b. Tiverton, 1790), Judge of the Queen's Bench, and editor of the *Quarterly Review* between the death of Gifford and the appointment of Lockhart in 1826. Sir John's son, the present Lord Coleridge, Lord Chief Justice of England, now resides at the family seat of Heath's Court.

Several notable Devonians were educated at Ottery grammar school. Two of the most distinguished, beyond the various members of the Coleridge family, were the martyred Bishop Pattison—whose life and labours are commemorated by the nave pulpit in Exeter Cathedral—and Richard Hurrell Froude. Henry VIII. appears to have contemplated that it should become a chief educational centre for the county; but that expectation has never been approached; and, until revived by a new scheme in 1883, it had dwindled into utter decay.

Ottery St. Mary has a very unimportant place in general history, though from its position on the main road into the county it was frequently visited by distinguished folk. The Parliamentary troops were quartered in the church for five weeks in 1645, when the pestilence began to rage, and they moved.

Thatch has caused Ottery several visitations of fire. The last was in 1866, when 111 houses were burned, and 500 persons rendered homeless.

CHAPTER VIII.

CULLOMPTON AND BRADNINCH.

THE valley of the Culme contains some of the earliest settlements of the Saxons in Devon; and seems to have formed the chief road by which the encroaching Wessex immigrants pressed on from Somerset after Devon had been reduced to Saxon sway. Even yet it retains a few distinctive characteristics.

Cullompton is the chief town in the valley. As a part of the royal demesne, the manor was bequeathed by Ælfred to his son Æðelweard; and in Saxon times there was founded here a collegiate church with five prebends, which the Conqueror gave to the Abbey of Battle; but which afterwards passed to the Priory of St. Nicholas in Exeter, and so continued until the Dissolution. The manor, granted by Richard I. to Richard de Clifford, afterwards came to the Redvers Earls of Devon, and the first grant of a market was made in 1278 to Earl Baldwin. Being one of the manors given by Isabella de Fortibus to the Abbey of Buckland, a further grant of market and fair was made to that fraternity in 1317. After the Dissolution, the manor was for some time in the St. Legers and Hillersdens, whose ancient seat of Hillersdon is in the parish.

Cullompton was one of the homes of the woollen trade, and to this fact the church owes its most notable feature.

The Lane Chapel, erected by John Lane in the early part of the sixteenth century, is one of the best Devonshire examples of florid Perpendicular. An inscription runs round the exterior of the aisle, which used mightily to puzzle the learned, seeing that it was supposed to confer on Lane the novel dignity of ' wapentaki custos lanuarius,' when all the while he only asked to be remembered ' with a paternoster and an ave.'

Uffculme, adjoining Cullompton on the north-east, appears to have had a more considerable trade in serges than either of the smaller towns in the vicinity; and had the grant of a market so far back as 1266. Advantage was taken of the river to erect machinery, driven by water-power; and the result was that about the middle of the last century the place flourished mightily. But decay followed close upon. The manor was part of the barony of Bampton. Bradfield House in this parish, though the manor chiefly lies in Cullompton, has been the seat of the Walronds since the reign of Henry III., when they succeeded a family of the Bradfield name. The house is one of the most interesting sixteenth-century mansions in the county, and the hall still retains its original roof and characteristics.

If the defensible element in the name have any special meaning, Culmstock, another ancient market-town and seat of the woollen manufacture, may be the oldest of the Saxon settlements on the Culm; but, beyond the statement that it was given by Æðelstan to his minster in Exeter in 938, it calls for no further remark.

The last of the Culme Valley villages in this direction is Hemyock, concerning which there must be much more to be known than has been learnt. The Hidons built a castle here, of which there are yet important remains, including the main gateway and its towers, and part of the general cincture. It is an edifice of great strength, and of some peculiar characteristics—Early Edwardian in general character; but of its history absolutely nothing seems to be known, save that it was garrisoned by the Roundheads, and used by them as a prison. The manor was long in the Dinhams.

The Abbey of Dunkeswell, sheltered among the neighbouring hills, was founded in 1201 by William Lord Briwere. Two years previously, he had acquired the manor of Dunkeswell, and this formed part of the endowment of the Abbey, with Briwere's lands in Wolford and at Uffculme. Dunkeswell was colonized by monks from Ford, and the convent of that place was liberal of its gifts to the daughter house. There were also other donors, so that the Abbey had a very fair start in life. Dunkeswell was chosen by the founder as his burial-place in 1227, and it is presumed that his wife was also buried there. Not long since, two stone coffins were found within the ruins of the Abbey Church, one containing the bones of a man, and the other those of a woman; and these are believed to have been the remains of Lord and Lady Briwere. All the bones were placed in one of the coffins, and reinterred. The annual value of the Abbey lands at the surrender was just £300. The history of this house was uneventful, and only a few fragments of the building remain.

Bradninch, south of Cullompton, is one of the oldest towns in Devon, so far as record goes; and in the later Saxon days must have been the most important centre from the source of the Culme to its junction with the Exe. Held by Brichtwold under the Confessor, and part of the demesne of William Chievre under the Conqueror, 'Domesday' enumerates thereon no less than 7 serfs, 42 villeins, and 16 bordars. Moreover, it had a mill, and its annual value was £14. Perhaps this importance was the reason which led to its being attached as an honour or barony to the earldom of Cornwall, in favour of his natural son Reginald, by Henry I. Appendant to the earldom when that merged into the dukedom, since then it has formed part of the duchy estates. The seal of the town bears the date 1136, which may be intended to indicate the year when it came into possession of Earl Reginald. It does not seem to have been chartered until 1208, when King John granted the burgesses all the liberties and free customs which the city of Exeter enjoyed. Under Edward II. members were returned to one Parliament. The town was first incorporated as a municipality by James I. in 1604; and the Mayor of Exeter, according to 'Bradneys lore,' has to hold the stirrup of the Mayor of Bradninch whenever the two dignitaries meet. Beyond being the headquarters of Charles in 1644, and of Fairfax in 1645, and being almost consumed by fire in 1665, there are no points in the long history of Bradninch worthy of special record.

Hele, now chiefly known for its paper-mills, was the original seat of the elder branch of the ancient Devonshire family of that name.

The church of the adjoining parish of Plymtree contains a screen, which has been described in a valuable volume by the late rector, the Rev. T. Mozley. The chief feature is a fine array of painted panels. One of the groups figured represents the Adoration of the Three Kings, and in this Mr. Mozley identifies the portraits of Henry VII., Prince Arthur, and Cardinal Morton, 'the most remarkable Englishman of his period,' of whom there is no likeness extant if this be not one.

Silverton Park, in the parish of Silverton (which once boasted a weekly market), is one of the seats of the family of Egremont. Among the portraits here is that which Reynolds painted of himself for the Corporation of Plympton, and which they sold for £150 when that borough was disfranchised.

CHAPTER IX.

TIVERTON.

TIVERTON is a very old town, taking name from its position at the junction of the rivers Exe and Loman, formerly the Suning. Tradition avers that in the reign of King Ælfred it was a village on a little hill, the capital of its hundred, and having twelve tithings, and governed by a portreeve. Legend also claims it as one of the places in which the Danes were massacred by order of Æðelred. Be all this as it may (or may not), it is pretty clear that a church was erected on the site of the present St. Peter soon after the Norman Conquest, and this is said to have been consecrated by Leofric in 1073. But this would not be the first place of worship Tiverton could boast, and possibly we have here a British ecclesiastical foundation—as certainly a Saxon. Before the Conquest Tiverton formed part of the royal demesne, with the hundred of which it was the head, Gytha holding it in the reign of Harold; and it was a place of such importance at the compilation of 'Domesday,' that it had an enumerated population of 68, while several of the adjacent manors seem to have been populous likewise.

In the reign of Henry I. the manor passed to the family of Redvers, and Richard de Redvers, about the year 1106, built the castle, which continued one of the principal seats of that powerful family for several generations. At the death of Baldwin de Redvers in 1245, his widow, Amicia, claimed the manor and lordship of Tiverton as part of her dower. It had then a weekly market and three fairs annually. Her daughter, Isabella de Fortibus, was a great benefactor to the town, giving an estate called Elmore for the pasturage of the cattle of the poor inhabitants; and being, it is said, the donor of the Town Leat, a stream of water conducted some five miles for the use of the townsfolk. The last of the family of Redvers that held the manor was Isabella's daughter Avelina, who married Edmund, Earl of Lancaster, second son of Henry III.; and Tiverton then passed to Hugh Courtenay, the first Earl of Devon of the Courtenay line. By the Courtenays Tiverton was held, with an interval under the Yorkist rule, when the Duke of Clarence was one of the lords and Sir Richard Ratcliffe another, until the attainder of the Marquis of Exeter.

Mary restored it to Edward Courtenay; but on his death it passed, with other estates of the house, into other families by the marriages of his coheiresses; and the Carews of Haccombe have been the dominant owners, in succession to the family of West, since 1759. The manor at one time was subdivided into forty parts, but nearly all became concentrated in the Carews.

The Courtenays were good lords to the town. The first earl, Hugh, divided the rectory into four portions. Westcote amusingly says that this arose from the greed of a chaplain who was not satisfied with the living as it stood, and complained to his patron. The earl told him that he would give him a living more proportionate to his deserts, if he would resign this. The chaplain resigning accordingly, the living was divided, and the fourth only offered to the late incumbent—' thereby fayrely taught to lyve by a crown that would not lyve by a pound.' Earl Hugh the first also gave the tolls of Tiverton market to the poor. His son obtained the name of 'the good earl,' and the inscription on his stately tomb in Tiverton church ran:

> 'Hoe hoe, who lyes here?
> 'Tis I, the goode Erle of Devonshere,
> With Kate my wyfe, to mee full dere;
> That wee spent wee hadde,
> That wee gave wee have,
> That wee lefte wee loste.'

Tiverton Castle has borne its share in the history of Devon, though not so prominently as its importance would suggest. It had part in the wars of Stephen, and was of some little note in those of the Roses, as a Lancastrian, and afterwards as a Yorkist stronghold. In after years it was the place where the Courtenays lived in their greatest splendour. It stood a siege, moreover, in the wars of the Commonwealth. Tiverton town leant strongly to the Parliament; but the castle was garrisoned for the King, the church being also occupied as an important outpost. In October, 1645, General Massey was detached by Fairfax to besiege the works, which were then under the command of Sir Gilbert Talbot. After battering awhile, the castle and church were taken by storm on Sunday the 19th, with much slaughter. The castle is now one of the residences of the Carews, and portions of Edwardian date still stand.

No town in Devon was at one time more actively engaged in the woollen manufacture than Tiverton, the city of Exeter hardly excepted. The trade seems to have begun so far back as the fourteenth century; and in the sixteenth it brought great wealth to those engaged in it. This prosperity continued with fluctuations until the latter half of the last century. Then decay set in, helped by quarrels between the employers and the workmen, which developed at times into serious riots. Tiverton is a manufacturing town of importance still, in consequence of the establishment of a flourishing lace factory there by Mr. Heathcoat just sixty years ago. He introduced the manufacture of lace net by machinery, and thus completely revolutionized this branch of trade. His patent was taken out in 1810, but the factory at Tiverton was not founded until 1816, when difficulties with his workpeople induced him to leave his former residence and settle in Devon.

Several of the old clothiers of Tiverton made good use of their wealth, notably Peter Blundell, by whose munificence Blundell's school, the chief of the public schools of Devon, was founded in 1604. Blundell was born in 1523, of parents who were so poor that he had to run errands and otherwise wait upon the carriers for his support. Saving a little money, he commenced business by sending a piece of cloth to London on sale by one of his friends and employers. Gradually he accumulated enough to go to London on his own account, and finally he began the manufacture of kerseys. Dying unmarried, he left the whole of a large fortune for the promotion of learning and various charitable purposes. His school was well endowed, and has acquired and maintains a very high reputation; and the old buildings have not long been abandoned for new and more commodious premises in a better situation. Among earlier benefactors to the town, connected with the same industry, was John Greenwaye, who erected the Greenwaye chapel and a set of almshouses, about the year 1517, the chapel being the most elaborate and notable portion of the Church of St. Peter. With John Greenwaye was associated his wife Joan. And so another set of almshouses were built by 'John Waldron and Richoard his wyfe,' in 1579. No town in Devon, and certainly very few in the kingdom in proportion to their size, had so many charitable bequests and gifts, and of such value, as Tiverton; but they had sadly depreciated when a century since worthy Martin Dunsford compiled the first account of them, and dedicated his 'Memoirs' of the town 'to all the virtuous and industrious poor of Tiverton.'

Tiverton has been noted, too, for the number and ravages of its fires. The first recorded was in April, 1598, when, in the course of an hour and a half, 400 houses and several public buildings were burnt, and £150,000 worth of property destroyed, while 33 persons lost their lives. This was a severe blow to the town, which only eight years previously had lost one in every nine of its population by the plague. But still worse was in store, for in August, 1612, the whole of the town was burnt, with the exception of the castle, church, school, and almshouses, and about thirty poor dwellings. Six hundred houses were then destroyed, and the total loss was estimated at £200,000.

It is stated to have been partially the result of this that a charter of incorporation was granted by James I. in 1615. From that date to 1885 Tiverton was a Parliamentary constituency; but there is a statement that a couple of burgesses had been previously returned to the first Parliament of James I. by the 'potwallopers.'

The next big fire was in November, 1661, when 45 houses were burnt; another in 1730 destroyed 15 dwellings, with loss of life; and in June, 1731, there was one of the older type—298 dwellings being consumed, and 2,000 persons rendered homeless. Towards the loss of £60,000 there were £11,000 contributed, the King giving £1,000. Twenty houses were burnt in 1762, 25 in 1773, 47 in 1785, 20 in 1788.

Blundell is the most notable of the worthies of Tiverton; but there is an old proverb which may refer to a real personage of even greater importance in his own day: 'Go to Tiverton and ask Mr. Able.' Hannah Cowley, the dramatist, born Parkhouse (1742-1809), was a native of Tiverton; and the town has produced several artists of high repute. Richard Cosway, R.A., a miniature painter of the greatest merit, who died in 1821, was the son of a master of Blundell's school; John Cross, historical painter (1819-1861), was son of the superintendent of the lace factory; Richard Crosse, though born at Knowle, near Cullompton, painter in enamel to George III. (1745-1810), a deaf mute, may also be named here. And Tiverton may finally claim, as a worthy by adoption, the late Lord Palmerston, seeing that he sat for this quiet little borough from 1835 until his death, the pride of both political parties.

A battle was fought at Cranmore Castle, near Collipriest, adjoining Tiverton, in 1549, in which a party of the insurgents who rose for the restoration of Roman Catholicism were defeated, and several hung and quartered.

There are several places of historical interest in the vicinity of Tiverton. Worth, in Washfield, is one of the three places in Devon which still remain the possession and residence of families of the same name, the Worths having been seated there since the thirteenth century. The other examples are Fulford of Fulford and Kelly of Kelly, of which more anon. The Exe Bickleigh was the birthplace of the notorious Bampfylde Moore Carew (1690-1758), 'the king of the beggars,' whose father, Theodore Carew, was sometime rector. Not far distant, on opposite sides of the Exe Valley, rise the rival heights of Cadbury and Dolbury, crowned by ancient earthworks, of which the rhyme runs, evidently archaic:

> 'If Cadbury Castle and Dolbury Hill dolven were
> Then Devon might plough with a golden coulter
> And eare with a gilded shere'—

so vast is the treasure that lies therein hidden under charge of a fiery dragon! Fairfax made Cadbury his rendezvous, December 26th, 1645.

Halberton church was given by William Earl of Gloucester to the Abbey of St. Augustine; and, with the manor of Halberton Abbot, or Halberton Dean, passed to the Dean and Chapter of Bristol. The adjacent village of Sampford Peverell, described in old records as a borough, had a somewhat considerable woollen manufacture. Named from its ancient lords, the Peverells, it was some time in the Dinhams and the Paulets. One of its owners was Margaret, Countess of Richmond, mother of Henry VII., who is said to have lived here, and built the south aisle of the church, which contains the defaced effigy of a crusader, supposed to be Sir Hugh Peverell, 1259.

CHAPTER X.

BAMPTON.

BAMPTON affords a notable instance of decadence. A very poor little market-town now, it was once the head of an honour held of the Conqueror by Walter de Douay. Previously it had formed part of the royal demesne. 'Domesday' records a population of 68, including 15 swineherds, rendering 106½ pigs, whose presence indicates the existence of extensive woods, set down as 320 acres. A hide adjacent to the manor had been held by five thanes, and here Walter had three tenants, with eight serfs, bordars, and villeins; while half a furlong was held by William de Moion, unjustly to the said Walter. There was also a mill; and the value of all Bampton was £18, but had been £21.

A chalybeate spring here led Polwhele to call Bampton a Roman station: his etymology for the river Batham, on which it stands, being *Bath-thermæ*—hot baths! But the Batham was originally no doubt the Baeth, and the town Baeth-ham-tun, unless the *ham* be, as Dr. Pring has suggested in 'hampton' suffixes, a corruption of the Keltic *avon*, through *aw* or *aun*. It has been claimed as the Beamdune where Kynegils defeated the Britons in 614; but that was Bampton in Oxfordshire.

Walter de Douay's son, Robert de Bampton, had an only daughter, who brought the manor to the Paganells;

and thence again it passed to the Cogans by the marriage of the Paganell heiress to Sir Milo Cogan, 'the great soldier and undertaker of the Irish Conquest.' Her descendant, Richard Cogan, had licence in 1336 to castellate his mansion house at Bampton, and to empark his wood and other lands at Uffculme. Every vestige of the castle has long disappeared. The Fitzwarrens, Hankfords, and Bourchiers were successively lords of the manor, and it was afterwards purchased by the ancestor of the present Earl of Portsmouth.

John de Bampton, the Aristotelian Carmelite (d. 1391) was born at Bampton. In the following century the church was made the subject of a singular exchange. It had belonged to the Prior of Bath; but was given, under an Act of Parliament in 1439, to the Abbot of Buckland, in compensation for surrendering his jurisdiction in Plymouth, as lord of the hundred of Roborough, the burgesses paying the Prior of Bath in his turn 10 marks annually.

The adjacent parish of Morebath (and the name affords additional evidence of the original name of the river) was once the property of the Abbey of Barlynch, of which a few traces yet remain within a short distance of Dulverton, in Somerset. Clayhanger claims notice as having been the property of the Knights Templars, who, according to Tanner, had a hospital there. The Knights Hospitallers are subsequently said to have held the church.

Wadham in Knowstone parish, the original residence of the Wadhams, is one of the few Devon manors noticed in 'Domesday,' as continuing in the same Saxon hands from the reign of the Confessor, and the Lysonses suggest it as not improbable that the holder, Ulf, may have been the ancestor of the Wadham family. There is at any rate nothing to militate against this hypothesis. Knowstone gave Devon a worthy in Sir John Berry, an eminent naval officer, and sometime Governor of Deal (1635-1691), born here while his father was vicar. He was of a younger branch of the Berrys of Berry Narber. His father, through adherence to Charles I., died in great poverty, and the son was at first apprenticed to a tradesman at Plymouth. His master failing, he walked to London, and obtained employment in a small vessel. By dint of ability and pluck, he speedily rose to the rank of captain in the navy. He served with the greatest distinction and success against both French and Dutch, and at length reached the highest honours of his profession, valued alike by the second Charles and James, and by William.

At Canonleigh, in Burlescombe, not far from the Somersetshire border, are the remains of a monastery, originally founded by Walter Claville, temp. Henry II., for a prior and Austin canons. Maud de Clare, Countess of Gloucester, converted it, however, in the reign of Edward I. into a nunnery for an abbess and canonesses of the same order. At the Dissolution, the house had a clear yearly rental of £197 3s. 1d. A market had been granted to it in 1286. The lands by exchange became the property of Sir George St. Leger. In Burlescombe parish is Ayshford, the seat of one of the oldest families of this part of Devon, now represented on the female side by the Ayshford Sandfords, of Nynehead.

Holcombe Rogus takes name from Rogo, its tenant under Baldwin the Sheriff, from whom it descended, through Chiseldon (Richard Chiseldon obtained a market in 1343), to the Bluetts. Colonel Francis Bluett, an active Cavalier, was killed at the siege of Lyme in 1644. Spurway, in Okeford, was the original seat of the family of that name.

CHAPTER XI.

SOUTH MOLTON.

SOUTH MOLTON is the principal centre in a district skirting the southern flank of Exmoor, which is singularly barren in features of historical interest. Probably the Melarnoni of the Ravennat; an ancient market-town of considerable importance; largely engaged in the serge and shalloon manufacture; represented in Parliament in the reign of Edward I.; incorporated by Elizabeth in 1640—never but once did it forsake the even tenor of its business way. And then it was rather by accident than design that John Penruddock and Hugh Grove here proclaimed Charles II. in 1655, and formally commenced a rising which, so far as they were concerned, never got further than words, but led to their execution at Exeter on the 16th of May following. Penruddock and Grove were Wiltshire Royalists, and with their followers were taken prisoners by a party of soldiers under Captain Crook.

The most interesting facts about South Molton are connected with the families of whose estates it formed part. Originally ancient demesne of the Crown (one virgate was held of the King by four priests in alms at the compilation of 'Domesday'), in the reign of Edward I it was held by Lord Martin, under the Earl of Gloucester, by the service of finding a bow with three arrows to attend the Earl when he should hunt in Gower. It was afterwards held by the Audleys, by the Hollands, and was granted for life to Margaret, Duchess of Richmond, in 1487. Other manors in the parish now belong to Earl Fortescue and Sir T. D. Acland.

The adjoining parish of North Molton is a mineral district, and has yielded small quantities of gold. The manor was part of the portion of Eadgytha, wife of the Confessor, and was given by John to Roger le Zouch. From the Zouches it passed to the St. Maurs, then to the Bampfyldes, and is now the property of Lord Poltimore. The church was given by Alan le Zouch, circa 1313, to the monastery of Lilleshull, in Shropshire. North Molton is also the ancient dwelling of the Parkers, now Earls of Morley; and the Lysonses suggest that before the Reformation they were tenants of this house. A holy well here still retains some reputation, Holy Thursday being the special day of visitation; and at Flitton is one of the most famous oaks in Devon, 33 feet in circumference close to the ground. Here, too, is the chief home of the leading strain of the famous native Devon cattle; while the rugged expanse of Exmoor adjoining is still tenanted by herds of the wild red-deer.

Molland, or Molland Bottreaux, had a dominant position in the hundreds of North Molton, Braunton, and Bampton, taking their third penny, and having the right to a third of the pasture of animals on the adjacent moors. Before the Conquest it belonged to Harold, and it passed to William. Shortly after the Conquest it came to the Bottreauxs, whence its second name, and continued in that ancient house until the reign of Henry VI. The church was given by William de Bottreaux to Hartland Abbey. The Bishop of Cloyne regarded Molland as a British town, and it certainly does lie upon an ancient trackway; but that it was the Roman station Termolus of Richard of Cirencester, which the

Bishop had 'no hesitation' in fixing, is an assertion that in the present day hardly needs to be controverted. Even if the authority were accepted, there is no trace whatever of the Roman in the neighbourhood.

Romansleigh, indeed, lying some miles to the southwest, has, on the strength of its name, been held to support the hypothesis of Roman occupation. It is really, however, Rumonsleigh, from St. Rumon, the patron saint of Tavistock Abbey, which had an estate here.

In Filleigh is Castle Hill, the seat of Earl Fortescue, the representative of this most ancient and distinguished family, whose surname, as in their motto, *Forte scutum, salus ducum,* is said to signify a 'strong shield.' The common ancestor was settled at Wimpston or Wymondeston in Modbury, which, according to the family tradition, was given to Richard le Forte, shield-bearer to the Conqueror, for his good services at Hastings. 'Domesday' disposes of this by showing that Wimpston (Winestane) was held by Reginald de Valletort under the Earl of Moreton. John Fortescue was, however, settled at Wimpston in 1209; and the elder branch continued to live there until early in the seventeenth century. The family branched out from Wimpston to Preston, Spriddleston, Shipham, Wood, Fallapit, Wear Giffard, Filleigh, and Buckland Filleigh in Devon, and settled also in Cornwall, Hertford, Essex, Buckingham, and Ireland.

Of its many distinguished members the most celebrated is Sir John Fortescue, Lord Chief Justice (1442) and Chancellor to Henry VI., who was born at Noreis in North Huish, and was author of the great work on jurisprudence—' De Laudibus Legum Angliæ.' From him descends the present Earl Fortescue. Other notable Fortescues are Sir John, Captain of Meux in France, temp. Henry V.; Sir Henry, Lord Chief Justice of Ireland;

Sir Adrian, who did service at Calais for Henry VII.; Sir Edmund, of Fallapit, High Sheriff for Charles I. and Governor of the Castle of Salcombe; Sir Faithful, who also rendered good service to Charles, whom he joined at Edgehill. The public services of the late Earl Fortescue are commemorated by a statue in the Castle Yard, Exeter.

The Fortescues obtained the manors both of Filleigh and of Wear Giffard by the marriage of Martin Fortescue, son of the Chief Justice, with the heiress of Densell, who represented the Giffards in the female line. Wear then became the chief seat of this branch of the Fortescues, and so continued for a considerable time. Castle Hill has, however, long been their residence, and in the early part of the last century was greatly improved and enlarged.

In the adjacent parish of West Buckland is the Devon County School, one of the earliest, if not the earliest, effort to provide good middle-class education upon modern lines for rural districts.

Swymbridge, according to Risdon, is the birthplace of St. Hieritha, a contemporary of Thomas à Becket.

CHAPTER XII.

CREDITON.

IT is in the year 909, and at Crediton, that the ecclesiastical history of Devon on the present order begins. Seven centuries before that date Christianity had reached these shores; and the existence of an organized Church among the Kelts can be traced very nearly thus far back. The British Church held its own in Devon down to the Saxon settlement of the county under Ecgberht; and retained the chief power in the further West, although in later years pressed hard by the Roman invaders, as the adherents of the elder system deemed them, until the approach of the tenth century. But its influence gradually waned, and in 909 the ecclesiastical order of Wessex was made complete by the consecration in one day of seven bishops. Of these Eadulph was one; and he became the first Saxon Bishop of Devon, with a partial rule in Cornwall, having assigned to him the manors of Pawton, Callington, and Lawhitton, that he might thrice yearly visit 'the Cornish race to extirpate their errors.' The fact that these three places are all in the east and north of Cornwall probably indicates a greater Saxon influence in that district of the county.

It has been shown that Crediton offered peculiar advantages for the establishment of the bishop's seat, which probably led to its selection in preference to the chief town of the shire—in the facts that it was 'central, not too large, free from secular interference; the *ton*, the place of the Saxon—hallowed by its associations with the great missionary, the earnest and devoted Wynfrid.' These considerations must have had their weight in the selection of a place of perhaps a couple of hundred inhabitants for this purpose (the enumerated population in 'Domesday' is but 407). It is further probable, however, that personal considerations, which it is now impossible to trace, had some influence in the choice.

The original Cathedral of Crediton was dedicated to the Virgin, and stood on or near the site of the present Collegiate Church of the Holy Cross. Leland, who says that the dedication was to St. Gregory, states that the old church stood by the side of its successor; but of this there is no distinct evidence. Nine bishops in succession ruled at Crediton, or Cridiantune, its Saxon name. Under the last but one, Lyfing, the Bishopric of Cornwall was united to that of Devon; and under his successor, Leofric, the seat of the see was transferred to Exeter, one of the chief reasons assigned being the defenceless state of the little 'tun' of the Creedy against the pirates, or Danes. The removal of the see was followed by what in effect became a removal of the minster—the Saxon Cathedral of St. Mary was replaced by the Norman Collegiate 'Church of the Holy Cross, and of the Mother of Him crucified thereon,' with its eight canons and eighteen vicars. Herein it is recorded that on the 1st of August, 1315, one Thomas Orey, of Keynesham, who had been totally blind, recovered his sight after spending two days in prayer before the altar of St. Nicholas. Bishop Stapledon, being satisfied of the truth of the miracle, ordered the bells to be rung and a solemn thanksgiving offered, and set forth the event in his 'Register.' The church is now in the hands of a corporation of governors.

In the time of the Confessor Crediton was the most

valuable manor belonging to the see, with the exception of Bishops Tawton; but when 'Domesday' was compiled it had a long way distanced all its competitors, the value having risen from twenty-one pounds to seventy-five. Originally taxed at 25 hides, it had 185 carucates. Six hides and 13 carucates were in demesne; there were 40 serfs, 264 villeins, and 73 bordars, with 172 carucates; and 30 swineherds, returning 150 swine yearly. There was a mill also, worth thirty pence. The woods, as may be judged from the number of swineherds, were very extensive—five miles long and half a mile broad.

The manor of Crediton, with a brief alienation, continued to belong to the See of Exeter, and the bishops retained there a residence and park. The palace is now represented simply by a buttress, and the park indicated by the name of the 'Lord's Meadow.' Under its episcopal lords the little town seems to have flourished; and the cloth trade, by which it mainly throve, is supposed to have been established under Bishop Grandisson. Crediton gained great fame for the fineness of its work, so that 'As fine as Kirton spinning' passed into a proverb, and Westcote avers that one of the sights of London, at the shop of 'Mr. Dunscombe, the Golden Bottle, in Watling Street,' was 140 threads of woollen yarn spun in Crediton, drawn through the eye of a tailor's needle.

There is ample proof, indeed, that Crediton was a place of considerable trading note so far back as the thirteenth century. Among documents relating to Crediton, entered upon a roll in the British Museum, is a letter of procuration from the Archdeacon of Totnes in 1249, stating that he will be unable to attend a meeting of the Chapter of Crediton and take part in 'treating and contracting with the merchants who frequent our church,' and appointing his brother Archdeacons of Exeter and Cornwall his proctors. The suggestion is that these merchants were 'contractors for the wool grown upon the estates belonging to the canons of Crediton, and that at this meeting the prices were fixed and the contracts settled.' This shows the importance of Crediton as a mart of the woollen trade six centuries since. There were several foreigners living in or near the town at this time—the Peytevin family, who were succeeded by the Widgers, 'Lord' Seer, a Knight of the Teutonic Order, one Richard Marchpain, and others.

Crediton was once a borough, and sent representatives to Parliament temp. Edward I. The old seal is still extant, dated in 1469: 'THE SELLE OF THE BOROWE TOWNE OF CREDYTON.' The device is a bishop in benediction, probably intended for Bishop Bothe, lord of the manor of Crediton at the date given. The association of Crediton with the Western Rebellion, which began at Sampford Courtenay, when 'The barns of Crediton' became a rallying-cry, has been treated under Exeter.

The earliest worthy of Crediton is also the earliest Devonian known to us by name—Wynfrid, St. Boniface, the Apostle of Germany. Born of Saxon parents at Crediton in 680, converted to the Roman form of Christianity—probably by travelling monks—first trained in a Saxon school at Exeter, and then at Nutschelle in Hampshire, he devoted all his working life to the conversion of Germany, and its reduction under the Roman rule. Eventually he became Archbishop of Mentz, and the spiritual head of the whole German kingdom, and was martyred in old age (75), when attempting to convert the still heathen portion of Friesland. No one of his day did more to spread Christianity among the heathen, or to destroy the influence of the elder British Church.

Crediton was occasionally occupied by both parties during the last Civil War, but saw no fighting. It was the headquarters of Prince Maurice for a time, in 1644; and in July of that year Charles was at Crediton, and reviewed his troops. Fairfax made it his headquarters more than once early in 1646.

The town had its 'great fire' in 1743, when 460 houses were burnt; and there was another serious one in 1769.

Several of the estates in and about Crediton are or have been connected with ancient families of the county. Downes, which once belonged to the Goulds, is now the property of the Bullers; Creedy of the Davies. Yewe, in the tithing of Yewton, is said to have been formerly held under the bishops by the barons of Okehampton, by the service of being stewards at their installation, for which they had all the vessels in which the bishop was served at the first course. This right was, however, claimed at the installation of Bishop Stapledon by Hugh Courtenay, as lord of the manor of Slapton, his fee being four silver dishes, two salts, one cup, one wine-pot, one spoon, and two basins. Higher Dunscombe was the seat of the Bodleys.

Shobrooke, now in the Shelleys, was long in the Ercedeknes, whose heiress brought it to Carew. Little Fulford was the seat of the Peryams, established there by Sir William Peryam, Lord Chief Baron. Raddon, in the same parish—which, after giving name to the family of Raddon, was in the Martyns and Audleys—in the reign of Henry VIII. was partially acquired by the Westcotes. Here, in 1567, was born Thomas Westcote, the antiquary, and author of the 'View of Devonshire in 1630.' Of the parishes of Stockleigh, distinguished by the affixes Pomeroy and English, the names of their ancient owners, it has been mistakenly held that the latter title indicates a descent in Saxon hands. This idea, however, 'Domesday' at once dispels. At Upcotts, in Poughill, was the scene of the murder of the Yorkist Radford by the Lancastrian Thomas Courtenay, already noted.

Newton St. Cyres was part of the ancient endowment of

the original cathedral, the Church of the Holy Cross at Crediton, which held it before the reign of the Confessor; and it passed, with Crediton, to the See of Exeter. In later days it came to Plympton Priory; and, after the Dissolution, the manor was divided, for several generations, between the Quickes and Northcotes, the former acquiring the whole in 1762. Hayne is the old Northcote seat.

At the meeting-point of the three parishes of Crediton, Colebrook, and Down St. Mary, stands a massive granite shaft, known as Coplestone Cross. The head, if it ever had any, has long been lost; but the shaft is perfect—ten feet six inches in height, and one foot six and a half inches in breadth at the top. It is four-square, and each side is covered with carving, the special feature of which is that twisted and interlaced ornament, generally held to be of Keltic origin, comparatively common in the North of England, but which occurs nowhere else in Devon, and is but rarely met with in Cornwall. Each side of the cross contains three panels, no two exactly alike; while on one face figures are introduced. There is no doubt that this monument dates at least from the earlier period of Saxon Christianity, when it was customary for the lords of land where there were no churches, to erect crosses of wood or of stone, to which outlying ceorls or serfs might repair to offer their prayers. It may be as old as the Crediton bishopric (909), and possibly is older. But it is not much, if at all, later, for it finds mention in a Saxon charter of 974, by which Eadgar grants three hides of land at Nymed to his faithful Ælfhere. The boundaries of these three hides begin and end at Copelanstan, and they agree with the present estate of Coplestone, which is about 160 acres in extent.

From the Copelanstan these three hides afterwards took name, and they were granted, as an endorsement on the original charter certifies, by the venerable priest Brihtric to the minster of Crediton, some time before the Norman Conquest. At an unknown but very early period, however, the estate passed into the hands of one of the oldest of Devonshire families, who thence took name, and who proudly held themselves to be descended from an English ancestor who kept his lands through the Conquest, the ancient rhyme running:

> 'Crocker, Cruwys, and Coplestone,
> When the Conqueror came were found at home.'

These families fill a prominent place in Devonian history; but neither can be linked on to any of the English thegns who retained their estates. The Coplestones held chief place of the three, and were called the 'Great Coplestones,' and 'Coplestones of the White Spur,' having, according to Westcote, the special grant of a silver collar, or chain of SS., and of silver spurs. Coplestone, however, is no longer theirs; though the Coplestone aisle remains in Colebrook church.

The Crockers have long ceased out of Lyneham, their ancient seat near Yealmpton, but the Cruwys remain connected, through the female line, with their old estates in Cruwys Morchard, which they have certainly held since the reign of King John.

The origin of the name Copelanstan is doubtful; but very likely it is the 'headland' or 'the chief stone.'

CHAPTER XIII.

CHULMLEIGH.

CHULMLEIGH, an ancient market-town, once enjoying the reputation of a borough, was a member of the barony of Okehampton, and long held by the Courtenays, who had a castle here, of which no trace remains. Garland is supposed by Prince to have been the birthplace of John de Garland, a poet of the eleventh century, and it continued in the Garlands until the close of the seventeenth century. Chulmleigh Church was once collegiate, with seven prebends, originally distinct from the rectory. The manner in which Westcote accounts for this is an amusing version of an old myth which has many forms, and which is most familiar in its assignment to the Guelphs. A poor man of Chulmleigh was troubled at the rapid increase of his family, and went on his travels for seven years. A year after his return, however, his wife was 'delivered of seven male children at one byrth, whiche made the poore man think himself utterly undone; and, thereby despairing, put them into a baskett, and hasteth to the river with intent to drowne.' 'The lady of the land,' however, happening to come that way, demanded 'what he carryed in his basket, who replied that he had whelpes, which she desired to see, proposing to choose one of them.' Finding, however, that they were children, she insisted on an explanation; and, that given, sharply rebuked him for his inhumanity, had the children put to nurse, then to school, 'and consequently being come to man's estate, provided a prebendship for every of them in this parishe.'

There was a little fighting at Chulmleigh in the Civil Wars, Colonel Okey defeating a party of Cavaliers in December, 1645; and on the February following, Fairfax rendezvoused at Ashreigny hard by.

Eggesford, also a possession of the family of Reigny, like the parish last named, passed by female heirs to the Coplestones and Chichesters; and Lord Chichester rebuilt the manor-house in the reign of James I. This was one of the mansions garrisoned for the King in the subsequent reign, but it was captured by Colonel Okey in December, 1645. From the Chichesters the manor came to the St. Legers; and of them it was bought early in the last century by Mr. Fellowes, ancestor of the present owner, the Earl of Portsmouth. The house, which has been rebuilt and enlarged at various times, is now the principal residence of the family; and one of the most important hunting centres in Devon.

The large and important manor of Umberleigh, extending over the parishes of Atherington and High Bickington, has been held by some notable families—chief the Willingtons (to whom it came from the Champernownes) and the Bassets, its owners from the sixteenth century. A mutilated figure in Atherington Church, brought from the Chapel of the Holy Trinity at Umberleigh when it was pulled down in 1800, is supposed to represent the last Champernowne seated here, temp. Henry III. The screen-work in this church is very fine; and the church of the adjoining parish of Chittlehampton has the reputation of possessing the finest tower in Devon, which looks, indeed, as if it had been transplanted from Somerset. St. Hieritha, said to have been born at Swymbridge, is also said to have been buried here. More certain is it that the church contains fourteenth-century brasses to the Cobleigh family. They succeeded by marriage a younger branch of the Fitzwarrens, who had taken the name of Brightley from their estate; and this was brought by the heiress of the Cobleighs to a younger branch of the Giffards of Halsbury, who held it for several descents. Hence the title of Lord Halsbury, taken by Sir Hardinge Giffard on his recent elevation to the Lord Chancellorship. Umberleigh in 'Domesday' is entered as the 'manor of the Church of the Holy Trinity at Caen,' whence, of course, the dedication of the chapel.

An interesting group of parishes, etymologically and thence historically, lies to the south of Chulmleigh. Nymet Tracy, commonly called Bow, after a decayed town of that name, which once had a market, granted to Henry Tracy in 1258, and which was the scene of a skirmish between Sir Hardress Waller and some Royalist troops, wherein the former was successful; Nymet Rowland; and Broad Nymet, which, in spite of its name, is the pettiest of the three, the smallest rural parish in Devon. With these are to be associated George, Kings, and Bishops Nympton, occasionally called Nymet also, grouped but a few miles distant to the south and west of South Molton. 'Newtake' is an expression used on Dartmoor for an enclosure from the waste; and, as Mr. R. J. King has shown, these 'Nymets' are precisely the same in meaning and in fact, *nymet* being the participle of the verb *nyman*, to take. They mark, therefore, the sites of ancient enclosures, or appropriations, long before the Norman Conquest.

CHAPTER XIV.

BARNSTAPLE.

NORTH DEVON is so thickly seamed with a network of ancient roads, still in use or long abandoned, as to show that it had in pre-Norman times, to distinguish no further, a fairly large population, dotted in numerous settlements. These ancient trackways are, as a rule, circuitous, and have been deeply worn by the traffic of ages—such being the main characteristics of the proverbial Devonshire lanes. A century since, they were described as 'rough and rocky; watery and miry in some places, deep and founderous in others; the hills precipitous, and the lanes everywhere narrow, with the hedges on each side too high to afford the traveller any prospect.' Better kept now than then, they still retain their leading features; and these very hedge-banks, ranging even to 30 feet in height, which in the old days had some value in screening the traveller from the sun in summer, and sheltering him from the driving storm in winter, grow more beautiful year by year in their floral carpeting.

Mr. J. R. Chanter has further pointed out that 'near Bratton, and at several other points north and east of Barnstaple, especially in the mining districts of North Molton and Combe Martin, and the ports and creeks of the Severn Sea, the pedestrian may still trace many deeply sunken lanes—mere clefts, which it is impossible to imagine can have been formed otherwise than by long-continued attrition of the feet of men and cattle for ages; and yet now they are never used nor traversed, and form concealed nooks thickly covered with vegetation, and ferns, particularly the scolopodendria, growing in the utmost luxuriance; and others which, though still in use, bear unmistakable marks of extreme antiquity.'

These roads were traversed by a purely local **breed of horses** called pack-horses, which carried their **burdens in panniers**, or on rough saddles known as 'crocks.' They were a very useful handy race, unfortunately now lost, though occasionally a strain makes its appearance here and there. Tradition ascribed them to a cross of the native pony of Dartmoor and Exmoor with a horse that escaped from the wreck of a vessel of the Armada. The story is more than doubtful, but the race had a **dash of** the thoroughbred. There are yet living **those who** recollect when it was a common thing to meet **long strings** of pack-horses, the best of the lot proudly leading **the way.**

Now since Barnstaple, *alias* Barum, the capital of North Devon, lies at the very heart of the densest network of these ancient roads, its high antiquity is clear, though there are no authoritative records of its origin. The suggestion that it may be the lost Artavia of Richard of Cirencester might have more weight if the authenticity of his so-called 'Itinerary' could be proved; though even then Hartland puts in a claim on the score of similarity of name, and Clovelly Dikes as presenting the most important relics of an ancient town in the district. Mr. Chanter has ingeniously shown that Artavia is near akin to Aber-Taw, which would be very good Welsh for the site of Barnstaple; and there can be little doubt it is the Vertevia of the Ravennat.

The borough appears to have grown up around a military settlement. This tradition, with somewhat more than its usual uncertainty, attributes to the Danes. It must once have had considerable strength. The ancient town stood in a rude triangle, bounded on two sides by the Taw and by its tributary the Yeo. Near the apex was the castle; landward the town was defended by a strong wall, the course of which is defined by the present Boutport Street (='About-port' street, port being used in its old sense of town). Of this wall there are no vestiges; the gates one after another have disappeared; and of the castle there only remains the mound. Æðelstan, the traditional founder of the castle, did probably translate it from earthen rampart into mural fortress, and at the same time restore and extend the cincture. Be that as it may, 'Domesday' describes Barnstaple as one of the four boroughs of Devon, having forty burgesses within the walls and nine without, and eleven that belonged to the Bishop of Coutances. It was then held by the King, but became the seat of a barony, sometime in the Tracys, Martyns, Audleys, and Hollands, among others.

Its first Norman lord was Judhel of Totnes, who founded a Cluniac Priory, dedicated to St. Mary Magdalene, valued at the Dissolution at £129 15s. 8d. One of the most curious antiquarian discoveries of recent years in Devon has been the finding of the remains of the twelfth-century chapel of this Priory in the main walls of a couple of ancient but much modernized dwellings, so perfect as to enable its plan, which is somewhat peculiar —on the basilica type—to be distinctly traced. The Priory lands were granted to Lord Howard of Effingham, and part was eventually purchased by the Rolles, whose present representative, the Hon. Mark Rolle, is Lord High Steward of the borough. A chapel dedicated to Thomas à Becket, which stood at the end of the bridge, is said to have been founded in expiation during the Tracy rule by William de Tracy, who took part in that prelate's murder. Like most of the Tracy traditions, this is doubtful.

The bridge, by the way, is historical. It is some six or

seven centuries old, but nothing is known with certainty as to its founder. In the thirty-sixth year of Henry VIII. the 'maior and maisters' sent out a begging letter to obtain money to improve the structure and its causeways, setting forth that the Taw was a 'great hugy, mighty, perylous, and dreadfull water, whereas salte water doth ebbe and flowe foure tymes in the day and the night,' and offering 'a gentle dirge and masse solemly songe' to all benefactors. It is amusing to contrast this description with the actual river. Perhaps the stream has learnt manners since an embankment was thrown up on the western shore by one of the Sir Bourchier Wreys of Tawstock, towards the close of the last century. Being the colonel of an infantry regiment stationed at Barnstaple, he employed the men in raising these earthworks and improving his foreshores. The Corporation didn't like it, and complained to headquarters. The authorities wrote, asking what was meant; Sir Bourchier replied that he was teaching his men 'practical engineering.' And there the matter dropped, possibly because the gallant colonel was a member of Parliament as well as an officer. Barnstaple Bridge is in the hands of a body of trustees, who hold considerable property. Their antiquity is fairly indicated by their seal, which is of fourteenth-century character and nearly three inches in diameter. It shows the bridge, the Chapel of St. Thomas, and a Calvary Cross, and between the latter an eagle displayed. The inscription sets forth that this is the seal of the 'long bridge' of Barnstaple.

The corporate and representative history of Barnstaple is of almost unique interest, in the controversies to which it has given rise. The Corporation proper dates from Philip and Mary, but the town had sustained its prescriptive right to a mayor two centuries before. The earliest charter extant is by Henry II. confirming a predecessor from Henry I. The latter has disappeared, but in certain proceedings taken in the time of the third

Edward, the burgesses asserted that they had a charter from Æðelstan which had been lost, and which not only gave them a right to choose a mayor, but to send representatives to the Witenagemot. It may seem strange now that either statement should ever have been seriously treated. Reeves Barnstaple no doubt did have before the Conquest, but certainly not mayors, and probably few will be found now to endorse Lord Lyttelton's opinion that Barnstaple was a representative borough of pre-Norman times, or even share in Turner's more cautious reference to the claim, as being entitled to considerable weight in determining the question of the representation of cities and burghs in the Witenagemot. It is a fact, however, that 500 years ago Barnstaple did claim Æðelstan as the author of its representative rights; and the borough returned members without intermission from twenty-third Edward I. to fatal 1885.

Notable traces of an early guild at Barnstaple have been discovered among the municipal records by Mr. J. R. Chanter. They consist of three rolls setting forth the names of the officers and members respectively in 1303, 1318, and 1329, and a few ancient deeds and fragments of accounts. The guild was that of St. Nicholas, but it is also spoken of as ' the Guild of the Liberty of the Borough of Barnstaple;' and its customs are declared to have been used and observed beyond memory of man. Moreover, its connection with the government of the town was most intimate, and the mayor was evidently its chief. At the same time it was not the corporate authority, for its members were scattered over the county; and after it was dissolved in 1549, the municipality acquired ' the site of the late Chapel of St. Nicholas, now a building called the Kay Hall,' by purchase. The Kay Hall, destroyed in 1852, was for centuries the ' common market,' and was in part of Norman architecture. The data are so few that it is difficult to decide what the precise object of this guild might be. The lists are not those of freemen, but of a distinct community. There seems also good evidence that it was not a mere trading guild, certainly not such a guild of sailors or seafaring men as the name might indicate; and it is clear also that it was not purely religious. Moreover, Mr. Chanter concludes (though the mayor exercised some authority) that comparatively few of the townsmen were members. This is shown both by the occurrence of the names of many who are specified as resident elsewhere, and by a comparison of the roll of the guildry with legal and other proceedings of the same period in the borough courts. The guild, indeed, chiefly consisted of the petty gentry, yeomen, and agriculturists of the neighbourhood, with a sprinkling of persons of higher rank, and from a distance.

The Priory of St. Mary at Pilton was reputedly founded by Æðelstan; and the ancient seal of the brotherhood bears testimony to the fact that no less an origin was claimed five centuries since. Actual records do not go beyond 1200. The seal bears on the obverse the figure of the Virgin Mary, to whom the Priory was dedicated; and on the reverse that of a king, evidently intended for Æðelstan, for the legend runs: 'HOC . ATHELSTANUS . AGO . QUOD . PRESENS . SIGNA . IMAGO.' It was a Benedictine house of small size, a cell to the great Abbey of Malmesbury, to which it gave a couple of abbots. It had an uneventful career, and at the Dissolution contained only three monks beside the prior, while its revenues amounted to but £56 12s. 8d.

Pilton, really an ancient suburb of Barnstaple, was, like it, largely engaged in textile manufactures, and had a 'shoddy' reputation in consequence of its make of coarse 'cottons' for linings. 'Woe unto ye Piltonians,' quotes Westcote, 'who make cloth without wool!'

Barnstaple bore its part in the maritime activity of the Elizabethan days, and contributed, as we shall see hereafter under Bideford, to the fleet fitted out against the Armada. Like nearly all the towns of Devon, it had strong Parliamentary sympathies, and a contingent thence took part in the defeat of Hopton at Modbury. It was, however, taken by Maurice in September, 1643. In the following July the townsfolk overpowered the garrison; and, with the aid of a contingent sent by the Earl of Essex, repulsed a party of Royalists despatched by Maurice to turn the scale. But the Roundheads did not hold it long, for in September, 1644, it had to yield to Goring, and then remained a Royal garrison until the close of the war, when Fairfax took it in April, 1646. There are still extant, specially at Fort Hill, a few lines of the defence and works of attack; and Puritan cannonading is *said* to have partially destroyed Pilton Tower.

Barnstaple was one of the western towns in which Huguenot refugees settled after the revocation of the Edict of Nantes. Quite dramatic is the account of their arrival and reception. The party left Rochelle in a small crowded vessel, and had a very tempestuous passage. At length they found themselves in Barnstaple Bay one Sunday morning, sailed over the bar and up the river, and landed on the quay during divine service. Utterly destitute, they ranged themselves in the market-place, and thither flocked the townsfolk when they left the churches. Happily, neither the good Samaritan nor his spirit was wanting. An old gentleman, whose name unfortunately is not preserved, took a couple of the refugees home to dinner, and recommended his example to his fellow-townsmen. In a few minutes the Huguenots were distributed throughout the town, their immediate wants supplied, and the foundation laid of a new period of commercial prosperity for the hospitable borough. Intelligent and industrious, and specially skilled in the woollen trade, these poor French folk proved well able to repay their benefactors. The Corporation gave them the Chapel of

St. Anne as a place of worship; and there French services continued to be performed until 1761, when the immigrants had become absorbed in the general population. Their descendants can still, however, be traced here, as at Exeter and Plymouth and Stonehouse, in the last of which towns a French congregation continued to meet until the present century.

This Chapel of St. Anne has for more than three centuries been used as a grammar school, the original foundation being presumably connected with the Guild of St. Nicholas. Barnstaple school has a long list of illustrious alumni. Bishop Jewell and his rival Harding; Jonathan Hamner, one of the most famous of the ejected divines of Devon; John Gay, the poet; Brancker, the Rosicrucian; Judge Doddridge; and the learned Dr. Musgrave—among the number.

Barnstaple is the seat of an important art pottery. Excellent pottery of what is commonly regarded as Roman type was made in Devon so far back as the Roman period; and some of the best clays of the county were then known and worked. Mr. Phillips, of Aller, believes that much that is commonly called Durobrivian ware is really of Devonshire manufacture; and that some of the so-called Samian found in the district, made on the wheel, is unquestionably of Devonshire make and clay. In the Middle Ages large quantities of encaustic tiles were made in various localities. The chief production appears to have been in the Barnstaple and Bideford districts, where potteries have been carried on, historically, from time immemorial. A mode of sgraffito ornamentation long since originated in North Devon, dated specimens existing over a century and a half old; and this has been developed recently with great effect. The decoration consists of 'washes of white clay, with incised patterns, and coloured glazes of flowing and pulsating lines.' The occurrence of beds of culm or anthracite in the Carboniferous rocks of the district may, by the provision of fuel, have stimulated the utilization of the clay.

Until the assertion was questioned by the late Dr. Oliver, Bishops Tawton, next Barnstaple, was commonly accepted as having been the primary seat of the See of Devonshire. It is now abundantly clear that Dr. Oliver was justified in his scepticism, for later research has shown that the belief rested entirely upon a statement made by Hoker, of Exeter, in his catalogue and memoirs of the Bishops of Devon down to 1583. Therein he states that 'Werstanus was the first who fixed the episcopal chair at Bishops Tawton,' in the year 905. No earlier writer than Hoker assigns a bishop to Bishops Tawton; such later writers as do, all follow Hoker; and, while no evidence confirmatory of this statement has anywhere been found, the difficulties in the way of its acceptance seem upon critical examination to be insuperable. There is, however, no reason to doubt, to quote the words of Dr. Oliver, that 'the manor of Bishops Tawton, with its members, Landkey and Swymbridge, formed a part of the original endowment of the see,' and was then regarded as its most profitable estate. ' Here the bishops occasionally resided, as they did at Clyst, in Farringdon parish; at Radway, in Bishops Teignton; at Place, in Chudleigh; and Paignton.' Some small remains of the ancient palace still continue.

The ancient manor was long since divided, though the bishops retained their residence down to the fifteenth century. The first important severance took place in 1225, when the church and rectory, with Landkey and Swymbridge, and the ecclesiastical manor, were appropriated as an endowment to the deanery by Bishop Brewer. The principal part of the manor was, however, conveyed by Bishop Veysey to the Russell family. By ancient practice the rectory was always granted to laymen, on freehold leases for three lives, the rector, as lord farmer, receiving all the tithes, exercising all the manorial rights, and granting leases on lives by copy of court roll. Originally, the lord farmer also appointed the incumbents of the three parishes.

A hamlet on the verge of Bishops Tawton, now a part of the borough of Barnstaple, was anciently the independent borough of Newport. The date of its foundation is uncertain, but the name shows it to be of later origin than the old 'port' of Barnstaple; and it may have been fostered by the bishops, and grown up under their protection. That it came to be called Newport Episcopi is but the natural result of the connection with Bishops Tawton parish. A market and fair were granted in 1294, and, either then or not long subsequently it had a corporate existence, for it is distinctly named the borough of Newport in 1307, and the names of mayors are recorded nearly as far back. Mayors were elected, indeed, but rather in form than fact, until the last century.

The distinguished natives of Barnstaple have been claimed to include Lord Chancellor Fortescue, author of 'De Laudibus Legum Angliæ,' who was, however, born, as already stated, in North Huish; Lord Audley (d. 1386), the foremost hero of Poictiers, who was certainly the owner of the barony in right of his mother, coheiress of the Martyns, and resided at the castle; Sir John Doddridge, Judge of the King's Bench under James I.; and John Gay, the fabulist. There is some doubt even as to Doddridge, who has been credited to South Molton. But Barnstaple was certainly his home; and when he died in 1628 at the age of seventy-three, his nephew succeeded to his property, and lived in the old town. Gay (1688-1732) has been attributed to the adjoining parish of Landkey; but there is no doubt that his parents were Barnstaple folk, and very little that he was born at their residence in Joy Street. An old armchair, sold many years since in Barnstaple, was found to contain a drawer with a number of unpublished poems by him.

Ralegh, Bishop of Winchester, 1244, was born at Ralegh, in the parish of Pilton, the original seat of this famous family. From the Raleghs it eventually passed to the Chichesters, another notable Devonshire house, of South Devon origin, but now chiefly settled in the North, at Arlington, Hall, and Youlston. A Chichester was Bishop of Exeter in 1128; but the most distinguished of the race was Arthur Chichester (d. 1620), born at Ralegh, knighted by Henri Quatre for his 'notable exploits' in arms, and created by James I., whom he served as Lord Deputy of Ireland, Baron Belfast.

Akland, in Landkey, near Barnstaple, is the first seat of the Acland family, and has been held by them from the twelfth century. Westcote gives a bad name to the ladies of a village nigh, called Newlands, who, if annoyed by the repetition of the phrase, 'Camp le tout, Newland,' would treat their aspersors so unsavourily, that 'he that travels that way a fortnight afterwards may smell what has been there done.'

Tawstock used, in the common talk of the countryside, to be regarded as having the finest manor, the richest rectory, and the most stately residence—at any rate in North Devon. If there is likelihood in the theory that the 'stocks' in a debatable land preceded the 'tuns,' then Tawstock may represent, as distinct from the Keltic town of Barnstaple, the first Saxon settlement of the Taw. However, we cannot trace it further than 'Domesday,' where it appears as one of the manors held by the King in succession to 'Harold the Earl,' and a place of note, having 18 serfs, 60 villeins, and 7 swineherds, with 5 houses in Exeter, and being worth £24 a year. William Lord Briwere held it in the reign of Henry II., and gave it to his daughter on her marriage with Robert, Earl of

Leicester. She, having no children, gave it to her niece Matilda, wife of Henry de Tracy. Thence it went in succession to the noble families of Martyn, Audley, and Fitzwarren, and through the Hankfords to the Bourchiers, Earls of Bath, now represented in the female line by its present possessors, the Bourchier Wreys. The fine old mansion of the Bourchiers, nearly all burnt in 1787, had been garrisoned during the Civil Wars. The park remains one of the oldest and finest in the county. The church has several monuments of the Bourchiers; and an oaken effigy, presumably a memorial of Thomasin, daughter of Sir W. Hankford, is of an unusual character.

Adjoining Tawstock is the ancient borough of Fremington, which sent burgesses to Parliament under Edward III., but has little other claim to notice. Like Tawstock, it had belonged to Harold, but was given by William to the Bishop of Coutances, who likewise had 7 houses and lands and 10 burgesses in Barnstaple itself. The population of Fremington was even greater than that of Tawstock —7 serfs, 40 villeins, 30 bordars, 13 swineherds, and 1 burgess in Barnstaple—but it was worth £2 less. This also was one of the manors that came to the Tracys, and, forming part of the barony of Barnstaple, passed through the Martyns to the Audleys. Coming to the Crown, it was granted by Richard II. to John Holland, Earl of Huntingdon, and was likewise one of the western manors granted to Margaret, Countess of Richmond.

Across the Taw lies Braunton, presumably derived from Brannock's 'tun,' Brannock being the patron saint; and the legend of the foundation of the church averring that he was directed to build it where he next saw a sow and her litter, in witness whereof sow and farrows are to be seen duly carven on a boss. Legend further affirms that he obtained the timber from a forest which then grew upon the site of the sandy waste fringing the Taw, now known as Braunton Burrows, and drew it to the spot by deer. And it would be a remarkable coincidence —if the remains had not suggested the tradition—that a submerged forest does exist in Barnstaple Bay near the point indicated, and that cervine bones and antlers have been found therein. On the cliffs at Croyde, hard by, flint chips are so numerous as to indicate the existence there of a prehistoric implement-manufactory. Braunton also figures in 'Domesday' as a populous manor in the demesne of the King; and, indeed, the character of the entries generally for this locality indicate a more thriving condition than that of the county as a whole. By a grant of Cœur de Lion, Braunton became the original Devonshire seat of the Carews, but was taken from them by John in favour of Robert de Seckville; while Henry III. gave two-thirds of the manor, with the lordship of the hundred, to the Abbey of Cleve, in Somerset. At the Dissolution, it was granted to the Earl of Westmoreland; and it was part of the property brought to the Courtenays by the marriage of Sir William Courtenay to the daughter of Sir William Waller and the heiress of the Reynells. The custom of the manor is noted by the Lysonses, following Chapple, as peculiar—some of the lands being held by the tenure of Borough English; while others passed to the elder son, and all were equally divided between daughters.

Heanton Punchardon preserves the name of a distinguished family, of whom the most prominent member, Sir Richard, served with great note in France under Edward III. Through Beaumonts the manor came to the Bassets; and Colonel Arthur Basset, born at Heanton Court in 1597, was one of the leading Royalists of Devon, and Governor of St. Michael's Mount when it surrendered to Colonel Hammond in 1646.

CHAPTER XV.

ILFRACOMBE AND LYNTON.

ILFRACOMBE, a little port of great antiquity, has developed, within the last quarter of a century, into a watering-place so thriving that it seems to have no history and to be all but bran-new. But the town is old enough to have some dozen names, varying from Ælfringcombe, through Ilford-combe, to the modern title; and to have been a harbour of some repute in the twelfth century, for the Welsh and the Irish traffic. In 1344 it was important enough to be cited to send representatives to a Shipping Council, while to the siege of Calais it contributed six ships to Liverpool's one! Perhaps the best evidence of its standing in the early Middle Ages is the quaint little chapel of St. Nicholas on the peaked hill overlooking the quays, still, as it probably always has been, the harbour lighthouse. There are many of these little half-sacred, half-secular cliff light-chapels along the southern and western coasts; but, so far as Devon is concerned, this alone retains its ancient uses. Moreover, it was a place of pilgrimage in the fifteenth century; and, though now sadly modernized, still has features of interest.

Like every western port, Ilfracombe was the scene of great activity during the Elizabethan era; and, though it does not occupy a prominent place in the annals of that time, evidently profited by the operations against the

Spaniards; and seems, by a few casual references, to
have kept up a regulâr traffic with the southern coast of
Ireland. Whenever war was onward Ilfracombe was
ready to do her share of privateering, or, to use the term
most in local favour, to engage in ' reprisals.'

The town was of little consequence in the Civil Wars of
the Commonwealth; though, like most of the Devonshire
centres, it had Puritan sympathies. It was captured by
Sir F. Doddington for the King in September, 1644, and
held by the Royalists until it fell into the hands of Fairfax,
soon after his capture of Barnstaple, in 1646. The isolated
position of Ilfracombe caused it to be selected as a refuge
by some of those who took part in the Penruddock rising in
1655. They were, however, taken; and history repeated itself
when in 1688 a party of refugees from Sedgmoor, headed by
Colonel Wade, seized and victualled a vessel at Ilfracombe
and put to sea, but were forced ashore by a couple of frigates.

The most curious incident in the later history of Ilfracombe is the fact that it was the intended scene of a
French invasion in 1797. On the 20th of February in
that year four French vessels came to an anchor to the
west of the port, and scuttled a few coasting craft. But
they made no attempt to land, for the North Devon
Volunteers manned the heights; and the Frenchmen set
sail for Wales. Here they disembarked 1,400 soldiers,
but surrendered without firing a shot to the militia under
Lord Cawdor, who is said to have dressed his miners in
their wives' red petticoats and frightened the invaders by
the demonstration of superior force. Be that as it may,
there is hardly a seaport in Devon which has not some
tradition of invaders being scared by a muster of old
women in red cloaks.

The Champernownes were once lords of a part of
Ilfracombe (held by Baldwin the Sheriff in 1086), and
obtained a grant of a market and fair in 1278; and among
their successors were the Bonviles, Nevilles, Greys, and

Gorges. Sir Philip Sydney, too, was one of its owners. This manor is now dismembered. Another, of which the harbour forms part, was a member of the barony of Barnstaple, passed from the Audleys to the Bourchiers, and has thence descended to the present owner, Sir H. Bourchier Wrey. By the Bourchiers and the Wreys the harbour-works have been several times improved and extended. The shipping trade of Ilfracombe is now, however, little more than local; and the modern importance of the town rests entirely upon its attractions as a watering-place, which have been developed with equal good taste and spirit. The healthiness of the site has, indeed, passed into a proverb: 'You may live in 'Combe as long as you like, but you must go somewhere else to die!' But there is a parish churchyard for all that.

Considering the antiquity of Ilfracombe, its personal relations are singularly scant. Its one notable is John Cutcliffe, whose name was Latinized into **Johannes de Rupecissa**, a reforming friar of the fourteenth century. He was born at Damage Farm in 1340, and died in prison at Avignon, where he had been cast for his opinions. He was a man of great earnestness and learning, but the influence of his labours and writings, as a contemporary of Wyclif, were chiefly confined to the Continent.

A far better known divine, John Jewel (1522-1571), the famous Bishop of Salisbury, was born at Bowden Farm in the adjoining parish of Berry Narbor, in an old house among the hills still standing. His 'Sermons,' in black-letter, may yet be seen chained up as of yore in some of the churches of the West. His stoutest opponent, Thomas Harding (died 1572), was born in the next parish of Combe Martin, and was Jewel's schoolfellow at Barnstaple Grammar School.

Sir William Herle, Chief Justice of the Common Pleas, 1316, certainly lived at Chambercombe, near Ilfracombe, but his birth there is doubtful.

Combe Martin.

Of Berry Narbor there is little more to say. Originally named after some old earthwork, 'burh' or 'bury,' it gave name in its turn to the family of Berry, from whom it passed to the Narberts or Narbors. Monuments of both families are in the old church; and hard by, fallen sadly from its high estate, is the old manor-house. Stowford in West Downe, and not Stowford in Berry, is the seat of the Stowfords of whom came Sir John de Stowford, Justice of the Common Pleas in 1343.

Combe Martin has a more formidable history. 'Milelong man stye,' as Kingsley called it, some antiquaries have seen in the little harbour wherewith the long Combe Valley terminates, a haunt of the Phœnician galleys. This is the purest speculation; but it must have been of some little note when it took its distinctive surname from the Martins of Tours, its Norman lords, to one of whom, Nicholas Fitz Martin, market and fair were granted in 1264; and its first importance seems to have been derived, not from its facilities for commerce, but its mineral wealth.

There is a vague tradition, for which Westcote appears to be responsible, that Combe Martin was a borough and sent representatives to Parliament; but the assertion is wholly unfounded. Its mines of silver lead, with those of Bere Alston, were unusually productive in the reigns of the first Edwards, the silver raised being turned to account in the prosecution of war with France. They were worked also under Henry V., and were then of little account until the days of Elizabeth. Adrian Gilbert, half brother of Sir Walter Ralegh, who had considerable skill in mining matters, led the way in the new venture; but Sir Bevis Bulmer carried forward the work, and with much success. He gave a cup of Combe Martin silver to the City of London—still among the Corporation plate—the cup and cover weighing 137 ounces; and another to the Earl of Bath (the manor of Combe Martin having then passed to the Bourchiers). Each bore a quaint inscription; but a portion of that on the City cup will suffice as a sample:

> 'Dispersed I in earth did lye
> Since alle beginninge olde
> In place called Combe, where Martin long
> Had hid mee in his molde.
> I dydd no service on the earth,
> And no manne sate mee free,
> Till Bulmer by his skill and charge
> Did frame mee this to be.'

Another attempt was made under Charles I. so late as the year 1648, but without much being done, though the project had his personal encouragement. In modern times the old mines have been worked and new ones opened, without any satisfactory result. Yet the ore is rich, yielding 140 and 150 ounces of silver to the ton.

Not fifty years since Combe Martin supplied a curious survival of history in a quaint custom of Ascension Day, called the 'Hunting of the Earl of Rone.' This part of Devon had a noted exceptional intercourse with Ireland through the Middle Ages, and, according to tradition, an Irish refugee, known as the Earl of Tyrone, was captured here by a body of soldiers in a place called Lady's Wood. This was the matter commemorated, with the addition of a few details of still older May-day mumming; if indeed the 'Earl of Rone' had not been grafted upon the more ancient ceremonial, and given it a new lease of life. The chief characters were the Earl of Rone, with mask and smock, and a chain of biscuits round his neck; the hobby-horse of the elder time, a decorated donkey; a fool; and a troop of grotesquely dressed grenadiers. The preliminaries lasted a week, which was devoted to processions; then the Earl was captured in Lady's Wood, led in mock triumph, shot at intervals, lamented by hobby-horse and fool; and the process repeated while contributions could be levied.

Lynton is the chief centre of a corner of Devon next Somerset, enclosed on one hand by the high land of Exmoor proper, and on the other by a spur which follows down to the sea to the east of Combe Martin from Bratton Down. To this comparative isolation is it due that the district retains much of its original old-world characteristics; and that it has had so casual a share in the general history of the county. This was not always so, and there is abundant evidence, in 'camps' and barrows and other memorials of antiquity, that the neighbourhood was well populated in Keltic times; and the next parish to Lynton, that of Countisbury, is clearly the 'bury or camp of the headland,' *Cant-ys-bury*, akin to Kinterbury, near Plymouth, and the Canterbury of Kent.

The Valley of Rocks, the most romantic feature of Lynton, with its grotesque piles of weathered stone and mimic natural masonry, has been held to indicate selection for the performance of druidical rites—a freak of pure fancy on the part of the elder antiquaries, without a vestige of evidence in its favour. Far more reasonable is the suggestion that Lynton was the scene of ancient raids and incursions on the coast by the Severn Sea, especially when Harold ravaged that district in 1052. This remote corner of Devon, too—probably from the natural strength of its position, belted by hills—appears to have formed a kind of refuge for the Saxons after the Conquest, for it is stated that William himself expelled the natives therefrom. The manors of Lynton, Crinton, and Countisbury all passed to William Chievre, and Lynton and Countisbury eventually came to the Tracys, and by them were given to Ford Abbey. After the Dissolution they passed to the family of Wichchalse, who are said to have been Protestant refugees of Dutch origin. The name occurs, however, in the records of St. Petrock, Exeter, at a date much earlier than that commonly assigned for their immigration.

Old Lynton—or rather Lynmouth, but the two are really one—was, in the main, a fishing port, with a bias towards smuggling. Westcote tells a story against the 'parson' of Lynton, how that when the herrings first resorted to the coast he 'vexed the poor fishermen for extraordinary unusual tithes.' The sympathetic herrings 'suddenly clean left the coast,' but—possibly on the 'parson' mending his way—' God be thanked, they began to resort hither again.' In the valley of Badgeworthy, or Badgery, on Exmoor, there are yet traces of the huts of the Doones, the last gang of professional banditti of a residential character in England. Their characters are strongly painted in 'Lorna Doone,' which is full of the local legends that have lingered long beyond their usual date in this quiet spot; now, under the name of 'the English Switzerland,' the increasing resort of the tourist tribe.

Occasionally used by both parties during the Civil War, Lynmouth was the final refuge of Major Wade, when, after his escape from Sedgmoor, he had to leave Ilfracombe; and he was captured in hiding at Farleigh, in Brendon. Lydcote Hall, on the flank of Bratton Down, has been assumed by many writers, following Sir Walter Scott, as the birthplace of the ill-fated Amy Robsart: this, however, is an error.

The little parish of Morthoe, which borders Morte Bay, on the other side of Ilfracombe, has a niche alike in history and in folk-lore. A tomb in Morthoe Church to 'Syr Wiliame de Tracey' was recorded by the elder historians as that of the Tracy murderer of À Becket. Risdon is confident upon the point; and Westcote jokes upon the assumption that some ill-affected persons stole the leaden sheets in which Sir William's body was wrapped, leaving him 'in danger of taking cold.' But Morthoe is an old Tracy seat, and a chantry in this very church was founded by a rector of Morthoe, William Tracy, who was undoubtedly buried here. This, coupled with the fact that the figure on the tombstone is that of a priest, and the frequent use in the Middle Ages of the prefix 'Sir' to indicate a parish clergyman, renders it probable that the whole of the tomb belongs to the rector, as a part admittedly does. According to West-Country tradition, after the murder of the Archbishop,

> 'The Tracys
> Had the wind in their faces'

wherever they went, or from whatever quarter it might blow; and, assuredly, high and rugged Morthoe was as likely a place as any to secure a remarkable fulfilment. Morthoe is 'High Morte,' and Mort is fancifully interpreted to mean 'death.' Beyond Morte Point is Morte Stone, the cause of many a shipwreck, which will be removed when it is taken in hand by a husband who can say from experience that the grey mare is *not* the better horse. There is, indeed, a version of the tradition which places the power in the hands of a number of wives who have the sovereignty, but adds sagely that enough have not been got together to produce the result. And Morthoe itself supplies material for yet another wise saw in the declaration that it is the place which 'God made last, and the devil will take first;' which may be matched in Northumberland at Elsdon, and probably in many other rugged neighbourhoods.

CHAPTER XVI.

LUNDY ISLAND.

LUNDY ISLAND has afforded ample proof of its settlement in far-back antiquity. Here in 1850 were found a couple of huge stone kists lying side by side, the larger of which contained an extended skeleton 8 feet 2 inches in length, while the other held the bones of a body which was several inches above the average height. Seven other skeletons of ordinary size, without coffins, were found in the same line; and then a burial-pit, containing a mass of bones of men, women, and children, with pottery, fragments of bronze, and beads. These remains belonged to two distinct periods—the 'giants' graves,' as they are locally called, dating from the Stone age. Another relic of the distant past was discovered in the following year —a huge earth-covered cromlech, the table-stone weighing about five tons. There are also traces of ancient cultivation, which show the presence, many centuries since, of a comparatively large population.

So much for the prehistoric days of this singular islet. It does not appear to have definitely found its way upon the historical record until the twelfth century, when it was the stronghold of Jordan de Marisco, who had married Agnes, daughter of Hamelin Plantagenet, natural brother of Henry II. His turbulence led to the forfeiture of Lundy, and its grant to the Knights Templars; but the family remained in possession notwithstanding, for in 1199 Jordan's son, William, followed in his father's steps, and forfeiture in favour of the Templars was then declared by John. Again was it found that to forfeit was one thing, and to seize another. Feeling secure in his island strength, Sir William defied alike Templars and King, levied contributions on the adjacent coast, and finally had to be besieged—a special hidage rate being levied in Devon and Cornwall to raise the funds. Whether he was even then ejected is by no means certain; for little conclusion can be drawn from the appointment by the Crown of keepers of Lundy; and it is known that the Templars never entered into possession.

Sir William, however, must have found it desirable to make an alliance with France, for he was among the prisoners taken by the English in the naval battle of August 24, 1217. He was speedily forgiven, and three months later Lundy was restored. The next Lord of Lundy, Jordan, or Geoffrey, de Marisco, was slain while engaged in a raid at Kilkenny in 1234; and his son William, having set on an assassin to murder Henry III. at Woodstock, was taken by stratagem, and hung, drawn, and quartered, while sixteen of his associates were dragged at the cart's-tail, and hanged. Thus for a time the Mariscos were at length effectually dispossessed. Bearing a noble name, and claiming to be men of high degree, they were really among the most pestilent piratical rascalry that ever fulfilled the sad words of the old chronicler, by filling their castles with 'devils and evil men.' There are several traces of their sway in the remains of their castle and other buildings; and it has been suggested that from this period date certain round towers, the foundations of which have considerable resemblance to those of Ireland.

Lundy was now in the possession of the Crown; and, as it was the common resort of the King's enemies, was placed in charge of a succession of governors, among whom were Henry de Tracy, Robert de Walerond, Ralph de Wyllyngton, Humphry de Bohun, and Geoffrey Dinant. Forty years had barely elapsed, however, before (1281) the Mariscos were back again. Next we find John de Wyllyngton keeping Lundy from Herbert de Marisco by force of arms; and the Mariscos were finally dispossessed in 1321 by the grant of the island, with the other estates of De Wyllyngton, to the King's favourite, Hugh, Lord le Despencer. This led in 1326 to the selection of Lundy by Edward II. as a place of refuge. But the winds were contrary, and the King had to land in Wales. With the fall of Le Despencer, and the accession of Edward III., Lundy again returned to the Crown, and was put in the keeping of Otho de Bodrigan. Subsequently it got back to the Wyllyngtons, and was sold by them to the Montacutes, Earls of Salisbury. In 1390, Lundy was held of the King in chief by Guy, Lord Bryan, and it descended from him through the Butlers, Earls of Wiltshire and Ormond, to the St. Legers of Annery; thence passing, by the marriage of Mary St. Leger with the gallant Sir Richard Grenville, to the Grenvilles. From the Grenvilles it went to the Leveson-Gowers; but was sold by the executors of the first Earl Gower, and since then has passed through several hands. It seems impossible to obtain a complete account of the holders and owners of the island; but, amidst much uncertainty, its importance in the Middle Ages is pretty plainly indicated by the number of prominent names associated with it.

The most romantic part of the history of Lundy extends through the seventeenth century. In the opening years of the reign of James I. it gradually grew into favour as a haunt of pirates, and had for 'king' one Captain Salkeld. He must have been expelled, if it be true that 'Judas' Stukely made it the place of his retreat; but in 1625 the island seems to have fallen into the hands of a Turkish squadron, and thenceforward for many years it was nothing if not piratical. In 1632 it was reported the headquarters of a buccaneer named Admiral Nutt, who required for his repression a fleet of some dozen vessels. But in the next year the island itself was plundered by a Spanish vessel; and it is somewhat doubtful how far the native inhabitants of Lundy, and of the adjacent coasts of the mainland, were clear from all participation in this special form of 'free trade.'

At the commencement of the Civil War, Lundy was garrisoned for the King by one Thomas Bushell, who was engaged in working the silver-lead mines of Combe Martin, and who fortified it at his own cost. But it saw no service; and having been acquired by Lord Saye and Sele, that nobleman, in February, 1646, called for its surrender. Bushell, not complying, was summoned by Sir Thomas Fairfax; but even then he declined to give way until he had laid the case before the King, and obtained his consent. Hence it was not until February 24th, 1647, that Lundy was given up to Colonel Richard Fiennes, and handed over to Lord Saye and Sele. There is a local tradition that his lordship died there, and was buried beneath the west window of the Chapel of St. Helen.

Under the Commonwealth the sea was too closely kept to allow of Lundy resuming its evil reputation; but with the Restoration the Lundy piracies cropped up again. In 1663 the island was actually held by French privateers; and so again in the reign of Queen Anne, to the serious damage of the colonial trade of Barnstaple and Bideford. There is no truth, however, in the story told by Grose of the capture of the island by a French vessel, the crew of whom gained an unopposed access by the pretence that they wished to bury their captain.

The last noteworthy thing about Lundy is its connection with a certain Thomas Benson, the descendant of a respectable merchant family of Bideford, and at one time member for Barnstaple. Having entered into a contract for the exportation of convicts to Virginia or Maryland in 1747, in 1748 he obtained a lease of the island from Lord Gower, and thereupon made that his convict station, employing his unhappy slaves in his improvements. Lundy or Virginia mattered not in his view, so that they were out of the kingdom. Benson was every way a great rascal. A smuggler, not far removed from a pirate, he had at length to fly the kingdom for an abominable fraud upon insurance offices, removing the insured cargoes of vessels, and then scuttling the ships.

Since Benson's time, Lundy has had no national concern, save the erection of a lighthouse on its highest point by the Trinity Board in 1819. It has, however, at various times been made the residence of its owners. Admiral Sir John Borlase Warren, who bought it of the executors of the first Earl Gower, continued there until the outbreak of the American War; and the late proprietor, Mr. Heaven, lived there up to the time of his death for nearly fifty years. The only attempt made to develop a trade at Lundy was the working of granite quarries, which he encouraged, but which did not prove successful. These quarries must, however, have been worked in former times, as the Lundy granite is largely used in many of the churches on the north coast of Devon and Cornwall.

CHAPTER XVII.

BIDEFORD.

BIDEFORD is generally interpreted to mean 'by the ford,' and in name, at any rate, is therefore Saxon. The 'ford,' however, is of far older date, being that by which the old British trackway, subsequently no doubt used by the Romans, crossed the Torridge. Bideford was a place of some importance when it belonged to Brictric, its last Saxon owner; for at the Domesday Survey, when, like most of the other manors of that unlucky thane, it passed to Matilda, it had an enumerated population of 52, while, as it then had a fishery worth 25s. a year, the germs of its maritime character already existed. The manor is remarkable for having remained for nearly seven centuries in one family. After Matilda died, William gave it to Richard Grenville; and by the Grenvilles it continued to be held until 1750. The first Grenville of Bideford was a cousin of the Conqueror, and in his way a conqueror himself; for he effected the reduction of Glamorganshire in the reign of Rufus. The Grenvilles occupy a distinguished position in English history; but the two most famous bearers of the name are the Grenville of Elizabeth and the Grenville of Charles. Most famous of all is the former, the Sir Richard Grenville (1540-1591) of whom Kingsley writes, one of the brightest stars in the Elizabethan naval galaxy, who closed a noble life in the stoutest sea-fight ever waged. Ralegh has told the story in noble prose, and Tennyson in heroic verse. Alone and unaided in his ship the *Revenge*, with but 103 men and many of them sick, he fought off Flores, in 1591, the whole Spanish fleet of 52 sail and 10,000 men, from three o'clock in the afternoon until daybreak the following morning, repulsing fifteen attacks of the enemy, who brought up two fresh vessels each time, sinking four of their ships, and killing 1,000 of their men. The *Revenge*, meantime, was shattered into a mere hulk, 800 cannon-shot piercing her through and through, killing 40 of her crew, and wounding nearly all the rest, Grenville among the number. When the sun rose on the scene of carnage, the *Revenge*, shattered and broken as she was, her decks streaming with blood, a veritable shambles, lay in the centre of a ring of baffled Spanish men-of-war, who dared come no nearer. Want of ammunition, not of pluck, compelled the crew to surrender, though Grenville himself wished the vessel to be blown up. Three days afterwards, Grenville died of his wounds, with a joyful and quiet mind; 'for that I have ended my life as a true soldier ought to do, that hath fought for his country, Queen, religion, and honour.' The *Revenge* was staunch to the last. After the battle she was filled with the Spanish wounded, and despatched for Spain; but a storm sprang up, and she was never heard of more, sinking with all hands.

Sir Bevil Grenville (1596-1643), whom Kingsley calls the 'handsomest and most gallant of his generation'—a Cavalier in whom lived the truest spirit of ancient chivalry—gained lasting fame for himself as one of the four great Royalist leaders of the West—the 'four wheels of Charles's wain.' Winning the day for his King at Lansdowne fight, he lost his life in the winning; and for a while the name of Grenville was dishonoured by the atrocities of his brother Richard, one of the most rapacious and unscrupulous of the Cavalier generals, as Bevil was the noblest.

It may fairly be assumed that it was to the Grenvilles, and notably to Sir Richard, that Bideford owed the rapid development of her maritime importance in the latter years of the sixteenth century. Sir Richard was concerned with Sir Walter Ralegh, his cousin, in the expeditions to colonize Virginia; and was General of the fleet which, in 1585, settled Roanoake. In the following year he was setting out again from Barnstaple to the relief of the infant colony, when his vessels were beneaped on the bar. The delay thus caused led the colonists to despair of relief, and to return home in a barque given them by Sir Francis Drake. This accident was, therefore, the direct cause of the breaking up of the first English settlement in America; and of the loss of fifteen North Devon men, whom Grenville left behind at Roanoake when his second voyage was made, and who were never heard of after, save that the Indians had vague tidings to tell of death and disaster.

It was with a fleet destined for the same service that North Devon participated in the fight with the Armada. Grenville had prepared an expedition for the relief of the colony planted by Ralegh in 1587, apparently consisting of three vessels, which was only waiting for a fair wind to put to sea, when the news came of the speedy advent of the Armada, and 'most of the ships of warre then in a readines in any hauen in England were stayed for seruice at home.' According to the contemporary Diary of Philip Wyot, town clerk of Barnstaple, five ships went over Barnstaple Bar to join Sir Francis Drake at Plymouth; but, while it has been held that three at least were furnished by Barnstaple, Bideford—in consequence of a statement in 'Westward Ho!' not, however, historical —has been credited with seven. Mr. R. W. Cotton, after an exhaustive analysis of all the evidence, is of opinion that the North Devon Armada fleet consisted of these five vessels only. The names of four have been preserved—the *Galeon Dudley, God save her,* and *Tyger,* entered as Barnstaple vessels, but probably forming Grenville's contingent; and the *John,* a Barnstaple vessel proper. The other was also in all likelihood a Barnstaple craft, possibly one of six 'reprisal ships' which are recorded as having belonged to that town.

That Bideford was the headquarters of the Ralegh-Grenville expedition, and so the chief contributor to the little squadron, there is every reason to believe; but Mr. Cotton has shown that eight years after the defeat of the Armada it was only assessed at one-fifth as much as Barnstaple, and that of itself it could by no means have supplied all the seamen needed. Bideford, therefore, was not one of the chief ports of England in the sixteenth century, as Kingsley states, though it bore a chief part in the Armada fight so far as North Devon is concerned. It was then, in fact, simply in the dawn of its prosperity; and had only been incorporated under Elizabeth.

When the commerce of the town began to rise, its extension was very rapid. The merchants of the port were quick to grasp the advantage of the traffic with America and Newfoundland; and this trade continued to extend until the commencement of the last century, when the export shipping to Newfoundland was exceeded by only two ports in the kingdom—London and Topsham; and the import trade by London only. Great was the harvest reaped in these days by the French and Spanish privateers, who preyed upon the ships of Bideford and Barnstaple to such an extent that the offing of the Taw and Torridge was named by them the 'Golden Bay.' But the American trade survived until the American war. For some years more tobacco was imported into Bideford than into London. These palmy days have long since flown; Barnstaple has once more recovered its superior position; and the shipping trade of the Torridge is mostly conducted, not at Bideford, but at Appledore.

Bideford, like Barnstaple, has a famous bridge. In fact, in Devonshire it is the bridge of bridges, and every true Bideford man feels a pride in the old structure, though he may not have seen it for half a century, and solicitously inquires for its welfare. Its origin is super natural; its history romantic; and its demeanour philanthropic. It is quite uncertain when it was built, the early records having been destroyed; but, as the oldest seal of the borough in existence, of fourteenth-century date, has the bridge for device, so old at least must Bideford Bridge be. According to tradition, no foundation could be laid until Sir Richard Gornard, or Gurney, the parish priest, dreamt that a rock had been rolled to the site to serve for that purpose, and, going there in the morning, found his dream accomplished; whereupon the work was soon completed. The seal to which reference has been made indicates the existence of buildings in association with the bridge that have long disappeared. A structure with a bell turret is on one side of the bridge, a church with a spire on the other, and the centre bears the Virgin and Child on a Maltese cross raised on a shaft. The bridge is wealthy; and the feoffees, in whose care it is, have been enabled from time to time to improve it materially, and to expend a handsome surplus in education and charity. Under the old regime the bridge was rather noted for its hospitality, being addicted to the giving of good dinners; but these days have fled before the presence of the Charity Commissioners.

Bideford, like Barnstaple, threw in its lot with the Parliament at the outbreak of the Wars of the Commonwealth, with more energy than staying-power. With their neighbours from Barnstaple, the Bideford band joined the rendezvous of the Devonshire Roundheads at Modbury in 1642, and took part in Sir Ralph Hopton's defeat.

This success inspired a confidence which led to their downfall. Colonel Digby held Torrington with a strong body of Cavaliers to keep the North Devon Parliamentarians in check. In August, 1643, he was assailed by the united forces of Bideford and Barnstaple, but their vanguard of musketeers, being suddenly charged by the colonel and a handful of his officers, were driven back upon the main body. Panic-stricken, they all fled, and were pursued by the Royalist cavalry until, as Clarendon states, 'their swords were blunted with slaughter, and their numbers overburdened with prisoners.' Those who escaped had lost their wits as well as the day; for when they reached Bideford they declared that no one had seen more than five or six of the enemy. Behind their walls and within their forts, however, they regained their courage, and, aided by Barnstaple, sustained a month's siege from Digby. They must then have stood to their guns well, for they did not surrender until they had promise of pardon, and guarantees of safety of person and property. Remains of the old fortifications still exist, East-the-Water.

Shebbeare, the author of 'Chrysal,' was a Bideford man; and here was first developed the genius of Edward Capern, the Devonshire Burns and postman poet, who is, however, a native of Tiverton.

Bideford is connected with the last execution for witchcraft in the West of England—the last but one in the kingdom. In 1682 there lived here 'three old women, ugly, poor, and discontented'—Temperance Lloyd, Susannah Edwards, Mary Trembles. Lloyd was a reputed witch, and the fact that she fell upon her knees in the street and thanked God for the recovery from illness of a certain Mistress Thomas seemed ground enough, when Thomas got worse again, to excite suspicion that Lloyd was the moving cause. Taxed with the witchcraft, she confessed. She confessed, moreover, that the devil attended her in the shape of a magpie, of a 'braget cat,' of a hobgoblin; and that she had killed by her witcheries four persons, whom she named. Hints let drop by her next led to the apprehension of Susannah Edwards and Mary Trembles. They, too, gave full confession. When Susannah Edwards made the acquaintance of the devil, he was 'like a gentleman.' Trembles was not so favoured. The devil had appeared to her 'like a Lyon.' The full text of these confessions is still extant, and is equally absurd and revolting. But the trio were convicted on their own testimony; and these three poor women, either mad or weary of life—described by an eye-witness as 'the most old, decrepid, despicable, miserable creatures that he ever saw'—were hanged at Heavitree, near Exeter, on the 25th of August, within two months of their apprehension. There were other trials for witchcraft in Devon and Cornwall in 1695-6; but though these ended in acquittal, it was not until 1716 that the last executions for this impossible offence took place, when a woman and her daughter were hanged at Huntingdon for selling their souls to the devil. It is an unpleasant commentary upon this that the belief in witchcraft is still widely prevalent in the rural districts of Devon, and leads to the cremation of multitudes of miserable toads, who are looked upon as the emissaries of the Evil One. However, if there are 'black witches' to do mischief, there are several 'white witches' who, for a consideration, will baulk their projects.

Northam is said to have been the scene of the landing of the Danes in 878; of their siege of Kenwith Castle, and of their repulse with great slaughter, the defeat of their chief, Hubba, and the capture of the Raven standard. Few identifications have been more disputed; yet the existence of the 'Hubbastow,' Hubba's traditional place of burial, and the assignment of the 'Bloody Corner' as the Danes' last stand, is evidence that cannot lightly be gainsaid. The manor had some importance so far back as 'Domesday,' when it belonged to St. Stephen, of Caen, in succession to Brictric; for it had then an enumerated population of 36, with two salt-works and a fishery. In 1252 it was confirmed as part of the possessions of the Priory of Frampton, in Dorset, a cell to St. Stephen; and when the possessions of the alien houses were seized, was given to the College of St. Mary Ottery. Ottery, in its turn, fell; and Elizabeth granted the manor to the Dean and Chapter of Windsor, so that it has almost continuously been under ecclesiastical lords.

The little town of Appledore had its rise in the early days of the Newfoundland fisheries, and developed a shipping trade of some importance. Appledore has been treated as Keltic, 'A-pwl-dwr,' the 'water-pool;' but it is really the Saxon 'Appletree.' Of late a new town has sprung up at the mouth of the Torridge, created and named by Kingsley's 'Westward Ho!' This faces the sea on the verge of the wide expanse of sandy dunes called Northam Burrows, which is defended against the encroachments of the waves by the natural breakwater ot Carboniferous pebbles, known as the 'Pebble Ridge.' Rights over the Burrows are exercised by the potwallopers, or householders, of Northam; and it is one of the few spots in England where the game of golf has been thoroughly naturalized.

On the opposite side of the river is Instow, really Johns-stow, and thus called in 'Domesday.'

Borough, in Northam, made ever famous by Kingsley in its association with his Sir Amyas Leigh, was the seat of a family of the same name, which produced at least two very eminent Devonshire seamen—Steven and William Borough. Steven Borough, though little known, is entitled to a very honourable place in the list of Devon worthies. Born in 1525, he was master of the largest vessel, the *Edward Bonaventure,* in Sir Hugh

Willoughby's luckless voyage to the Arctic Seas, planned by Cabot, and which would have been an utter failure had not Borough and his comrade, Richard Chancellor, the pilot-major of the fleet, determined to prosecute their voyage after they had been separated from Willoughby by a storm. Keeping northward until they found no night at all, naming the North Cape on their way, they sailed into the White Sea—the first vessel that had ever entered its wide waste of waters—thus, as it was afterwards said in all earnestness, 'discovering' Russia. Chancellor proceeded to Moscow, there obtained important trading privileges, and laid the foundations of the important Muscovy Company. In 1556, Borough went again to the Northern Seas in a pinnace, to carry forward the intentions of the original expedition, and to find a way by the north-east to Cathay. He made the most remarkable voyage in the annals of Arctic exploration. The little vessel drew only four feet of water. She had for crew only the brothers Borough and eight others; yet she entered the Kara Sea, and reached a point beyond which no navigator went until our own days—English, Dutch, and Russian failing each in turn. Borough made sundry other voyages, and won such reputation that, in January, 1563, he was appointed by Elizabeth Chief Pilot of England, and one of the four Masters of the Navy. For twenty years he toiled in official harness, and he was buried in Chatham Church in 1584. William Borough, also a seaman of distinction, wrote a treatise on the magnet, and became Comptroller of the Navy.

Horwood, for many years the chief residence of the Pollards, of whom one notable monument still remains in the church—a fifteenth-century effigy of a lady, with three children in the folds of her robe—claims mention historically from the fact that a shoe nailed on the church door was reputed to have been placed there by Michael Joseph, the Cornish blacksmith, who headed the insurrection of 1497, and marched through Horwood on the way to his defeat at Blackheath.

Abbotsham was anciently part of the estates of the Abbey of Tavistock, whence its name; but early in the seventeenth century belonged to the Coffin family, who have been seated at Portledge, in the adjoining parish of Alwington, almost from the time of the Conquest, and who continued there in the male line until the death of Richard Coffin in 1766. The family has produced many men of note, Sir William Coffin, Master of the Horse at the coronation of Anne Boleyn, and a prominent participator in the Field of the Cloth of Gold, being of the number. He is said to have been a leading cause of the reform of mortuary fees by threatening to bury a priest— who had declined to read the service over the body of a poor man in Bideford churchyard until he had received the dead man's cow in payment—in the grave which had been prepared. The disturbance thus created—for Sir William proceeded to actual business—led to inquiry and regulation. The present branch of the family bear the name of Pine-Coffin. The Coffins spread also into the adjoining parish of Parkham.

Buckland Brewer has name from the Briweres; and, by the gift of William Lord Briwere, formed part of the endowments of the Abbeys of Dunkeswell and Torre.

On the hill above the quaint little port of Clovelly, the most 'upright' village in its structural relations in England, are the gigantic earthworks of Clovelly Dikes. Not only are they the finest in Devon, but they are fairly comparable with the remains of such ancient cities as Old Sarum or the Dorchester Maiden Castle. It is certain that here was the capital of a powerful tribe. No remains in Devon more strongly emphasize the common error of calling all earthworks 'camps,' and treating them as relics of active warfare. Nevertheless the 'Dikes' are a masterpiece of ancient defensive skill, and must have required the long-continued labours of even a numerous population. There are three complete circumvallations, the ramparts ranging from 15 to 25 feet in height, with outworks or fragmentary cinctures.

Visibly connecting the Dikes with 'cliff-cleft' Clovelly, are the remains of an ancient paved road, which has been cited in proof of presumed Roman origin. It may very well have been that the Romans used this landing-place, seeing that traces of a Roman villa have been found in Hartland parish adjoining, and that the coast here was skirted by one of the old trackways; but there is nothing about Clovelly Roman in its character; and though the name has been ingeniously derived from Clausa Vallis, the 'hidden glen,' there does not seem to be any reason to regard it as being anything but Saxon—the 'cliff-place' —Cleaveleigh. The little town is really a sharp notch in the cliff range, with a steep step road, lined with houses on each side, running down to a beach and pier. There is every appearance of considerable antiquity in this.

Clovelly, indeed, finds a place in 'Domesday' as one of the manors that passed from Brictric to Matilda, and had then an enumerated population of 37, so that it has fully maintained its relative importance. At a very early date it was in the hands of the Giffards; but in the reign of Richard II. came to the Carys, who continued to hold it until this branch of that distinguished family died out in 1724. One of the chief members of the Clovelly Carys was Sir John, Chief Baron of the Exchequer in 1387, who died in banishment at Waterford. His son John was, it is said, nominated Bishop of Exeter in 1419 by the Pope while in Italy, but only lived six weeks afterwards, and was never installed. George Cary, Dean of Exeter (1644-1680), is recorded in his epitaph to have twice refused a bishopric. The church is said to have been made collegiate by Sir William Cary in 1387.

Clovelly, for centuries a fishing village, has acquired reputation as a seaside resort.

Hartland, or Harton, is the westernmost town in Devon, and the extensive parish in which it lies occupies nearly the whole of the north-west angle of the county. Hartland Point is named by Ptolemy after Hercules; and the Romans left unmistakable traces of their presence in this remote corner. In Saxon times it was evidently a county centre of considerable importance, for the population recorded in 'Domesday' exceeds that of any other Northern manor—30 serfs, 60 villeins, and 45 bordars. Moreover, it was worth £48 a year. The name in 'Domesday' is Hertitone, agreeing with the modern Harton, but the form Hartland is probably of as great antiquity, since the affix 'land' is constantly employed in the Devon Survey as signifying a district of a promontorial character, somewhat akin in usage to the Kornu-Keltic *lan*.

The last Saxon holder of the manor was Gytha, mother of Harold, and by her was founded what afterwards became Hartland Abbey, for canons secular, in gratitude, it is said, for the preservation of her husband, Earl Godwin, from shipwreck. Her foundation was dedicated to St. Nectan, the patron saint of the parish church of Stoke St. Nectan, reputedly buried here. The abbey was refounded for Augustine canons by Geoffrey de Dynham, or Dinant, in the reign of Henry II., and by him re-endowed. It had benefactors also in the Tracys, Peverells, and Boterells, and Richard I. gave it the right of gallows. At the Dissolution its revenues were valued at £306 3s. 4d.

It was to Oliver de Dinant that the market was granted to 'Harton borough' in 1280. The Dinants held Hartland until the last male of the name, created Lord Dinham by Edward IV. in 1466, died without issue, and his estates passed through his sisters to the families of Carew, Arundell, Fitzwarine, and Zouch. There is some little confusion as to the further descent of the various manors; but the Abbey, in the basement of which there remain portions of the Early English cloisters, belongs to Sir George Stucley, who represents, in the female line, the Stukelys of Afton, several members of whom figure prominently in Devonshire history. Thomas Stukely undertook the plantation of Florida, but turned to something like piracy instead, and died at Alcazar in Africa, fighting side by side with Sebastian of Portugal, in 1578. He it was who told Elizabeth that he would rather be the sovereign of a molehill than the highest subject to the greatest king in Christendom. It was Sir Lewis Stukely, afterwards named 'Judas,' who arrested Ralegh on his return from his last voyage; and in later days Puritanism and the Parliament had few more earnest advocates in word and deed than another Lewis Stukely, the Independent minister of Exeter.

A more striking illustration of the comparative isolation of Hartland in the sixteenth century can hardly be afforded than the fact that it was evidently overlooked by the commissioners of Edward and Elizabeth in their visitations for the reform of religion. The church of Stoke St. Nectan is not only one of singular architectural merit, especially for so remote a situation, but it contains its screen in perfect preservation, and, what is far more noteworthy, its stone altar standing in its original place.

There are stated to have been anciently eleven chapels in this extensive parish. The parish documents are unusually numerous and interesting, and have been reported on by the Historical Manuscripts Commission. Dr. Moreman, born at Hartland in 1529, vicar of Menheniot, is reputed to have been the first who used the English language in public worship in Cornwall—teaching his parishioners the Creed, Commandments, and Lord's Prayer in that tongue.

CHAPTER XVIII.

GREAT TORRINGTON.

WHAT is now Great Torrington was of old Cheping (= Market) Torrington. There are several Torringtons entered in 'Domesday,' and the need of distinction was early felt. Now we have Great Torrington, Little Torrington close by, and Black Torrington some miles higher up the river. Of these the only one that has a history is the first. Gytha held lands in one of the Torringtons, but probably not the 'great' manor of that name. Under the Normans Great Torrington became the head of an honour containing twenty-nine knights' fees, which were eventually divided among the five daughters of Matthew de Torrington, married respectively to Merton, Wallis, Tracy, Sully, and Umfraville. This seriously complicates the descent of the barony and manor. In 1228, however, the Castle of Torrington belonged to Henry de Tracy, and the Sheriff of Devon was directed to cause it to be thrown down. A return to a writ of inquiry under Edward I. shows Thomas de Merton possessed of two parts, Walter de Sully of one part, John Umfraville of one part, and Galfride de Kamville, by the death of Henry de Tracy, of one part. The names of De Brian, St. John, and Cary afterwards come into the succession, and when John de Cary was attainted 2 Henry IV. his estates passed to Robert Chalons. The castle was rebuilt in 1340 by

Robert de Merton. Little more than the name of Castle Hill continues. It was at Torrington the Sessions were held in 1484, at which the Marquis of Dorset, Sir Edward Courtenay, Bishop Peter Courtenay, and 500 other noblemen and gentlemen, were outlawed for treason against Richard III.; while Sir Thomas St. Leger, who had married Richard's sister, and Thomas Rayme, were found guilty of high treason, and beheaded at Exeter. Margaret of Richmond was one of the chief residents of Torrington, and gave her manor-house as a residence for the vicar. Torrington no doubt was Lancastrian. Torrington has had two illustrious vicars. Cardinal Wolsey, who held the incumbency until his promotion to the See of Lincoln in 1514, and gave the church to his new foundation of Christ Church, Oxford. And John Howe, chaplain to the Protector, who was ejected in 1662.

The church figures prominently in the one event which links Torrington with the later history of the kingdom. The town was held for the King by Sir John Digby in August, 1643, when the Bideford and Barnstaple men made their unsuccessful assault, and in the hands of the Royalists it chiefly remained. In February, 1646, it was the headquarters of Lord Hopton, who had been making preparations for the relief of Exeter. Fairfax soon advanced against him, marching from Crediton to Chulmleigh on the 14th, and mustering all his forces at Ashreigney on the 16th. Although he had an army of 9,500 men, Hopton was unaware of his approach until attack was imminent; and the preparations for defence were necessarily of a hurried character. Nevertheless, the advance of the Parliamentary troops was so obstructed by skirmishing behind the hedges and by blocking the roads with trees, that, although they left Ashreigney at seven in the morning, it was eight in the evening before Torrington was reached, Stevenstone House having been taken on the way. Even then, although Hopton had no more than 5,000 troops,

his position might almost have been deemed impregnable.
Standing upon a hill among hills, all but girdled with
deep valleys, the place is one of great natural strength;
and Hopton had made good disposition of his forces.
Fairfax was content with what had been already done for
the day, and prepared for an assault in the morning.
About midnight, however, as he and Cromwell were going
their rounds, they heard sounds that led them to imagine
the enemy were in retreat. To test the point a small
body of dragoons was ordered to approach the first
barricade and fire over. They met with such a warm
reception that others had to be sent to their relief; and
then the reserve, thinking that an attack had been commenced, came running up without waiting for orders.
An assault in force was now inevitable; and, after an
hour's desperate fighting, the place was won. Hopton
himself was wounded and barely escaped. The Royalist
losses were very heavy. More than 600 prisoners were
taken; and, though Fairfax did little in the way of
pursuit, there was another sharp conflict at Hembury
Fort, near Buckland Brewer, where the Cavaliers took
refuge within the earthworks of the ancient camp.

The capture of Torrington was the real end to the war
in the West. It was signalized, moreover, by a great
catastrophe. The Royalists had converted the church
into a powder-magazine. The Roundheads, ignorant of
this, drove into it 200 of their prisoners. Whether by
accident or by design the powder was fired, and the
church blew up, killing prisoners, guards, and townsfolk,
and destroying scores of houses. Fairfax nearly fell a
victim; but it was noted as an evidence of miraculous
interposition with the 'hellish plot'—a '*mira non mirabilia*'
—that 'though the Books of Common Prayer were blowne
up or burnt, the blessed Bible was preserved and not
obliterated, although it were blowne away.' Hugh Peters
preached a thanksgiving sermon for the capture in the

market-place, and a more formal thanksgiving was appointed by the Parliament. In addition to the prisoners, 3,000 stand of arms and the whole of the baggage and money of the Royal army were taken.

The inhabitants of Great Torrington have extensive and peculiar rights over the common lands adjoining their town, which are said by Risdon to date from the time of Richard I. The documentary history extends to the reign of Elizabeth. Over the unenclosed commons of 370 acres 'all occupiers of ancient messuages,' locally called 'pot-boilers,' claim the right to common of pasture without stint. Over another 163 acres of 'common fields' similar rights are claimed, subject to a right of tillage in the owner of the fee. The ancient custom was to remove the gates of these fields annually after harvest, and stock the land with cattle from the adjacent open commons until the customary time for the next year's tillage. In 1835 this plan was modified by an agreement on the part of the occupiers to pay, and the commoners to receive, 'quiet possession rents,' in consideration of which the fields are allowed to be cultivated in any way thought proper. Still more recently fresh disputes have arisen between the commoners and the lord of the manor, the Hon. Mark Rolle.

Considering the antiquity and early importance of Torrington, and the large number of important families resident in the neighbourhood, it may seem somewhat singular that Torrington should not have had a more prominent place in the national life. Two causes probably, however, contributed to this—one, the fact that notwithstanding its antiquity and trade, it lay in an isolated part of the country, outside the run of ordinary traffic; the other, its successful endeavour in 1368 to rid itself of the burden of sending burgesses to Parliament, on the score of its poverty. It was represented 23rd Edward I. to 45th Edward III. The present incorporation of the town as a municipality dates from Mary; but the seal of 'Chipyngtoriton' is certainly of older date. The market is held by prescription, and possibly has a Saxon origin. The town was largely engaged in the woollen manufacture; it is now chiefly occupied in gloving, of which it is a very important centre.

Frithelstock, an adjoining parish to Great Torrington, held by Ordulf before the Conquest, then passing to the Earl of Moreton, is chiefly noteworthy here as having been the site of a small priory of Austin canons, founded, 1220, by Sir Roger de Beauchamp. Portions of the original Early English structure are still standing. The Priory was settled by monks from Hartland, and the two houses were always so far connected that the prior of each had a voice in the election of the head of the other. The revenues at the Dissolution were valued at £127 2s. 0½d.; and the estate was granted by Henry VII. to Arthur, Viscount Lisle, afterwards passing into the family of Rolle, and descending to the Earl of Orford and Lord Clinton. The advowson of Ashwater was given by Richard de Braylegh, temp. Edward III., to the prior and convent of Frithelstock for certain charities.

Monkleigh was given to the Priory of Montacute in Somerset by its founder, William, Earl Moreton, in the reign of Henry I., and after the Dissolution passed to the family of Coffin. Here is the ancient seat and park of Annery, once the home of the Stapledons, then by marriage of the Hankfords. This was the residence of Sir William Hankford, born at Hankford, in Bulkworthy, and created in 1413 Lord Chief Justice of the King's Bench; the judge who traditionally disputes with Gascoigne and Hody the credit of having committed Henry V., as Prince of Wales, to prison for striking him a blow on the Bench. Another tradition, probably of equal authority, is connected with Hankford alone.

Having returned to Annery, and being weary of his life, he accused his park-keeper of want of care in the preservation of his deer, and ordered him to shoot anyone whom he might meet in his rounds at night, and who did not answer upon being challenged. Having so provided, he himself walked in the park, met his keeper, refused to reply to the challenge, and, as he hoped and intended, was shot by a quarrel from the keeper's cross-bow. A tree is still pointed out as that under which Hankford was standing at the time; and there is yet a little dread in the country-side of meeting the ghost of the Lord Chief Justice. All the ancient accounts of the transaction differ so materially that speculation seems almost idle. Hankford was, however, buried at Monkleigh, where his mutilated monument remains. His descendants married into the families of Fitzwarine, St. Leger, and Bourchier, Grenville, Stukely, and Tremayne. Anne Bullen was granddaughter of Anne, daughter and heiress of Sir Richard Hankford, thus enabling the county to claim Queen Elizabeth as in part of Devonshire kindred.

Wear Giffard has already been mentioned as one of the seats of the once wide-spread and powerful family of Giffard, and later of the Fortescues, whose manor-house has one of the noblest halls of its period still left, the roof being reckoned among the finest examples of Perpendicular woodwork in England.

Then we have, on the east of Torrington, the extensive parish of St. Giles-in-the-Wood, so called to distinguish it from St. Giles-in-the-Heath, which lies on the borders of Cornwall, and which contains the manor of Cary, reputedly the original home of the Cary family. The church of St. Giles was originally a chapel to Torrington. Stevenstone here, now the property of the Hon. Mark Rolle, in the time of Henry II. belonged to Richard St. Michael, thence passing to Basset, De la Ley, Grant, and Moyle; and finally, in the reign of Henry VIII., being bought by George Rolle, an eminent London merchant. Way passed from the Ways to the Pollards and Wyllingtons. Winscott from the Barrys came to Risdon, the chorographer (1580-1640), now represented by Sir Stafford Northcote, and is the seat of Mr. J. C. Moore-Stevens, a descendant of one of the wealthy townsfolk and benefactors of Torrington, William Stevens. There are also Dodescot, which belonged to the Howards; and Whitsleigh, held by Dynants, Durants, Kellaways, Drakes, and Woollacombes.

The parish of Merton is celebrated as containing the manor of Potheridge, the home for many descents of the family of Monk, made illustrious in their descendant, the famous General. There is some little confusion as to the exact place of Monk's birth (1608), arising from the fact that he was baptized, not at Merton, but at Landcross, a parish some miles distant, adjoining Bideford. Hence he has been variously regarded as being born at Potheridge and at Landcross. However, Potheridge was both the seat of his family and became his own chief residence. The mansion was rebuilt by him for that purpose; but in greater part was destroyed after the death of the widow of his son Christopher, the second and last duke, in 1734. Monk was one of those men, so characteristic of the period in which he lived, who were equally at home at sea or on land; and his first service was marine. Afterwards he saw much active duty in Scotland and Ireland, originally as a partizan of Charles I.; but subsequently in command of the Roundhead forces under Cromwell. In Ireland he dispersed the forces of O'Neale; and in Scotland he quenched the hopes of the Royalists by the capture of Edinburgh and Stirling Castles. Then he became 'general at sea,' and defeated the Dutch in two great engagements; after which, for a while, he took up his residence at Dalkeith. Here he was living when Cromwell died; and hence he marched into England with a small army, and took the leadership of affairs, and the direction of the movement which led to the restoration of Charles II. The King was grateful. Monk was made Captain-General, Baron Potheridge, Earl of Torrington, and Duke of Albemarle. Thenceforward, until his death in 1670, he held the foremost position in the kingdom in all matters connected with the national defence. His last service of importance was the defeat of the Dutch in conjunction with Prince Rupert.

Concerning Merton itself, it may be noted that at the Conquest it passed to Geoffrey, Bishop of Coutances, having been held by Torquil. The 'Domesday' entry gives it all the characteristics of a wild woodland manor; for to a population of 23 serfs, villeins, and bordars, it had no fewer than 9 swineherds. A much smaller manor of the same name was held by Richard, under Baldwin the Sheriff. Baldwin was likewise the lord of Porridge, in which we may in all probability identify Potheridge. This had been the land of Ulf, and was held under Baldwin by Alberic. There seems to have been some connection between Potheridge and Merton, possibly derived from ancient common ownership, as the rector of Merton was entitled to a dinner every Sunday and the keep of his grey mare out of the barton of Potheridge, which eventually was commuted for a modus of £3 per annum. At least, so say the Lysonses, following Chapple. Merton, which was for a while in the Stawells (following the Mertons) and the Rolles, passed to the Trefusises, Barons Clinton.

CHAPTER XIX.

HOLSWORTHY AND HATHERLEIGH.

THERE is no more uninteresting part of Devon historically than the corner next the Cornish border, of which the chief centres are Holsworthy and Hatherleigh; and yet it is precisely here that almost the only trace of Roman influence on the nomenclature of Devon, outside Exeter, is to be found. Near North Lew—a bleak upland parish, where, according to the local proverb, 'the devil died of the cold'—are Chester Moor, Scobchester, and Wickchester; and it does not seem possible to evade the conclusion that these names mark the localities of Roman castra, and point to some sort of Roman, perhaps frontier, occupation.

Hatherleigh formed part of the original endowment of Tavistock Abbey, and appears in 'Domesday' under the name of Adrelie. The entry has some interesting features. The Abbey held in demesne 6 serfs, 26 villeins, and 6 coscets; and there were 4 tenants under the abbey—Nigel, Walter, Geoffrey, and Ralph, who had 4 serfs, 12 villeins, 4 bordars, and 5 coscets. Geoffrey, moreover, had a mill upon his lands. This tenancy—itself continuing in all likelihood older divisions—probably originated the subsequent manorial apportionments of the parish. After the Dissolution the chief manor, Hatherleigh proper, passed to the Arscotts. Hatherleigh Moor, the manor waste, belongs to the inhabitants, and it is the common belief among them that this comes of the gift of John of Gaunt, who executed the conveyance in the rhyme :

> 'I, John of Gaunt,
> Do give and do grant
> Hatherleigh Moor
> To Hatherleigh poor
> For evermore.'

And this is all that there is to be said of Hatherleigh, beyond the fact that it gave birth to John Mayne, dramatist and theologian (1604-72).

Holsworthy, the other town of the district, has a somewhat better claim to notice. The market is one of great antiquity; and the chief fair was recorded in the time of Edward I. as having belonged to the ancestors of William Martyn from time immemorial. Holsworthy was held for the King in 1646, and occupied by Fairfax, after his capture of Torrington; but apparently without a contest. Probably the Haldeword, which Harold held before the Conquest and William afterwards, it had even then an enumerated population of 75. There is evidence also that it must have been of much greater importance in the Middle Ages than it has been since, in the fact that it had 600 houseling people in 1547. The manor has been the property of several distinguished families. Henry II. gave it to Fulk Paganell, until he should be able to recover his own lands in Normandy. Afterwards it came to the Chaworths, thence to the Tracys, the Martyns, and the Audleys. Then it reverted to the Crown, and was held by royal grant in succession by John of Gaunt (and this may have been the association that linked his name with Hatherleigh tradition) John Holland, Duke of Exeter, and Margaret, Countess of Richmond. For a while it was in the Specotts and Prideauxes, and was sold by the latter to Thomas Pitt, Lord Londonderry, from whom it has descended to its present owner, Lord Stanhope. At Thorne a family of that name were seated from the reign of King John till the early part of the seventeenth century. Here also is Arscott, which gave name to that ancient house, later of Tetcott. The 'church town' of Holsworthy is now a thriving agricultural centre.

Few of the adjoining parishes call for special mention. Ashbury has been the seat of the Morth-Woollcombes for some two centuries; at Beaworthy a park was made about 1366 by Sir Nigel Loring, one of the first Knights of the Garter; Abbots Bickington takes its distinctive name from being given by Geoffrey de Dinant to Hartland Abbey; Bradworthy Church was the gift of Lord Briwere to the Abbey of Torre; Bratton Clovelly disputes with Bratton Fleming, and Bracton Court near Minehead in Somerset, the honour of being the birthplace of Henry de Bracton, Chief Justiciary under Henry III., the celebrated writer on the laws and customs of England— 'De Legibus et Consuetudinibus Angliæ' (d. *circa* 1268)— who lies buried in Exeter Cathedral; Bridgerule is really Bridge Raoul, from its Norman owner, Ruald Adobed; Broadwood Widger, named from the once prominent family of that name, belonged subsequently to Frithelstock Priory, while the manor of Mere Malherbe was given by Fitz Stephen to the Hospital of St. John of Jerusalem, and by its prior conveyed to the Abbey of Buckland in Somerset; Hollacombe, like Newton St. Petrock (the gift of Æðelstan), was the property of Bodmin Priory; Honeychurch gave name to a family which has ceased to be connected with it, but has only recently, if yet, become extinct; Iddesleigh was anciently the seat of the Sullys, the last of whom was Sir John Sully, who served at Halidon, Cressy, Poictiers, and in Spain, and at the reputed age of 105 (1387) gave evidence at his residence in the Scrope and Grosvenor controversy—he died soon after, and is said to have been buried at Crediton, but a figure of a Crusader at Iddesleigh is also assigned to him; Inwardleigh was an early settlement of the family of

Coffin; Jacobstow, as Jacobescherche, is remarkable as being not only one of the 'Devenescire' manors which did not change hands at the Conquest, but as belonging to a Saxon lady, Alveva, and as being the seat of a Saxon church; Pancrasweek, which anciently belonged to the Briweres, was given by William Lord Briwere to Torre Abbey, and, like the next manor, recalls a dedication of the British Church; Petrockstow was part of the possessions of the Abbey of Buckfast, mentioned as such in 'Domesday'—the park of Heanton Satchville belongs to Lord Clinton, whose seat is in the adjoining parish of Huish, once possessed by the bearers of that ancient name; Shebbear was formerly in the Nevilles, and John Alvethol held lands here by the service of holding the King's stirrup whenever he should come into the lordship; Sheepwash, adjoining, was of old a market-town; Tetcott was the last seat of the family of Arscott, who died out in the male line in 1788, and were succeeded by the Molesworths; Werrington was the chief manor of the Abbey of Tavistock..

Winkleigh has claims to a more detailed notice. In the first place, the parish forms a hundred of itself; and in the second, it was part of the honour of Gloucester. Before the Conquest, it was held by Brictric, who succeeded his father, Algar, in the Gloucester earldom; and, like other possessions of that unlucky Saxon, passed to William's Queen. 'Domesday' notes it an important manor, with 40 ploughlands, and an enumerated population of 76. Moreover, it contained the only park entered for Devon. Upon Matilda's death, Rufus became the lord; and, shortly after his accession, gave the manor to Robert Fitz Hamon. By the marriage of Fitz Hamon's daughter, Mabel, to Robert Fitzroy, illegitimate son of Henry I., the estates of the earldom of Gloucester passed to him, and the title followed. Winkleigh was early divided into the two manors of Winkleigh Keynes and

Winkleigh Tracy, named from their respective owners. The Earls of Gloucester still continued, however, to retain some interest—at least, down to the fourteenth century. Risdon speaks of the existence of two castles here ; but there is no trace of either now, beyond a couple of mounds, which *may* have been the foundations ; and both manors were eventually for a time reunited in the family of Lethbridge. It is quite possible that one of those 'castles' may have been the mansion at Up Holecombe, which Richard Inglish had the licence of the King to castellate about 1361, especially as one of the mounds above mentioned is very doubtful. And as William de Portu Mortuo obtained a charter for a market at Hollacombe village in 1260, the place must then have been of some little consequence. Indeed, Winkleigh is sometimes called a borough town. Southcote, another estate in the parish, appears to have given name to the Southcote family. Winkleigh Church was given to the Abbey of Tewkesbury by one of the Fitzroys, and it had a Guild of St. Nicholas. The Rev. Wm. Davey, who died vicar of Winkleigh in 1826, is remarkable for having, while curate of Lustleigh, written and printed with his own hands a system of divinity in twenty-six volumes, working fourteen copies only.

CHAPTER XX.

OKEHAMPTON.

INSIGNIFICANT as Okehampton has been for many a long year, deriving its sole importance since the days of the Stuarts from its position on the high-road into Cornwall, and losing even that when the construction of the Great Western Railway diverted the course of traffic, there are few towns in Devon associated with more distinguished names. It is signalized in 'Domesday' as the one manor in Devon stated to possess a castle. Moreover, it had a mill and a market; and, in addition to 50 villeins, serfs, and bordars, 4 burgesses. Though not one of the four boroughs of the county, it had, therefore, a definitely town-like character in the modern sense. How much of this importance it enjoyed under its Saxon lord, Offers, is doubtful; for, though his timbered 'strength' may have been the nucleus, there is no ancient town in Devon that seems more thoroughly the creation of its castle, the only really defensible spot it possessed.

Baldwin the Sheriff, or Baldwin de Redvers (otherwise De Sap, or De Brioniis), was the most important feudal lord in Devon. No fewer than 181 manors fell to his share in this county alone; and from among them all he selected 'Ochementone' (far more closely preserved in the still current 'Ockington' of the natives than in the polite and utterly unetymological Okehampton) for his chief residence. Ninety-two fees were held of this barony. Here in the centre of his domains, in the very heart of Devon, commanding the passes to the north and west of Dartmoor, and dominating the district far away to the Severn Sea, he reared his castle. None of his masonry remains; but the site is that which he chose, the mound is that which he scarped and isolated from the hillside, of which it formed a rocky spur; and the surroundings have changed little from the day when the square Norman keep first frowned upon the brawling waters of the rapid Ockment in the valley below.

For a time the house of Redvers flourished. Not only did they hold the chief barony of Devon in Okehampton, not only were they hereditary castellans of Exeter, and sheriffs of the county; but Richard, son of Baldwin, by his faithful adherence to Henry I., gained the town of Tiverton, and the honour of Plympton. His son, Baldwin, espoused the cause of Matilda, and was driven from the kingdom, with the loss of all his great possessions. Yet it was not long ere the De Redverses were reinstated in their honours and estates; and it was by marriage with Mary, daughter of William de Verona, sixth Redvers Earl, the coheiress of that great family, that the historic house of Courtenay became not only lords of Okehampton, but eventually obtained the earldom of Devon they again so worthily enjoy. With occasional intermissions of forfeiture, the Courtenays held Okehampton, from the death of Isabella de Fortibus in 1292, until the death of Edward Courtenay in 1556.

Robert de Courtenay is said to have made Okehampton a free borough in the reign of Henry III. He can only, however, have affirmed and extended pre-existing rights. Representatives were sent to Parliament as early as 28th Edward I.; but the town was not incorporated by royal charter until 1623, and portreeve and mayor long existed side by side, the custom being for the same burgess to be chosen to fill both offices. From 7th Edward II. until 1640 the town ceased to elect members; then it resumed and continued until finally extinguished in 1832. There are two corporate seals. One, presumably attached to the office of portreeve, bears for device a triple towered castle; the municipal seal has a cornucopia, charged with an escutcheon, bearing the Redvers arms. A new corporation was chartered in 1885.

Brightley was the original seat of the Cistercians of Ford Abbey, which they found it impossible to colonize successfully.

The value of Okehampton as a strategic point entailed many inconveniences and no little loss in the course of the wars between Charles and the Parliament. Troops of both parties occupied in turn, and it was never free long together from the presence of one or the other. Charles himself, Maurice, Essex, Goring, Richard Grenville, Fairfax, and several minor commanders, held possession at various times; but it was never the scene of actual conflict. The nearest fighting was a hotly contested affair in May, 1643, between Chudleigh and Hopton and Grenville, at Meldon, in Bridestowe, memorable for being fought by night in a storm of wind and rain. Chudleigh had somewhat the advantage; but the defeat of the Earl of Stamford followed too closely to render the victory of any avail. Okehampton Castle had been dismantled by Henry VIII., or in all probability an effort would have been made to hold it. Okehampton Park is still the name of the ancient demesne skirting Dartmoor; but it was disparked and alienated by Henry VIII.

Bridestowe, the adjoining parish to the south-west, was held at the time of the Domesday Survey by Ralph de Pomeroy, ancestor of the great house of Pomeroy, under Baldwin. The name is really a corruption of Bridgetstowe, the church being dedicated to that saint, and thus marking the site of a pre-Norman foundation. Sampford Courtenay, which lies to the north-east, has been already noted as the place where the Western Rebellion for the restoration of Roman Catholicism had its rise. It was a parcel of the barony of Okehampton.

North Tawton, a market-town of considerable antiquity and of old time a borough, retained its portreeve as a memorial of former importance, though the prefix has long been dropped which gave it claim to rank with Great Torrington as a Saxon market—Cheping or Chipping Tawton. This may be taken as some guide to its identification in 'Domesday.' It was certainly held by William; but whether it was the Tavyetone which had 3 serfs, 31 villeins, and 33 bordars, or the Tavetone which had belonged to Gytha, with its 12 serfs, 50 villeins, and 30 bordars, there is very little direct evidence. The greater importance of the latter would indeed seem to make it likely that this was North Tawton, and Tavyetone South Tawton; but though at first sight the former identification would appear almost certain from the fact that while Tavetone is associated in 'Domesday' with the smaller manor of Ashe, there is still extant in North Tawton the estate of *Ash*ridge; oddly enough, we find that at South Tawton we have the alias of Eastash.

North Tawton was one of the possessions of the famous family of Valletort, to whom a market-grant was made in 1270. It came by coheiresses to the Champernownes, from whom it descended to the St. Legers and Woods (or Atwoods) who lived at Ashridge several generations.

The barton of Bath is associated with a notable piece of folk-lore. It was the name, place, and seat of the family of Bath, De Bath, or Bathon—a house sometime of much note. Of this stock was Sir Henry Bath, Justice Itinerant to Henry III., who was charged with corruption in his office, and respecting whom Henry is said to have declared at his trial, 'Whosoever shall kill Henry de Bath shall be quit of his death, and I do hereby acquit him.' However, Bath was fortunate enough not only to be taken into favour again, but to be made Chief Justice of the King's Bench. He died in 1261. The point of folk-lore raised is not unique, which makes it the more curious. There is at Bath a large pit or excavation, which under ordinary circumstances is perfectly dry, but becomes filled with water, by an intermittent spring, before any great national event or family calamity. This is said to have occurred in recent days, immediately before the death of the Duke of Wellington. As Bath is the Saxon *baeth*, 'water,' probably this phenomenon has continued for many centuries, and gave name to the estate.

North Tawton is one of the very few centres of the woollen manufacture which retains its trade. It possesses a very large woollen factory which has always kept pace with the times, and thus illustrates what might have been done if masters and men had been everywhere equally well advised to keep the ancient trade in the county.

The leading manor of South Tawton was once in the Beaumonts, being granted by Henry I. to Roselm Beaumont, Viscount de Mayne, whose granddaughter brought it to Roger de Tony. This family appear to have made the village of South Zeal (=Saxon, *sell*, a dwelling) the borough which it is occasionally described as being, for Robert de Tony had a grant of a market and fairs there in 1298. Tantifer, Chiseldon, and Wadham are also ancient names in connection with the descent of South Tawton Manor.

A far more remarkable piece of Devonshire folk-lore than that just noted is associated with this parish of South Tawton—'the Oxenham omen'—every fact in relation to which has recently been collected with the minutest care by Mr. R. W. Cotton. Oxenham here gave name to a family of repute, one of whose members was John Oxenham, of Plymouth, the first Englishman who sailed on the Pacific, a comrade of Drake at Nombre de Dios, who eventually fell into the hands of the Spaniards and was by them executed as a pirate—one of the bravest and most unfortunate of the great seamen of Elizabethan Devon. The 'omen' consists in the appearance of a 'bird with a white breast,' or of a white bird, before the deaths of members of the family. The earliest record of this apparition refers to the year 1618; but in 1641 what is now a rare pamphlet was published, detailing four appearances before the deaths of four members of a branch of the Oxenhams, settled at Zeal Monachorum, in 1635. The tradition continues in the family, where the reality of the appearances is not doubted, though 'no decided conviction obtains as to their cause.' Recent instances of the 'omen' are quoted in connection, the most remarkable of which was the appearance of a white bird outside the windows of a house in Kensington a week before the death of Mr. G. N. Oxenham, then head of the family, in 1873. The bird refused for some minutes to be driven away, and a sound like the fluttering of wings is stated to have been heard in the bedroom. Probably this belief in the white bird of the Oxenhams is associated in some way with the wide-spread superstition that the flying of birds around a house and tapping against the window, or resting on the sill, portends death. Mr. Cotton inclines to the belief that the solution of the problem may be 'physiological . . . and that *heredity*, of the force and effects of which we have probably little conception, and the marvellous instincts of animals, of which we know so little, are the keys to it.' Zeal Monachorum, by the way, takes its distinctive name from having been given by Cnut to Buckfastleigh Abbey.

CHAPTER XXI.

LYDFORD.

UBI LAPSUS, QUID FECI ? might well be the motto of the little town of Lydford, one of the oldest boroughs in all broad Devon, populous and wealthy long before the Norman Conquest—almost the rival of Exeter, as we see it first emerging from the mists of antiquity—now the mere shadow of a shade. Some scattered houses, a few green mounds, a crumbling ruin—these are modern Lydford—all we have left beside a few legends and tattered memories of former greatness: a few scattered entries that make up the sum-total of a history which extends over more than ten centuries. No town or village in the West teaches the mournful lesson—*vanitas vanitatum*—so thoroughly as Lydford. We are even left to guess at the cause of its fall.

Like Exeter, we have in Lydford an ancient British settlement; but, unlike Exeter, one cast down from its high estate. Approach it from any quarter, save where the bridge of later days spans the chasm of the Lyd, and the strength of the position is seen at once. So environed is it with moor and bog, with hill and ravine, that in ancient days there was but one mode of access, and that most exposed and circuitous. The village stands upon a tongue of land, bounded and defended towards the south by the deep and, in old days, impassable gorge of the Lyd;

on the north by the ravine of a tributary of that river. Northward and southward therefore, and on the angle to the west, the natural strength of the position in days of primitive warfare was enormous; and all that was needed was to guard the approach from the higher ground to the east. This was done by the construction of a line of earthworks, yet traceable, though never observed until their existence was recorded by the writer, from one valley or ravine to the other.

Although Lydford finds no place in history until Anglo-Saxon times, it then appears as a town that had some antiquity to boast. Its importance is shown by the fact that it was the seat of a Saxon mint, sharing that honour in Devon with Exeter and Totnes. Lydford pennies are extant of the reign of Æðelred the Unready, Cnut, Harold Harefoot, and possibly of Eadweard the Confessor and the second Harold. Its earlier antiquity is indicated not only by the earthworks of the Kelts, but by the Keltic dedication of its church to St. Petrock; and, while the font in the existing church is probably Saxon, there is some reason to regard the north wall of that fabric as of at least equal age.

It is under the reign of Æðelred that Lydford first appears in the pages of history. The 'Saxon Chronicle' records how, in 997, the Danes made a raid up the Tamar and Tavy until they came to Hlidaforda, burning and slaying everything they met; burning Ordulf's minster at Ætefingstoc (Tavistock), and bringing back to their ships incalculable plunder. Whether the passage implies the capture of Lydford by the Norsemen, to whom its mint must have been a great attraction, or whether we are to infer that it proved the barrier to their inroad, is not certain. If taken and spoiled, recovery must have been speedy, for 'Domesday' ranks Lydford one of the four Saxon boroughs of Devon—with Exeter, Barnstaple, and Totnes—and as doing equal service. The most significant

'Domesday' entry, however, is the statement that forty houses had been laid waste in Lydford since the Conqueror came to England. Prior to 1066, therefore, it is evident that Lydford must have been the most populous centre in Devon, Exeter alone excepted.

History is silent as to the cause of this devastation of Lydford, but there seems every reason to believe that it was connected in some way with the Conquest, and that it probably arose from the resistance which the sturdy little borough offered to the Norman arms. Exeter, while resisting, as we have seen, gave way in time, and was spared. William may have deemed it desirable to make an example of Lydford, though more merciful even here than in the Northern counties.

Lydford never thoroughly recovered this blow; though, as it remained the head of the Forest of Dartmoor, and was subsequently appointed the prison of the Stannaries of Devon, it retained some importance in the Middle Ages, particularly in the early part of the thirteenth century. Thus, when Edward I. summoned his first Parliament, Lydford was one of the boroughs to which writs were directed.

The Castle of Lydford, in part at least Late Norman, dates from the latter part of the twelfth century. The Keltic earthworks were continued as defences by the Saxons. There was no place within the circuit of supreme command whereon to plant a citadel to dominate the whole. Okehampton traces its origin to the castle near which it grew—here the castle is the child of the town. The building is a true keep, wholly differing in character from the shell keeps which, as at Plympton and Totnes, were planted by the Normans upon the mounds of the elder 'strengths'; and it was of peculiar importance as one of the border fortresses by which the roads skirting Dartmoor were commanded. The earliest traceable mention of the castle in history is its grant, July 31st, 1216, to William Briwere to be held during pleasure. A century later (1305) it is named as the prison of the Stannaries.

Lydford law has the same bad proverbial reputation as *Jeddart justice;* and the rhymes of William Browne of Tavistock, one of the sweetest of English pastoral poets, are familiar far beyond the precincts of the county:

> 'I oft have heard of Lydford law,
>   How in the morn they hang and draw,
>   And sit in judgment after.
>   At first I wondered at it much,
>   But now I find their reason such
>   That it deserves no laughter.'

The piece is one of the most humorous topographical poems in existence. The castle is likened to

> 'An old windmill,
> The vanes blown off by weather.
>   *   *   *   *   *
> 'If any could devise by art
> To get it up into a cart,
>   'Twere fit to carry lions!'

Besides the castle we are told

> 'There is a bridge, there is a church,
>   Seven ashes and an oak;
> Three houses standing and ten down.
>   *   *   *   *   *
> 'One told me, "In King Cæsar's time
> The town was built of stone and lime"—
>   But sure the walls were clay;
> For they are fall'n for aught I see,
> And since the houses are got free,
>   The town is run away.'

As to the neighbourhood and its denizens:

> 'This town's enclosed with desert moors,
> But where no bear nor lion roars,
>   And nought can live but hogs;
> For all o'erturned by Noah's flood,
> Of fourscore miles scarce one foot's good,
>   And hills are wholly bogs.

> 'And near hereto's the Gubbins' cave,
> A people that no knowledge have
> Of law, of God, or men :
> Whom Cæsar never yet subdued ;
> Who lawless live, of manners rude,
> All savage in their den.'

Fuller gives a description of these Gubbinses, utilized by Kingsley in 'Westward Ho!' and the surname survives in the district, and in the saying ' Greedy Gubbins.'

Many have been the attempts to account for the origin of 'Lydford law.' Local tradition avers that it originated in the cruelty of Jeffries during the Bloody Assize, and that his ghost haunts the castle in the shape of a black pig. But the Bloody Assize stopped short of Lydford, and the saying is far older than the days of Monmouth. Browne wrote his rhymes when he visited Lydford to see his friend, the Roundhead Colonel Hals, imprisoned there by the brutal Sir Richard Grenville. But Browne had *often* heard of the proverb, and it did not originate with him. It has been usual to trace it to the practice of the Stannary Courts, and to connect it with the case of Richard Strode, imprisoned at Lydford as an offender against the Stannary Laws in the reign of Henry VIII.; but Strode was certainly incarcerated by process of law, and by no means ' hung first and tried after.' Moreover, there seems to be very fair ground for holding that, in the line of action which led to his imprisonment, Strode was actuated rather by personal motives, and was not, as most of the county historians have assumed without inquiring into the facts, a martyr for the public good. Be that as it may, his detention in the ' hainous, contagious, and detestable' dungeon pit of Lydford, now open to the day within the castle walls, led to the declaration of the right of Parliamentary free speech. Strode was member for Plympton ; the sentence against him was annulled by Act of Parliament, on the assumption that he was prosecuted for preventing the tinners from injuring creeks and harbours; and it was declared in that statute that all proceedings against members of Parliament 'for any bill, speaking, reasoning, or declaring of any matters' in Parliament, should be void and of none effect.

In any case the experience of Strode could not originate 'Lydford law;' for the expression occurs in a poem, assigned by Mr. T. Wright, on internal evidence, to 1399:

> ' Now be the law of Lydfford
> in londe ne in water.'

We thus get an antiquity of at least five hundred years, and come too near to the establishment of the Stannary Prison to look to the maladministration of the Stannary Laws for the origin of the phrase. It is highly probable, therefore, that we must seek it in the fact that the Forest Courts of Dartmoor were held at Lydford, and the intolerable Forest Laws there administered. From the peculiar character of these laws, it was quite possible for the Chief Warden—whose post, as Sir C. S. Maine notes, was executive rather than judicial—to inflict summary punishment, and yet for the case to be inquired into at the Court of Swainmote, and not adjudicated on for three years at the Court of Justice Seat.

From the time of the Commonwealth down to the early part of the last century, the castle was in ruins. It was then restored, and used as a prison and as the meeting-place of the Manor and Borough Courts until the foundation of Princetown. But Sir Thomas Tyrwhitt moved the courts to his new capital of the Moor, and Lydford Castle fell into deeper decay than ever.

As a municipal borough, Lydford continued to possess and exercise many rights and privileges until comparatively recent times. The election of mayor ceased about the middle of the last century, and the corporate insignia have disappeared. The borough coroner was invariably ' the oldest and most grey-headed man in the place.'

CHAPTER XXII.

TAVISTOCK.

FEW places in Devon have a greater antiquity than Tavistock, if we take the Saxon period into chief account. The 'stock' of the Tavy was the most important settlement made by the Saxons on that river, and long before the Conquest it assumed the characteristics of a provincial centre of population and wealth. It was remarkable, until 1885, as being the only Parliamentary existing borough in the county not municipal; for it had never received any charter of incorporation, although it had been represented since the 23rd of Edward I.; and it retained as its chief officer the ancient Saxon portreeve, elected by the voices of his fellow-freeholders. The old village commune of the earliest Teutonic settlers had therefore direct succession in Tavistock. But even this does not fully indicate the antiquity of organized human settlement in the vicinity.

It is a fact that must have a meaning, if this can only be defined, that nearly all the ancient inscribed stones of Devon are found upon one parallel in the south-west of the county, between Stowford on the north and Yealmpton on the south, the line passing through Tavistock as a kind of centre. These all give token of ecclesiastical influence; and two, by the Ogham writing which they bear, proof also of Irish intercourse. They probably indicate therefore a period of active mission-work on the part of the Irish Church, somewhere about the latter part of the fifth and first half of the sixth century.

Of six such monuments found upon the line noted, three will be found within the vicarage garden at Tavistock, placed there by an enthusiastic antiquary of the past generation—the Rev. E. A. Bray. Two of these stones came from Buckland Monachorum. One, which stood in a field, bears the inscription in Roman characters —'DOBUNNI FABRII FILI ENABARRI,' or simply 'NABARR' —the reading adopted by Mr. C. Spence Bate. This latter word is repeated as 'Nabarr' in Ogham, and it is a singular fact that the stone supplied the last letter wanting—'b'—to the completion of Dr. Ferguson's South British Ogham alphabet. The second Buckland Monachorum stone was found by Mr. Bray in use as the support of the roof of a blacksmith's shop. Here the legend is, 'SABINI FILI MACCODECHETI.' The third, which had been adapted as a foot-bridge over a little stream near Tavistock, appears to run, 'NEPRANI FILI CONBEVI,' though the last word has been read 'CONDEVI.'

Of the other three inscribed stones of this group the most interesting was found lying across a brook near Fardel, Cornwood, and is now in the British Museum. This is also bilingual, with the legend both in Roman and in Ogham characters, slightly varied. It was the first stone found in England with an Ogham inscription. The legend runs, 'SANGRANVI FANONI MAQVIRINI.'

The Stowford stone stands in Stowford churchyard, a sepulchral monument, which appears to commemorate a certain 'GUNIGLEI.' The lettering is very rude and peculiar, and the reading quite uncertain. This version, by Mr. C. Spence Bate, seems, however, the most probable; and certainly commends itself much more than the 'GURGLES' of Professor Hubner. The chief interest about this stone lies in the fact that, like the kindred memorial at Yealmpton to 'TOREVS' or 'GOREVS' (of which more anon), we find it in a churchyard; and, so far as appears, upon its original site. Lustleigh, as we shall see, affords another illustration of this; though, from the fact that the stone there has been diverted from its original purpose, by no means of so marked a character.

But the history of Tavistock itself begins with the establishment of the Abbey of St. Rumon. Ordulf, son of Orgar, Ealdorman of Devon, is the reputed founder. He is one of the semi-mythic heroes of the Saxon race who may be found in almost every county, a man of amazing strength—a giant, whose sport it was to stride a stream and cut off with one blow of his hunting-knife the heads of animals brought him for the purpose. He was commanded to build the Abbey in a vision, and his wife was guided by an angel to the site. There is thus ample room for discriminating criticism as to the circumstances attending the foundation, even if we ignore the counter tradition that it was the joint work of Ordulf's father, Orgar, and himself. This much, however, does seem certain, that the Abbey was founded about the year 961; and that in 997 it was destroyed by the Danes during the inroad in which they carried fire and sword from the mouth of the Tamar to Lydford. The monastery must then have been of great size and very wealthy, though we may reject the statement that Ordulf's magnificence made it large enough for 1,000 men. It had, however, come under royal patronage. Ordulf's sister was that Ælfryth (or Elfrida) whose career forms one of the most notable features of Anglo-Saxon annals. Though familiar, her story forms part of Devonian history, and falls into place here. Eadgar, hearing of the beauty of Elfrida, sent Æðelwold to view, with instructions to report if rumour spoke truth, to the intent that if it did he might make her his queen. Instead of securing her for his master the unlucky noble fell in love with her himself, and, disparaging her to the King, easily gained his monarch's consent. At length Eadgar visited Devon, and Æðelwold, fearing the consequences of his deceit, implored his wife to besmirch her loveliness for awhile. She, finding that whereas she was simply the wife of a noble she might have been a queen, resented the fraud, and heightened her attractions to the utmost of her power. The King came, saw, and was overcome. Æðelwold was conveniently killed by accident while hunting the following day with the monarch, we may presume on Dartmoor, and his widow mounted the throne. Her sons were Eadmund and Æðelred, and after the murder of his half-brother, Eadweard the Martyr, by Elfrida's orders, at Corfe Castle, the latter succeeded to the crown, and became the liberal patron of the Abbey of Tavistock. To this connection was due the fact that after its destruction by the Danes the Abbey was rebuilt with so much greater grandeur that it eclipsed every religious house in Devon, in the extent, convenience, and magnificence of its buildings.

It was fortunate, too, in its early heads. Lyfing, who from his eloquence obtained the title of 'Wordsnotera,' and in whom the Sees of Devon and Cornwall were united at Crediton, was one of them. His successor was Ældred, afterwards Archbishop of York, who crowned William the Conqueror. The final dedication was to St. Mary and St. Rumon.

'Domesday' places Tavistock Abbey far at the head of the religious houses in Devon, in the extent and value of its estates. Fourteen manors, besides a house at Exeter, were its landed possessions; and the total annual value is set down at £71 10s. 7d. A noteworthy fact also is that the Abbey had several military tenants, some of whom may have been among the thanes by whom the lands so held were occupied in Saxon times. Tavistock itself had an enumerated population, exclusive of the monks and their five military tenants, of 79, and was therefore the most populous place in the district at the time the Survey was taken. To make its importance fully apparent, however, other manors immediately adjacent would have to be taken into account. There were a dozen residents on that of Wrdiete, now Hurdwick, close to the town; while the next manor of Mideltone, now Milton Abbot, had another fifty. Thus liberally endowed at the time of the Conquest, the Abbey throve even more mightily afterwards, for its possessions were so enlarged by several liberal benefactors, that, while they do not seem to have been always stewarded most heedfully—and in fact the monks in the fourteenth century bore a bad reputation for luxury, gluttony, and laziness—its revenues were valued at the Dissolution at £902 5s. 7d.

In 1458 the abbot was mitred, and in 1514 Henry VIII. put the finishing-touch to the Abbey's glories by calling its head, Richard Banham, to the House of Lords as Baron Hurdwick, while Pope Leo X. granted the same dignitary a bull exempting the Abbey from episcopal jurisdiction. A quarter of a century later came the surrender; and the site of the Abbey and its estates passed to John Russell, ancestor of the Earls and Dukes of Bedford, by whom they have ever since been enjoyed.

That Devonshire should be one of the first counties in England into which the art of printing was introduced, is due to the enterprise and zeal for learning of the monks of Tavistock, in their later mended ways. Only two works from this early Tavistock press now exist; but as the first of these is dated 1525, and the second 1534, they must have produced much more than these two fragments. The earliest is a copy of Bœthius's 'Consolations of Philosophy,' as translated by Walton of Osney: 'Emprented in the exempt monastery of Tauestok, in Denshyre, By me, Dan Thomas Rychard, Monke of the sayde Monastery. To the instant desire of the ryght Worshypful esquyer, Mayster Robert Langdon.' Langdon was a

Cornishman, of Keverell, in St. Martins-by-Looe. The other extant publication of the Tavistock press is a copy of the 'Statutes of the Stannaries.'

The remains of the Abbey are far from affording any adequate idea of its former magnificence, thanks chiefly to the iconoclastic work of a last century vandal named Saunders, who built on part of the site, and with the materials, the Abbey House, which is now the Bedford Hotel. The east gate—essentially of late twelfth-century work, with fifteenth-century additions, however—still remains, with the western gateway, commonly called Betsy Grimbal's Tower, the tradition being that a nun of that name was murdered there. There are also the refectory, now used as the Unitarian chapel, its groined porch being converted into a dairy attached to the Bedford Hotel; a fragment of the north wall of the great Abbey Church, sometimes called Ordulph's Tomb, and at other times Childe's (of whom more anon); and the boundary walls next the Tavy, with a tower which has always been known as the Still House. The fragment of the Abbey Church is in the churchyard of the parish church of St. Eustatius; but the site of the Abbey Church itself is now part of the public street.

The Russells have ever been the most liberal of landlords. Every improvement made in Tavistock has been carried out by the Duke for the time being, 'regardless of expense,' with a taste as well as a liberality that have resulted in making the little town—so far as its main thoroughfares go—the handsomest of its size in the West of England. The venerable parish church, and the yet more venerable Abbey, have governed the style adopted in the erection of the chief public buildings, which are all gathered to one centre; and much expense has been incurred in the removal of structures which did not harmonize with the prevailing mediæval character. At the same time all that was worthy of preservation has been fully kept.

The gatehouse of the mansion of the Fitzes of Fitzford, noted in local history as the scene of a duel between Sir John Fitz and Sir Nicholas Slanning, in which the latter was killed, had to be removed, but it was carefully rebuilt; and close by now stands the latest gift to the town of its ducal lords, a magnificent statue of Tavistock's most distinguished son, Sir Francis Drake, by Boehm. Most of the new public edifices, too, are built of the same material as the old, a free-working green volcanic ash from Hurdwick. This is seen to special advantage in the buildings of the Kelly College, founded on a site given by the Russells, from a bequest of the late Admiral Kelly.

Tavistock is the chief mining centre in Devon, and was one of the Stannary towns. Near it are the Devon Consols Mines, which commenced with a capital of £1,000, reworking an abandoned shaft, and immediately struck a lode of copper so rich that nearly a million and a quarter were paid in dividends. Not far off is Hingston Down, of which it was said in old time:

'Hingston Down, well y-wrought,
Is worth London town, dear y-bought.'

But the modern operations in its mines have not borne out the promise of the rhyme. Hingston was the scene of the defeat of the Danes and their Cornish allies by Eadgar, and of this it is said in Tavistock:

'The blood that flowed down West Street
Would heave a stone a pound weight.'

Tavistock threw in its lot with the Parliament in the Civil War of the seventeenth century. A town which had chosen the famous Pym for representative, and which had the Earl of Bedford for lord, would hardly do other. At the commencement of the struggle in the West, Sir George Chudleigh raised some troops here; and after the defeat of Ruthven at Bradock Down, Stamford retired on Tavistock, but left it for Plymouth on the approach of the

Royalist forces, who in their turn made it their headquarters. Having no defences, it was never made a garrison, but served as a convenient station on the way to Cornwall, for whichever side might for the time be uppermost.

Prince Charles held a council here in December, 1645, which proved the last attempt of the Cavaliers to make head in the West. Exeter was then besieged by the Roundheads; but the Puritans of Plymouth were kept in check by a blockade under Colonel Digby; and, on the arrival of a large reinforcement of trained bands from Cornwall, it was agreed to march upon Totnes, and use that town as a base of operations for the relief of Exeter. The march was about to commence when news came of the advance of Fairfax and Cromwell, and a hasty retreat was beat to Launceston.

The Royalist leader most closely connected with Tavistock was Sir Richard Grenville. His first association with Tavistock was as the claimant of Fitzford House, in right of Lady Howard, his wife, the heiress of the Fitz family. This house was the occasion of the only fighting Tavistock at this time saw; being held for the King and taken by Essex on his way into Cornwall in 1644. The defeat of Essex proved Sir Richard's opportunity; for he added to his wife's estates of Fitzford and Walreddon those of the Earl of Bedford and Sir Francis Drake, confiscated by Charles, so that not only Tavistock itself but a wide extent of surrounding country fell into his hands. His wife, however, contrived to rescue her portion; and the Bedford and Drake estates went back to their original owners when the Parliament gained the upper hand.

Lady Howard had been married three times, before the Duke of Buckingham prevailed with her on behalf of Grenville; and she was so well alive to her own interests, that she settled her estates beyond the power of Grenville to control. His violence when he discovered this led to his being fined heavily in the Star Chamber, and in default committed to the Fleet, whence he escaped to Holland. On the breaking out of the Civil War, he naturally took the Royalist side, as his wife inclined to the Parliament, and, as a first reward of his loyalty, had a sequestration of her estates. The meanness of his character is illustrated by the fate of the unfortunate lawyer who had conducted the suit against him—Francis Brabant; for he hung him as a spy.

Tavistock sent two notable men to St. Stephen's. One, the great Pym, already mentioned; who, with Strode —one of the family of Newnham, Plympton—Hampden, Holles, and Hazelrig, Charles I. sought to send to the Tower for their fearless defence of the rights of the people. The other, the unfortunate Lord William Russell, who perished on the scaffold in 1683, a martyr to the popular cause. Portraits of Pym and Russell, painted by Lady Arthur Russell, adorn the New Hall of the town, which contains the portraits of other local worthies by the same lady.

For its size, Tavistock has produced more distinguished men than any town in the county; and the neighbourhood contains the ancient seats of many leading families of olden time.

Chief of the worthies of Tavistock is the renowned Sir Francis Drake, born in a cottage at Crowndale, probably in the year 1539; but the date is uncertain, and all that is known of Drake's parentage is that his father was a clergyman. Drake is by no means an uncommon name in the neighbourhood and throughout South Devon, and all attempts to connect the Drakes of Tavistock with the line of Ashe have failed. The Tavistock Drakes appear to have been of the burgher class. The name occurs among the monks, and while Sir Francis's father was a clergyman, a contemporary William Drake was vicar of Whitchurch. Clerical position was, however, in those days no proof of family, and the nearest evidence of station we have is the record of a William Drake of Tavistock—temp. Henry VII.—who was a smith. The register of the name of Francis Drake as a Plymouth freeman, in 1570, shows that no claim was then made to descent or arms, the distinctions of rank being most scrupulously observed in that record.

Francis Drake took to the sea, and made his first important voyages under his kinsman, John Hawkins, afterwards the famous Sir John. Joint sufferers from the Spanish treachery at San Juan de Ulloa, in 1568, from that moment they waged unceasing war against Spain on their own account. Drake's first independent expedition was in 1572, when he took Nombre de Dios, Vera Cruz, and acquired great booty. In 1577 he sailed from Plymouth Sound on the most remarkable voyage ever undertaken by an English sailor. He had seen the Pacific while blocking up 'the gulf of Mexico, for two years glorious with continual defeats,' and had resolved to sail thereon. So, with a squadron of five vessels, the largest the *Pelican* of 120 tons, he started to circumnavigate the globe. Nearly three years elapsed ere he returned. Desertion and disaffection broke up his little fleet; but he persevered, and brought his vessel back to Plymouth, laden with treasure, on the 26th of September, 1580. Great was the rejoicing, and great the glory, for he had the honour of entertaining Elizabeth on board his famous ship at Deptford, and of receiving knighthood at her hands. In 1585 he did great damage to the Spaniards in the West Indies with a fleet of twenty-five sail; and in 1587 performed the exploit which he jocularly called 'singeing the King of Spain's beard'—with his fleet so ravaging the Spanish coast as to delay the sailing of the Armada for a year. When the Armada came he was the vice-admiral of the fleet which assembled in Plymouth Sound to await them, and which hounded the unlucky braggart Spaniards to their destruction up

Channel. In August, 1595, Drake and John Hawkins sailed together from Plymouth in joint command of a fleet intended for the West Indies, which from the first was destined to failure. Hawkins died a few weeks after the ships sailed—partly of old age, partly of chagrin. Two months had not elapsed before Drake followed, from dysentery, produced in the first instance by the disasters which attended the expedition.

William Browne, the poet, author of 'Britannia's Pastorals,' was born at Tavistock in 1590.

Kilworthy, now sadly modernized, is the ancient seat of the Glanvilles, of whom the first distinguished member is Sir John, Judge of the Common Pleas under Elizabeth. Either by him, or by his son, Kilworthy was built. A daughter of Judge Glanville has been regarded as the heroine of the once popular Elizabethan drama—'Page of Plymouth'—founded unhappily upon fact. Ulalia Glanville was attached to one George Strangwidge, but was married by her parents to an old and wealthy merchant of Plymouth, named Page. This unequal match led to the murder of the husband, and the wife and the lover and their accomplices were executed for the crime at Barnstaple. The event was made the theme of ballads and tales as well as of the play; and the horror of the deed was heightened in the popular mind by the tradition that Judge Glanville himself pronounced the fatal sentence. It is a sufficient answer to this to show that Glanville did not become a judge until seven years after the murder; but beyond this, Ulalia Page was not the daughter of the Judge, but of another member of the Glanville family who had removed from Tavistock to Plymouth; and from whom, in all probability, the once famous. author of 'Saducismus Triumphatus'—Joseph Glanvill, Prebendary and F.R.S., born at Plymouth in 1636 (died 1680)—was descended.

Judge Glanville's second son John was another Tavistock worthy, who sat for several years in the House of Commons as member for Plymouth, and filled the difficult post of Speaker in the Parliament of 1640. When all hopes of a peaceful understanding were at an end, Glanville withdrew with the King to Oxford; and, when the conflict was over, paid the penalty of his loyalty in imprisonment and fine. He lost a son, Francis Glanville, in the defence of Bridgewater in 1645. After the Restoration he was appointed King's Serjeant, and died in 1661. By the failure of the male line Kilworthy came to the Manatons, who are now also extinct.

Another Tavistock worthy of the law was Sir John Maynard, said to have been born in a house that stood on the site of the Abbey. He was a man of note throughout the stirring days of the Stuarts and the Commonwealth, his long life covering the whole of the Stuart reigns until the final expulsion of the family and the accession of William of Orange. Born in 1602, he did not die until 1690. William remarked, when he was presented at Court, that he must have outlived all the judges and eminent men of his day. 'Yes,' rejoined Maynard, 'and I should have outlived the laws too, had it not been for the happy arrival of your Majesty.' Maynard was elected to the Long Parliament for Totnes and for Newport in Cornwall, but preferred Totnes, and took a prominent part in the debates of the house. He was engaged in the impeachments of Strafford and Laud, and sat in the Assembly of Divines; but was sent to the Tower in 1647 and 1653 for opposing Parliamentary measures. He pleaded strongly for the life of the King, and was too moderate a man for the temper of the times; but was elected in 1657 for Plymouth, of which town he had become recorder, in succession to his townsman Glanville, in 1640. At the Restoration he was again elected for Plymouth, and unseated as having been elected by the Mayor and Corporation, and not by the freemen.

Charles II. then made him Serjeant-at-law, and knighted him; and in 1679 he was returned for Plymouth unquestioned, and continued to sit for the town until the accession of James II., though displaced from the recordership by Charles in 1684 in favour of John Grenville, Earl of Bath. Thenceforward, in spite of his age, Maynard proved a vigorous opponent of the royal policy—refused to take part in the persecution of the Seven Bishops, and became an ardent promoter of the Revolution.

Brent Tor is a remarkable eminence, of volcanic aspect and origin, crowned by a quaint little church dedicated to St. Michael. This is said to have been erected by a merchant, who, in peril at sea, vowed, if saved, to build a church on the first point of land he saw. It is also associated with a local version of the common legend, that the site of the church was to have been at the bottom of the hill, but that in the night the materials were carried to the top. In some versions of this myth the conditions are reversed; and in all likelihood it is simply a survival of the antagonism between the old heathen faith in high places, grafted on a nominal Christianity, and the more definite religious idea which would have nothing to do with places that had been profaned by idolatrous rites. The form of the legend would naturally depend upon the party who succeeded. As the Tor belonged to the Abbey of Tavistock, we may assume that the church was founded by the monks.

And here a curious question arises. The manor of Liddaton, as Lideltone, belonged to the Abbey at the compilation of 'Domesday;' and this was in Brent Tor parish. But the Abbey had another manor called Bernintone, which has not been identified; and this also may be associated with Brent. The one name seems to echo the other. Moreover, this manor of Bernintone was not only extensive and fairly populous, containing thirty-five ploughlands and an enumerated population of forty-eight; but, in addition to serfs, villeins, bordars, and swineherds, it had four bures and a quantity of 'common pasture.'

In the adjoining parish of Marystow the Abbey held from Saxon times the manor of Radone or Raddon. Sydenham, which gave name to a family long extinct, had come to the Wises so early as the reign of Henry IV.; and their many-gabled house, now that of the Tremaynes, is the best preserved Elizabethan mansion in this part of the county, although it was garrisoned for the King under Colonel Holbourn in 1645. Built by Sir Thomas Wise, it passed from his name in the next generation; for his only son died unmarried, and his granddaughter, Bridget Hatherleigh, brought it to the Tremaynes, in whom it has ever since remained. Prior to this marriage, the Tremaynes had been seated at Collacombe in Lamerton for several generations. They had the estate of Collacombe by marriage from the Trenchards; but the house was erected by the Tremaynes in the latter part of the sixteenth century, and retains many picturesque features. Here were born the twin Tremaynes, Nicholas and Andrew, of whose likeness and sympathy Prince tells some wonderful tales, and who both fell at the siege of Newhaven in 1563. Among the Tremayne memorials in Lamerton Church is one recording how

> 'One of both sore wounded lost his health,
> And t'other slain, revenging brother's death.'

Lifton, which adjoins Marystow, one of the frontier parishes of Devon next Cornwall, passed from the Crown, by the grant of King John in 1199, to Agatha, who had been nurse to Eleanor his mother. By Edward I. the manor, hundred, and advowson were given to Thomas of Woodstock, and descended thence through the Hollands to the Nevilles. Then the Harrises had it a couple of centuries, and next came the Arundells.

The Lysonses state that it was held of the chapel of

Berkhampstead by the annual render of a pound of incense.

Kelly is noteworthy as affording one of the few continuing local instances of families seated on the estates whence they take name. The Kellys of Kelly have held this manor from the time of Henry II. at least.

Milton Abbot, already mentioned, contains the lovely Devonshire seat of the Dukes of Bedford—Endsleigh. Edgcumbe, here, is the original home of the family of Edgcumbe, and has continued in the possession of the elder branch from the reign of Edward III. The younger branch is ennobled as Earls Mount Edgcumbe.

There is additional testimony to the importance of the valley of the Tavy in the early days of Saxon settlement, in the fact that Whitchurch parish—Wicerce in 'Domesday'—by its name indicates the existence here of a church in pre-Norman times. Like the other parishes around Tavistock, in later days it testified to the importance of that ancient town by giving home to several families of ancient gentry. A younger branch of the Courtenays was long settled at Walreddon; Halwell was a seat of the Glanvilles for some three centuries before they removed to Kilworthy; Grenofen, now belonging to the Chichesters, was long in the Pollards; Britsworthy ong continued in the Mewys, Moortown in the Mooringes, and Sortridge in the Pengellys. Whitchurch was once an archpresbytery, on the foundation of Robert Champeaux, abbot of Tavistock about the year 1300, the rector being archpriest and having three fellows.

CHAPTER XXIII.

BUCKLAND MONACHORUM.

One of the hundreds of the Exon 'Domesday,' which neither the Lysonses nor any other general writers on Devonian history identified, is that of Walchentone, which appears again in the 'Exchequer Domesday' as Wachetone, with the appendant manors of Svdtone (now Plymouth), Tanbretone (Tamerton), and Macretone (Maker), all part of the royal demesne. **Walchentone** hundred is now represented by the hundred of Roborough; and Walchentone itself is to be found in the moorland parish of Walkhampton, the identification being easy to anyone acquainted with the ancient and indeed current pronunciation—'Wackington.' Nowhere in Devon has so great a change taken place in the relationships of manors — Walkhampton being quite an insignificant parish, important only in its association with Buckland Abbey, and Sutton the site of the largest town of the West.

The Cistercian Abbey of Buckland was founded by Amicia, the widowed countess of Baldwin, seventh Earl of Devon, and the mother of Isabella de Fortibus. She acquired in 1273 lands for the purpose by purchase or gift from her daughter, and in 1280 signed the foundation deed, vesting in the monks and their successors the manors of Buckland, Bickleigh, and Walkhampton, with the advowsons, and the hundred of Roborough, for the use of the Abbey dedicated in honour of God and the blessed Mary, mother of God, and the blessed Benedict. The monks came from the Abbey of Quarr in the Isle of Wight, founded by Baldwin, second Earl of Devon, and Robert was the first abbot. They were unfortunate enough to start by incurring episcopal censure, celebrating divine offices without the consent of the parish priest or the bishop's license, and Bishop Bronescombe therefore laid them under interdict. This was relaxed at the solicitation of Queen Eleanor, and speedily removed.

The data for the history of Buckland are very scanty. Soon after the foundation the title of the Abbey to the hundred was questioned, and judgment given for the King. Yet the abbot continued to exercise the jurisdiction, and in that right successfully resisted the attempt of Edward II. to grant a charter to the town of Plymouth, which came within his authority. When Plymouth was incorporated the Abbey was compensated with the church of Bampton. In 1336 the royal license was granted to crenellate the Abbey, Plymouth and its vicinity being at this time in constant peril from foreign descent. Having asserted their rights against the King, the convent were not likely to allow them to be infringed by a plain squire. James Derneford, lord of the manor of East Stonehouse, set up a pillory and tumbrel in his manor, and held a court of frankpledge there. This was resisted by the monks, and eventually referred to the arbitration of William Hylle, Prior of Plympton, and James Chudlegh. They, in 1448, decided in favour of the Abbey, and Derneford, besides removing the pillory and tumbrel, had to pay £20 as a fine.

Thirty years later the monks themselves were cast. They were sued at Lydford for encroachments upon the rights of the duchy of Cornwall within the forest of Dartmoor, and were found to have offended.

None of the sixteen abbots of Buckland was a man of note; but Thomas Olyver, who succeeded in 1463, was a warm supporter of the Earl of Richmond, afterwards Henry VII., and was proscribed, without result, by Richard. The last abbot was John Toker. At the Dissolution the revenues were no more than £241 17s. 9½d.; but then Toker had been mindful of 'those of his own household,' and just prior to the surrender had leased the rectorial tithes of Buckland, Walkhampton, Bickleigh, Sheepstor, and Bampton, to his brother Robert, and his nephews William and Hugh Toker.

The Abbey passed through various lay hands with unusual rapidity. George Pollard, of London, had a lease granted in 1539 for twenty-one years. In 1542 Sir Richard Grenville had a grant of the reversion. In 1580 the Grenvilles sold the property to John Hele and Christopher Harris, and nine months later it was conveyed to Sir Francis Drake, to whose representatives it still belongs. With the exception of the manor of Buckland, the Abbey lands at Bickleigh, Walkhampton, and elsewhere in the neighbourhood were purchased in 1546 by John Slanning. Buckland was bought by a London haberdasher, named Richard Crymes, in the same year; but in 1660 it also was sold to the Slannings. From the Slannings, through heiresses, the estates passed to the Heywoods; from them, by purchase, to Sir Masseh Manasseh Lopes; and they are now the property of his grandson, Sir Massey Lopes.

What is yet known as Buckland Abbey is really the Abbey Church, converted by Grenville into a dwelling-house. The chief interest of the place lies in its connection with the great sailor into whose hands it subsequently came. There are portraits of Drake and of his captive, Don Pedro de Valdez, Vice-Admiral of the Armada, for whom the Abbey became a prison pending the payment of his ransom; shields of arms of the Drake and allied families; and personal relics of Sir Francis—as his drum, his Bible, sword, and shield! Another noted warrior with whom Buckland is associated is General Elliot, Lord Heathfield, defender of Gibraltar, whose monument is in the church.

Buckland parish, now from the Abbey known as Buckland Monachorum, was in 'Domesday' the most populous manor between Tavistock and the sea—held by William de Pollei, in succession to Brismar—and had both a saltwork and a fishery. Brismar had also held, and William had succeeded to, the adjacent manors of Bickleigh and Sampford, now Sampford Spiney. The added name, in this latter case, is said to have been derived from its possession by the family of Spinet or De Spineto; but as the neighbouring parish of Shaugh takes its title from the Saxon *sceacga*, 'rough coppice,' it is quite as probable that the Spiney here may be simply the allied word *spinney*. Between Sampford and Shaugh lies the parish of Meavy, made up of four Domesday manors of that name, all of which passed from their Saxon holders to Judhel of Totnes. To this fact is probably due the foundation of a Norman church here, whereof some trace yet remains in the present edifice. Either one of the Meavys (the ancient form is Mewi, and the river, whence the name is taken, is called the Mew in the older records), or an unidentified manor of Metwi, is in all probability the modern parish of Sheepstor; but one of them has been identified by Mr. Davidson in half a mansa granted by Cnut in 1031 to a thane named Ætheric. The boundaries can still be traced, even to a *cleaca* or set of stepping-stones across the river.

Sheepstor alone of all the group, apart from Buckland, has any historical connection. It was the ancient home of the Elfords, and one of these, a staunch Royalist, is said to have found refuge from his enemies in a cavity amidst the confused heap or 'clatter' of detached rocks that clothes the precipitous side of Sheepstor Hill, and possibly named it Schittis or Schattis Tor—the older form—from its shattered aspect. The cavity is now commonly called the Pixies' Hole. Elford is said to have employed his time in painting its rocky sides, but of this there is no trace.

At Bickleigh there still remains the old house of the Slannings, as at Sheepstor, its daughter parish, that of the Elfords, and at Meavy the manor-house of the Strodes and Drakes. South Devon has a large number of ancient mansions, degraded to farms. Of the Slannings, who were somewhat intimately connected with Plymouth, and who were settled at Shaugh before Bickleigh, the most distinguished member was Sir Nicholas, one of the 'four wheels of Charles's wain,' who was killed at the siege of Bristol, 1643.

Two important parishes lie at the junction of the Tavy with the Tamar, one on either side—Beer Ferrers and Tamerton Foliott. Beer is the Birland which before the Conquest belonged to Ordulf, and is entered in 'Domesday' as held by Reginald de Valletort under the Count of Moreton. It was a very extensive manor, and had seven salt-works. Henry, the common ancestor of the Ferrerses, whence its distinctive name, held it as early as the reign of Henry II. Sir William de Ferrers had a license for castellating his house here in 1337; but before the end of that century the coheiress of the Ferrerses brought the manor to the Champernownes, and they to the Willoughbys, Lords Broke. In the latter half of the fifteenth century one of this family was Lord High Steward of Plymouth, and engaged in sharp controversy with his neighbours the Edgcumbes at Cotehele, concerning which some amusing records are still extant. Curiously enough the Earl of Mount Edgcumbe is now the owner of this property, by descent from the coheiress of the Earls of Buckinghamshire; they in their turn had it by descent in the female line from Sir John Maynard, who purchased it of the Broke successors. Ley, here, is said to have been the original seat of the Leys, Earls of Marlborough.

So far back as the reign of Edward I., and probably much earlier, it had been discovered that Beer contained mineral treasures of no little value; and there are extant records of 1298 which show that Edward I. was then working silver lead-mines in Byr or Birlond on his own account, and that the process of extracting and refining the silver was well understood. The mines have been worked at intervals ever since; and were in extensive operation when the principal workings were drowned out by the Tamar breaking through its bed. 140 ounces of silver have been extracted per ton of lead; and 6,000 ounces of silver are said to have been produced in six weeks.

It was probably in consequence of mining prosperity that the little town of Beer Alston in Beer Ferrers gradually acquired importance. It had a market granted about 1294, and was made a Parliamentary borough by Elizabeth. It returned two members in right of certain burgage tenures until 1832. Risdon derives the distinctive name Alston from Alençon, to whom he says the manor was given by the Conqueror; but as the latter statement is wrong, the former need not trouble us.

Beer Ferrers Church was rebuilt by William de Ferrers, and contains his monument, with other memorials of the family. He also founded here a collegiate chantry.

Matthew Tindal, the Deist, was born here in 1657, his father being rector of the parish.

For something like a century at least Beer Ferrers has been noted for its orchards and fruit-gardens, and it sends away enormous quantities of fruit every season by rail.

Tamerton Foliott, once a market-town and occasionally called a borough, takes name from the Foliotts, who had their residence at Warleigh. The heiress of the Foliotts brought it to the Gorges, and from them it passed, by female heirs, to Bonvile, Coplestone, and Bampfylde. For some century and a half it has been the seat of the Radcliffes. The Coplestone oak, which stood on the green by the church, was the traditional scene of a murder by one of the Coplestones, the 'fatal oak' of Mrs. Bray's 'Warleigh.' Gilbert Foliott, successively Abbot of Gloucester, Bishop of Hereford (1149), and Bishop of London (1161), was a native of Tamerton. One of the most learned men of his day, he was also a steady opponent of À Becket, and was excommunicated by that primate and the Pope accordingly, but relieved by a synod which he called. He held the See of London twenty years.

Maristow in this parish, the seat of Sir Massey Lopes, was the site of the ancient chapel of St. Martin (whence the name) belonging to the canons of Plympton. After the Dissolution it came to the Champernownes, who sold it in 1550 to John Slanning of Shaugh. Thence it descended with the rest of the Slanning estates, and was bought by Sir Masseh Manasseh Lopes in 1798. It seems probable that Maristow was the chapel of St. Martin de Blakestane (the next Domesday manor to Tamerton), held by the Priory temp. Henry I., and given by Paganel. It is also said to have been the gift of William de Pin and his daughter Sibella.

CHAPTER XXIV.

PLYMOUTH, DEVONPORT, AND STONEHOUSE.

THE recorded history of Plymouth cannot be traced much farther than the Norman Conquest. The town finds no mention in the 'Saxon Chronicle.' Risdon, indeed, citing the life of St. Indractus, tells us that by the Saxons it was named Tamarweorth, which is much more likely, if the reference has any historic value, to be the Saxon name of what is now Drake's Island—'the Island of the Tamar.' Leland also asserts that much of what afterwards came to be called Plymouth was held by the canons of the ancient Saxon college of Plympton, which Bishop Warelwast made the foundation of the famous Plympton Priory. But these statements have no authority; and the earliest undoubted and distinct mention we have of Plymouth is as the Sutton of 'Domesday,' held by William in succession to the Confessor, an insignificant manor, with an enumerated population of 7 only. It was many a long year after this that the manor was granted by the Crown to the Valletorts, and by them in part to the monks of Plympton; and that mainly by the fostering care of the prior and his brethren, though largely as the result of independent effort, the foundations of the chief centre of population of the West were laid.

'Domesday' affords the materials for a striking comparison between past and present. The eight manors, which included what is now the great triple community of the three towns of Plymouth, Devonport, and Stonehouse, with their suburban area, had in 1086 an enumerated population of 61, and were valued at £7 15s. annually. The population is now 150,000, and the annual value £380,000. In eight centuries the population has increased 2,500 times, and the value nearly 5,000. This is the most remarkable contrast Devon has to show.

But the tale of the early days of Plymouth would be incomplete if we stopped here. Plymouth herself may be this mere infant of some eight centuries' growth; but the magnificent harbour to which she owes her birth had played its part in the national life, such as that was, many a long year before the Norman Conquest; and for the first settlement on its shores we must go back at least to the days of the ancient Keltic civilization, which preceded the coming of the Roman, and in the West was never supplanted by him. The eastern shores of Plymouth Sound, in the neighbourhood of Staddon Heights, have yielded abundant traces of the presence of a comparatively dense and cultured population. Mount Batten has produced examples of the earliest and latest British coinage in gold, silver, and copper; and in an ancient cemetery hard by were found a number of articles of bronze—the final and most finished illustrations of the elder pre-Roman civilization of the land. Here was the *Stadio Deuentia* of the Ravennat. Nay, the prehistoric dates go farther yet. Not only are worked flints of rude type found on the heights on either side of Plymouth Sound, but there was found beneath an ancient house in one of the oldest streets of Plymouth the remains of a kitchen-midden, and below them a singular example of urn burial. Again, the oldest name of the promontorial district to the east of Plymouth, now called Cattedown, is Hingston, or Hangstone—Stonehenge reversed; and the rude sketch-map of the coasts, made in the reign of Henry VIII. in connection with his schemes of fortification, depicts what appears intended for a 'hanging stone,' or cromlech.

There is no evidence of the position of Plymouth in the Roman era. With the exception of a few scattered coins, hardly a score in all, found at various points in the neighbourhood, the Romans have left no traces of their visits here. True, the remains of a Roman galley are said to have been found silted up near Plympton, but the authority for its identification is not clear. There is no means whatever of linking on the Saxon Sutton of 'Domesday' with the Keltic settlement of Staddon (the direct Saxon continuant of which was probably the once fortified village of Plymstock), unless we are content to fall back upon myth and legend, and these will carry us very much farther afield.

There seems no reason for questioning the honesty of Geoffrey of Monmouth when he states that he is reproducing an ancient record brought from Brittany; and while he did not invent the story of Brutus the Trojan, there must have been some reason for associating the Hoe at Plymouth with the legendary combat of Corinæus and Goemagot, and perpetuating the memory of the association by cutting the 'effigies' of the two champions in the greensward there, renewed for centuries at the cost of the Corporation. But while either Geoffrey or one of his editors erred seriously in identifying the Hamo's Port, which finds such frequent mention in his 'Chronicle' as the chief port of Western Britain, with Southampton, on the single score of the 'ham' common to both, these references do appear to point somewhat definitely to a regular use in the Keltic period of the estuary of the Tamar for British maritime expeditions, seeing that it has descended to us at the present day as the Hamoaze. Hamo's Port is made the fitting centre by Geoffrey of some of the most stirring scenes in the traditional national life, and it is the Hamoaze that best suits the references.

Plymouth has been treated as one of the ports to which the Phœnicians traded in quest of tin. It may have been so, but there is no proof. It has been suggested further that the many-named little islet in the Sound, probably the true Tamarweorth, subsequently St. Michael's, Tristram's, St. Nicholas's, and now Drake's Island, was the Ictis of Diodorus Siculus. To that we may give a distinct denial. Thus, all we really know with certainty of the origin of Plymouth—this important factor in the general history of the country—is, that whilst the shores of the Sound have been peopled, perhaps continuously, from far-distant prehistoric times, at the date of the Norman Conquest its place was occupied by a tiny hamlet of the name of Sutton. There is, indeed, good evidence that the neighbourhood, if not the actual site, was even then of some importance. Plymouth is the only locality in Devon that has so far yielded traces of the Teutonic 'mark'—certain lands within the borough which retained a very complicated ownership until the present day, being noted in ancient deeds as 'landscore lands,' and as held in landscore tenure. Moreover, while the borders of the Sound do not appear to have afforded any special spoil to the Danes when they sailed up the Tamar and Tavy and burnt Tavistock—Wembury, on its eastern shore, at the mouth of the Yealm, seems the most likely scene of the Danish defeat in 851 by the Ealderman of Devon; though Okenbury on the Erme, and Wickaborough in Berry Pomeroy, are also candidates for identification as the place which has come down to us in the 'Saxon Chronicle' as Wiganbeorche.

Why the infant Plymouth was called Sutton=Southtown, has never been clearly made out; but the older part o the borough, which still bears the name of 'Old Town,' preserved in Old Town Street, was apparently known by the same title. It was not until the year 1439 that the familiar Plymouth supplanted the older form, though it had been in occasional use at least a century before. The growth of the community was very rapid. Leland states that in the latter part of the twelfth century it was still 'a mene thing as an Inhabitation for fischars.' And an official inquiry made in 1318 by the Sheriff of the county, records that prior to the foundation of the 'ville of Sutton,' there was a place on the shores of the ancient creek, now harbour, of Sutton Pool, where the fishermen used to sell their fish. This must have been long anterior to the present market rights, which date from 1254. Not until the manor passed from the Crown to the Valletorts did the town begin to grow. They made it their occasional residence, and gave freely of their land to the Priory of Plympton. Successive priors then encouraged settlement, and hence by the side of the original 'Old Town,' distinguished as Sutton Valletort or Vawter, there grew up the new town of Sutton Prior, which speedily distanced its elder sister. Rapid was the growth when prosperity fairly set in.

While the original foundation of the mother church of St. Andrew certainly dates well back in the twelfth century, the Carmelites established themselves in the town in 1313, the Franciscans were not very much later, and the Dominicans were also speedily represented. To the siege of Calais in 1346, Plymouth sent more ships and men than any other town save Dartmouth, Yarmouth, and Fowey. And the latter part of the fourteenth century found Plymouth one of the best known and most thriving ports in England, with a corporation of some kind bearing rule, and with so large a population that the Subsidy Roll of 1377 records a taxable inhabitancy of 4,837, and thus gives it the rank of the fourth town in the kingdom, London, York, and Bristol alone preceding. In these early days of the national life no town advanced with such rapid strides; in later centuries no provincial community has had more important links with the national history.

But all was not quiet progress. The need of defensive works was recognised at least as early as the reign of Richard II.; and the 'Town Ligger' records that the place was burnt three times by the French and Bretons, in 1377, 1400, and 1403. But these were not the only occasions on which it was assailed; nor need this excite wonder, seeing that the port was made the headquarters of so many hostile armaments in the thirteenth and fourteenth centuries. The first great fleet recorded as sailing from its waters is one of 325 vessels, in 1287, for Guienne. The Black Prince made Plymouth the centre of his operations against France, and sailed thence in 1355 on the expedition which was crowned by the victory of Poictiers. Retaliation was therefore natural; and the attempts were even more frequent than the municipal annals record. Thus, in 1339, the French fired the town, but were repulsed by Hugh Courtenay, Earl of Devon; in 1350 they tried again, but were only able to destroy some 'farms and fair places.' In 1400, the fleet of James de Bourbon, after doing considerable damage, was assailed and partially destroyed by a violent storm. The worst invasion, and the last, was that of a body of Bretons under the Sieur du Chastel, in 1403. No less than 600 houses were then burnt, the greater part of the town sacked, and many of the inhabitants taken prisoners. The chief scene of the ravages of the invaders has been distinguished to this day by the name of Briton Side.

There is good evidence, although successive fires have destroyed all the earlier records of the town, that after this the prosperity of Plymouth waned. In 1439-40, however, the town was formally incorporated by Act of Parliament, and again began to thrive. The incorporation was really the extension of a much older corporation, possibly originating with the Valletorts, for names of prepositi or mayors occur as early as 1310, and the Parliamentary representation commenced in 1298. What the Act did was to relieve the community from its dependence on the Priory; and the burgesses thenceforth prided themselves upon belonging to the 'Kinge's towne of Plymothe,' as their ancient seal testifies.

While there is no direct proof that the town took any active part in the Wars of the Roses, there is no reason to doubt that its sympathies were Lancastrian; for here, in 1470, did the Duke of Clarence, with the Earls of Pembroke, Warwick, and Oxford, land to excite the revolt which led to the temporary restoration of Henry VI.; and here, too, in the following year, disembarked Margaret of Anjou, on her ill-starred way to share in the final disaster of Tewkesbury. Nevertheless, Henry VII. could not land at Plymouth in 1483, because of the close guard kept. The attitude of the townsfolk towards the Warbeckian insurrection is shown by two or three entries of corporate expenditure, which speak of a party being sent into Cornwall to 'dfend Pkyn'—defend being used in the old and now forgotten sense of opposition. The commerce of Plymouth with France and Spain was so great at the close of this century, that the selection of the town for the disembarkation of Katherine of Aragon, in 1501, was but natural. Right heartily was she welcomed. During her stay she was the guest of a rich merchant prince named Paynter; and the Receiver's Accounts record, among other matters, how the Corporation gave her six oxen, five-and-twenty sheep, three hogsheads of 'Gaston' and claret wine, and a pipe of 'Meskedell;' while 'my lady pryncs ys amner' (almoner) had ten shillings to 'wryte oure supplicacion yn Spaynysch and in latyn, and to be oure salucyt.' Thus early did the burghers of Plymouth establish a precedent for the now inevitable address.

In the opening years of the sixteenth century Plymouth began to fit herself for her leading share in the glories of the reign of Elizabeth; and the pioneer in this work was one William Hawkins, the first prominent member of the greatest family of merchant seamen and heroes England has known. For his 'skill in sea causes' this William Hawkins the elder was much esteemed by Henry VIII., and he was the first Englishman who sailed a ship into the Southern Seas. He had two worthy sons. The first, another William Hawkins, was the most influential resident of Elizabethan Plymouth—a merchant and a sailor, the holder of a commission under the Prince of Conde, and, like the rest of his kinsfolk, quite as ready to fight as to trade. His son, a third William, was the founder of the East India Company's first trading-house at Surat, and an ambassador to the Great Mogul at Agra.

The most famous of the family was the second son of Henry VIII.'s favourite captain—the renowned **Sir John Hawkins**; the first Englishman to take a ship into the Bay of Mexico; the early friend of his relative, the redoubtable Sir Francis Drake; converted from an adventurous trader into the heroic scourge of Spain by Spanish treachery at San Juan de Ulloa; for many a long weary year the Treasurer of the Navy and the man to whom is due all the credit of preparing the Royal Fleet to meet the Armada; the first true friend of the British sailor; and not only the ablest captain, but the best shipwright of his time. Probably born in 1532, he died at sea in 1595 (while engaged with Drake in the expedition which proved fatal to both these great seamen), worn out by years and toil, and heartbroken by failure and by the captivity of his son, Sir Richard Hawkins—he who gained the honourable epithet of 'the complete seaman,' and who lingered for ten years in a Spanish prison ere he obtained that release which his father had hoped to achieve.

William Hawkins the elder, both his sons William and

John, and his grandson Richard, represented Plymouth in Parliament, besides filling the leading places in the municipality; and while they form the most distinguished family of Elizabethan Devon, Sir John is unmistakably the chief worthy of their native Plymouth.

Plymouth was attacked, though not besieged, by the Western rebels for the restoration of Roman Catholicism in 1549. The details preserved are but meagre; and from the fact that the assault was made on the 15th of August, ten days after the defeat of the insurgents at St. Mary's Clyst, it must have been either by an independent body or by a party of the Cornishmen on their retreat. However that may be, the town records state that they were driven out of the town on this day, with a loss of eighty prisoners. They did, however, one notable piece of damage—'Then was our steeple burnt with all the townes evydence in the same.' The greater portion, though not the whole, of the borough muniments were thus destroyed. The Plymouth men chased their foes into Cornwall, and brought back an unfortunate wretch with them, called in the accounts 'the traytour of Cornewall,' who was hung, drawn, and quartered on the Hoe— the central figure of a great public holiday.

The mere recital of the naval expeditions which had their origin in Plymouth in the reign of Elizabeth, and of their results, would fill a volume.

It was from Plymouth that Drake sailed in 1572 on his expedition to Nombre de Dios. When he returned one Sunday in August in the following year, the news reached St. Andrew Church while the people were assembled in worship, and straightway the preacher was deserted and the good folks ran to the seaside to welcome their hero home. Still more hearty were the rejoicings when he returned after 'ploughing up a furrow round the world,' his vessel laden with great store of 'gold and silver in blocks'—solid facts which were greatly appreciated by the business-like Plymouthians. At the earliest opportunity he was made mayor; and a few years later sat in Parliament for the town.

From Plymouth, too, Drake sailed in 1587 to 'singe the King of Spain's beard,' while in August, 1595, he and Hawkins sailed together on the fatal expedition to the West Indies from which neither returned. Drake is connected with the modern life of Plymouth, by his construction of the leat or water-course through which the town is still supplied with water from the river Meavy. There was a tradition that he did this at his own cost; but recent discoveries of long-lost documents show that the work was initiated by the Corporation, planned by one Robert Lampen, and carried out at their charges, and that Drake's relation to the scheme was that of a contractor, paid partly in cash and partly by a lease for sixty-seven years of mills erected on the line of the new leat or stream. His memory is drank at the annual inspection of the waterworks by the Corporation, as that of the man—to adopt the lines under his portrait in the Guildhall—

> 'Who with fresh streams refresht this Towne that first,
> Though kist with waters, yet did pine for thirst.'

Plymouth—according to Prince a 'port so famous that it hath a kind of invitation from the commodiousness thereof to maritime noble actions'—was the place whence Sir Walter Ralegh sent forth his fleets for the settlement of Virginia, and to which he returned broken-hearted from his last fatal expedition after the golden city of Manoa, and was apprehended by 'Judas' Stukely. It was the port, too, whence Sir Humphry Gilbert sailed on that voyage to Newfoundland from which he never came back; but which has left us the rich legacy of his dying words, 'Heaven is as near by sea as by land.' Hence in 1589 set forth the expedition under Drake and Norris, intended to place Don Antonio on the throne of Portugal. And hence went the memorable expedition against Cadiz in 1596, of which Howard and Essex were the chief commanders, while the last of the plentiful ' Knights of Cales ' was made in Plymouth streets on the return, ' as the Lords General came from the sermon!'

But, indeed, in these days there was, to apply the words of Carew, an 'infinite swarm' of expeditions of one kind and another. Now and again large fleets and powerful squadrons set forth, and single ships almost daily; so we pass on to the central incident of these stirring times, the defeat of the Armada.

Twice had Spanish invasion been averted by the astuteness and daring of two Plymouth seamen—for Drake, if Tavistockian by birth, was Plymouthian by adoption. Once Philip's schemes were counteracted by the pretended treachery of Sir John Hawkins, who applied the money paid him by the Spanish King to bring over his fleet in works of defence. Once again Philip's preparations were destroyed by Drake harrying one Spanish port after another. And when the time of trial could no longer be delayed, again it was Plymouth, and Plymouth men, that took the foremost place. There are extant some most graphic descriptions by William Hawkins the second, who was mayor in the eventful Armada year, of the repair of vessels by night, torch-lights and cressets flaring fitfully in a gale of wind. His brother John had worked for years to bring the royal navy to efficiency; and the ships which he collected in Plymouth harbour were 'in such a condition,' as Mr. Froude says, 'hull, rigging, spars, and running rope, that they had no match in the world.' They were the nucleus of a much larger gathering of volunteer craft from many a port throughout the kingdom, but chiefly from the maritime towns of the West and South. Of 190 vessels which waited in Plymouth waters to resist the boastful Spaniard, 34 only belonged to the Queen. To the volunteer levy, Plymouth supplied seven ships and a fly-boat. Though nominally under the command of Howard of Effingham, the two chief captains were Drake and Hawkins—Drake being vice-admiral, and in charge of the volunteers; Hawkins rear-admiral, with special relations to the royal squadron.

There is a much-cherished tradition that when Captain Fleming brought the news of the approach of the Armada, the leading captains were playing bowls, and that Drake insisted on the set being finished, pithily remarking, 'There's time enough to play the game out first, and thrash the Spaniards afterwards.' No contemporary authority exists for the tradition, and even the site of the bowling-green which Plymouth undoubtedly possessed at that time is disputed; but the story so fathers itself, that we may accept it heartily without too strict an inquiry into pedigree. There *was* time enough to play the game, and thrash the Spaniards; and this, although contrary winds made it a work of some difficulty to get the ships to sea.

It was about four o'clock on the afternoon of the 19th of July, 1588, that news of the approach of the Armada came; and that night some of the English ships were warped out of harbour. But the Spanish fleet did not appear in sight until noon of the following day; and then began that great battle of nations which was not to end until the pride of Spain was hopelessly crushed. The only man of note who fell on the side of the English was a Plymouth sailor, Captain Cock, who joined the fleet in a vessel of his own, captured a Spaniard, and died in the moment of victory—'cock of the game,' as Fuller calls him.

The defeat of the Armada was commemorated until within living memory in Plymouth, by the ringing of a merry peal from the bells of the old church of St. Andrew on the Saturday night preceding the 25th of

July; and on the Sunday the Corporation used to walk to church in state.

Charles I. came to Plymouth in September, 1625, for the purpose of inspecting the troops gathered for the abortive expedition to Cadiz. It was an unfortunate business for the town. The fact that the King's servants received £33 3s. 4d. in fees was a very small matter. The great evil was that the place was crowded with the impressed soldiery to the number of some 10,000, while many had to be billeted in the neighbouring villages. Four hundred men were impressed in Devon—to a large extent the sort of scum that Falstaff so graphically describes; and whether they were good, bad, or indifferent, were so ill looked after by the authorities, that the greater part were but half clothed, while the want of money made them wholly starving. Most miserable was the condition of soldiery and townsfolk alike; and right glad were the Plymouthians when the King had reviewed his 'ragged regiments,' and set out on his return; and when the expedition finally set sail. Worse remained behind: overcrowding and filth begat the plague, and a third of the population was swept away.

Plymouth formed the centre of the operations for the settlement of New England and the foundation of the United States. The 'Plymouth Company,' for the colonization of North America, had its origin in the patents granted by Elizabeth to Ralegh to settle Virginia. £40,000 were spent by him ineffectually; and five times he sent to search for the missing colonists whom he had planted at the 'City of Ralegh' in 1587, the settlement having been destroyed, and the survivors adopted, according to tradition, into the Hatteras tribe. His failures led, however, to other attempts, and eventually to the incorporation by James I. of two companies—the London Company for the colonization of 'South Virginia,' and the Plymouth Company for the colonization of 'North Virginia'—

Virginia being used as a general term for the North American coast. The London Company settled Jamestown in 1607; the attempt of the Plymouth Company to plant a colony at the mouth of the Kennebec failed, and thenceforward its members confined themselves to trading and fishing. In 1620, however, a new charter was granted them, whereby the Duke of Lennox, the Marquis of Buckingham, the Earls of Arundel and Warwick, Sir Ferdinando Gorges, and thirty-four others, were incorporated as 'the first modern and present Council established at Plymouth, in the county of Devon, for the planting, ruling, and governing of New England in America.' The grant gave the patentees all property and control over all North America from the Atlantic to the Pacific, between the 40th and 48th degrees of north latitude. The ruling spirit of this second organization was Sir Ferdinando Gorges, long Governor of Plymouth and connected with the Gorges of St. Bude. The monopoly was too huge for realization. The pretensions of the patentees were laughed to scorn and ignored. Their vast designs dwindled into a scramble for individual interests and proprietorships; and the real settlement of New England was effected without their knowledge or intervention. The 'Council of Plymouth' does not therefore fill a very important place in history. The only really notable thing it did was to grant the charter of Massachusetts, which proved so troublesome a child, that in 1635 the Council surrendered their charter, its members first passing particular patents to themselves 'of such parts along the sea-coast as might be sufficient for them.' Gorges interpreted this liberally, for he appropriated what is now Maine; and his comrade, Mason, New Hampshire. The dissolution of the Company was really an incident in the earlier phase of the conflict between Charles and his Parliament—Massachusetts being strongly Puritan and welcoming the Puritanically disaffected; and the leaders of the Company being Royalists and Episcopalians, absolutists by charter, and above all things mindful of the duty of strictly attending to their own pockets. As Sir Edward Coke told Gorges to his face, 'the ends of private gain were concealed under cover of planting a colony.'

Before the Plymouth Company had begun its later operation, 'on the 6th day of September, 1620, thirteen years after the first colonization of Virginia, two months before the concession of the grand charter of Plymouth, without any warrant from the sovereign of England, without any useful charter from a corporate body, the passengers in the *Mayflower* set sail from the waters of Plymouth Sound for a new world.' Bound for the Hudson, in the territory of the London Company, they landed, Nov. 9, in the domains of the Plymouth Association, and there founded New Plymouth, the first permanent settlement in New England. The Huguenots were then at Port Royal or Annapolis (founded 1604), the London Company at Jamestown (1607), the Dutch at New York (1614). It is a singular coincidence, if nothing more, that the spot where the Pilgrims landed is called Plymouth in 1616, in Smith's map of New England. Probably it had therefore been early frequented by Plymouth ships. Whether the Pilgrims continued the old name or gave it anew cannot now be ascertained.

A singular error, and one which it seems almost impossible to overtake, has sprung from the departure of the Pilgrim Fathers from Plymouth. It has been again and again either stated or assumed that the little band of the *Mayflower* were, if not Plymouth people, at least Devonians. There is, however, not the least evidence that any one of them belonged to the West of England, and the amplest proof that the great majority did not. Nevertheless some Plymouth and Devonshire men did play an important part in the work of actual settlement. Gorges had a plantation on the island of Mohegan in 1621 or 1622, which was afterwards bought by Abraham Jennings, a Plymouth merchant. Moses Goodyear, son-in-law of Jennings, and Robert Trelawny, afterwards member for the town, two other Plymouth merchants, laid the foundation of the town of Portland; and of actual Plymouth settlers we have John Winter, long Trelawny's agent, and George Cleeves, a man of great note in the new country, and as staunch a Republican as Trelawny was a Royalist.

Massachusetts, moreover, was largely peopled from Devon and Cornwall; and, although originating in Dorchester, had important connections with Plymouth. Thus in 1630 a number of intending emigrants to Massachusetts met in the Hospital of the Poor's Portion at Plymouth, a recent Puritan foundation, and there formed a Congregational church under 'Master John Warham, a famous preacher of Exeter, and Master John Maverick.' A ship which sailed from Plymouth in 1622 took over eighty emigrants. In Western Maine and the lower districts of Massachusetts, the population still largely retains the characteristics of the men of Devon, Cornwall, Somerset, and Dorset, and is spoken of as 'the pure English race.' 'The importation in the first place was made by English proprietors, who sent the farmers, mechanics, and adventurers, who lived in and about Devonshire, to cultivate and improve their large and vacant grants.' Massachusetts generally, however, drew from a wider field. One Roger Clap, of Salcombe, claims notice, as having become captain of Boston Castle.

Since the siege of Exeter by the Conqueror, there has been no similar event in the West of equal importance to the siege of Plymouth by the Cavaliers. It marks an epoch of the first importance in national as well as local history. It was the longest and fiercest siege of these times, and it was endured successfully to the end. After the surrender of the army of Essex in 1644, Plymouth was the only place that remained true to the Parliament in the entire Western Peninsula; and had the Royalist soldiery employed in besieging it been set free by its capture, it is certain that the struggle between the two parties would have been greatly protracted. It is even possible it might have had another issue. Plymouth was the key to a good deal more than the fortunes of Devon and Cornwall.

Although it had elected a staunch Royalist in Robert Trelawny to the Long Parliament, the town declared on the popular side the moment there was a prospect of war. As early as November, 1642, such preparations had been made by the mayor, Philip Francis, that the earthen line, 'weak and irregular,' cast up about the town under his directions, enabled Colonel Ruthen, or Ruthven, to repulse an attack in force by Sir Ralph Hopton. Retiring to Modbury, the Royalists were routed; and this success led to Ruthven's marching into Cornwall, to carry the war into the enemy's country, and to his utter defeat in turn by Hopton at the battle of Bradock Down. This was on the 19th of January. In the following month, Hopton besieged Plymouth again, this time in much greater force; and having with him such distinguished Royalist leaders as Sir Bevil Grenville, Sir Nicholas Slanning, Colonel Trevanion, and Lord Mohun. He was again compelled to retire, however, by a second defeat at Modbury, on which the Parliamentary troops of the county had concentrated; and efforts were made, but unavailingly, to arrange a treaty of peace for Devon and Cornwall, and let the rest of the kingdom fight the quarrel out for themselves. For a while there followed a petty border warfare between Royalist Cornwall and Roundhead Devon, which was brought to a sudden close by the defeat of the Earl of Stamford at Stratton, and by the consequent eastward expedition of the Cornishmen, which ended so fatally for their leaders—Grenville being killed at Lansdowne, Trevanion and Slanning at

Bristol, and Sidney Godolphin at Chagford. Plymouth took advantage of this period of comparative peace to strengthen its defences.

They were soon needed. In August, 1643, the town was thoroughly blockaded by Colonel Digby, who did his work so well that no provisions could be brought in. Moreover, Sir Alexander Carew, who held command of the fort and island, the chief defences of the port, was detected in treaty for their surrender, sent to London, and subsequently executed. Prince Maurice took Exeter on the 4th of September, and marched on to reduce Plymouth. Stopping on his road to take Dartmouth, after the method of old-fashioned warfare, the Parliament found time to throw some 500 soldiers into Plymouth, under Colonel Wardlaw, who proved a commander of decision, and against whom Maurice, when he did arrive, found it hopeless to contend. The only advantage the Cavaliers gained was the capture, after three weeks' independent leaguer, of an outlying and, as it proved, useless work called 'Mount Stamford.' Maurice was incessant in his efforts to reduce the obstinate town, for well-nigh two months making almost daily assaults; and on Sunday, the 3rd of December, all but succeeded. The stoutness of the defence, however, was too much for him. The Cavaliers, some of whom had pushed on to within pistol-shot of the walls, were routed to the cry of 'God with us!' Hence for many a long year the bells of St. Andrew rang in memory of the 'Sabbath-day fight;' and sermons were preached, on the foundation of a pious Puritan widow, to hold the deliverance in lasting remembrance. The town motto, 'Turris fortissima est nomen Jehova!' of which Plymouth is as proud as Exeter of its 'Semper fidelis'—dates from this period.

Maurice raised the siege on Christmas Day, prompted thereto partly by the appearance among his troops of the fatal 'camp disease;' but Digby continued the blockade, until placed *hors de combat* by a rapier-wound in the eye. He was succeeded by Sir Richard Grenville. In like manner, Colonel Wardlaw, worn out, was followed for a short time in command of the garrison by Colonel Gould. The latter died early in 1644; and then came Colonel Martin, a most energetic officer, who again was followed, on his death in harness, by Colonel Kerr.

The march of Essex into the West caused the siege to be raised; but four days after the surrender of his forces at Boconnoc, the King himself summoned Plymouth, and on the 10th of September sat down before the town with a gallant armament 15,000 strong. Lord Robartes, who had escaped with Essex and a few others in a boat from Fowey to Plymouth, was appointed Governor on the following day, on which the royal troops made a desperate but unavailing assault. Neither by persuasion, threats, nor force could Charles win his way within the stubborn town, and accordingly he and Maurice speedily marched off, leaving the conduct of the blockade once more in the hands of Grenville. There was not much fighting at Plymouth itself during the remainder of 1644; but 1645 was a very active year, and there is a valuable contemporary record of its proceedings, so far as they have a financial bearing, in the accounts of the Committee of Defence, yet in the possession of the Plymouth Corporation. This committee held the governorship in commission when Robartes was removed by the Self-Denying Ordinance, Colonel Kerr having chief military command.

The most desperate attempt made by Grenville was in January, 1645. He appears at first to have captured three of the great outworks, and to have made his footing good for a while in one. His attack was in force along the line; but when he had been repulsed at all points, save the scene of his temporary success, the captured work was stormed from every quarter by the Plymouth men and taken, and all who were within killed or made prisoners. Probably nearly a fourth of Grenville's whole force of 6,000 men was killed, wounded, or captured. Another fight at Fort Stamford, where the garrison also had the advantage, brought the siege practically to an end. True, it continued in name, after Grenville's defeat, first under Sir John Berkeley, and then under General Digby; but towards the close of the year we find the garrison assuming the offensive, taking St. Budeaux Church, which had been turned into a Cavalier garrison, after an hour and a half's hard fighting, in December; surprising Kinterbury; and storming Saltash and Buckland Abbey. On the 28th of January, 1646, the Royalists decamped in such a hurry at the advance of Fairfax, that they left guns, arms, and ammunition behind. The last Cavalier garrisons in the neighbourhood were Mount Edgcumbe, which had been held most gallantly by Colonel Edgcumbe against repeated attacks, and which, only when all hope was lost, surrendered to Colonel Hammond; and Ince House, which resisted until the 29th of March. Then the 'scorn' was taken out of the Cavaliers who held it, by the planting in position of some big guns.

The siege cost the town dear, though the battle had been won. During the three years that it lasted the parish registers record the deaths of about 1,000 soldiers, and of 2,000 of the townsfolk beyond the death-rate of that time. These figures do not, however, include the losses to the garrison of those who were buried where they fell; nor those of the besiegers, whether in the field or by the still more fatal 'camp disease.' There were many occasions when more than 100 fell in an assault; one, at least, when the loss was over 300. The population of Plymouth at this date did not exceed 7,000; the deaths due to the siege approximated at least 8,000. In three years, therefore, a number greater than the population of the town was swept away. The whole history of the

Civil War fails to supply a parallel. Moreover, the trade of the town was ruined, and scores of families reduced to the greatest distress and misery. As a partial relief the Plymouth duties were for a while taken off.

It was the undaunted spirit the town had shown that led Charles II. to prepare for possible eventualities by erecting the citadel—one of the finest specimens of seventeenth-century fortification now extant in England —upon Plymouth Hoe. And it was the merest irony of Fate that led to the revival of the old temper under James, and that caused Plymouth to be the first municipality in the kingdom to declare for William of Orange, and this very citadel to be the first stronghold put into his hands by its Governor, the Earl of Bath.

For something like 200 years—ever since, in fact, the waters of the Tamar were chosen as the site of a royal arsenal—Plymouth has mingled the characteristics of war and trade, though at times one has predominated and then the other. It was chiefly in consequence of the trading importance of the port that first Winstanley's (1696), then Rudyerd's (1706), Smeaton's (1756), and lastly, Douglass's (1882) lighthouses were erected in turn upon the Eddystone Reef, which lies a few miles off the entrance of Plymouth Sound. The construction of the great breakwater (1812-41) which stretches for a mile across the roadstead between the opposite heights of Maker and of Staddon, was, however, carried out for the express purpose of protecting the vessels of the fleet. And the forts which line the shores of the harbour, and form a cincture round the whole of the three towns, also bore reference to the public works, and not to any private interests. So absorbed, however, did the town become in privateering in the days of the great French war, that for the time almost all legitimate trade died out, and it required years of untiring energy to recover lost ground. One of the first steps taken was the formation of what is now the oldest Chamber of Commerce in the kingdom; and since then wharves and piers have been formed and docks built, and in addition to a good foreign and large coasting trade, Plymouth has become one of the chief mail ports in the kingdom. The growth of the town in the present century has been very rapid. The population is more than five times what it was in 1801; and in the last forty years it has considerably more than doubled. Growth has been accompanied by reconstruction, and there is very little left to mark the age of the community save the fine old mother church of St. Andrew, close by which now stands the noblest pile of municipal buildings in the West of England. The windows of the great hall are filled with stained glass illustrating the richly storied past of the old town; and among the prized possessions of the Corporation is an old portrait of Drake, placed in the ancient Guildhall not many years after his death. Many local antiquities of interest are preserved in the Museum of the Plymouth Institution, including those of Keltic date.

Plymouth has been very rich in worthies. The Hawkinses have been already named. Sir Thomas Edmonds, son of the 'customer' at Plymouth (1562-1639) became the ambassador for James I. to Brussels and Paris, and subsequently Comptroller of the Household. John Quick, a celebrated Puritan divine (died 1706), and Joseph Glanvill, Prebendary of Worcester, author of 'Saducismus Triumphatus' (already noted), were born at Plymouth in 1636. It was likewise the birthplace of Dr. James Yonge (1647-1721), an early member of the Royal Society; of Bryant the Mythologist (1715-1804), and of Kitto (1804-1854), the deaf author.

William Elford Leach, Curator of the British Museum, the greatest zoologist Devonshire has produced, was born at Plymouth in 1790, and died in 1836. A year later was born Sir William Snow Harris (died 1867), the inventor of the system of applying lightning-conductors to ships;

and another Plymouth electrician, Jonathan Hearder (1810-76), was blind nearly all through his scientific career. But it is in connection with Art that the chief personal excellence of modern Plymouth has been reached. Here was born (1746-1831) James Northcote, R.A., pupil and biographer of Reynolds, himself a native of what is now a Plymouth suburb. Here Samuel Prout (1783-1852), the most distinguished water-colour artist of the West, and in his peculiar gifts unrivalled in the kingdom. Here the unfortunate Benjamin Robert Haydon (1786-1846), the true founder of Schools of Art; here Samuel Hart, R.A. (1806-1881), Professor of Painting, and Librarian of the Royal Academy. And here also first saw the light Sir Charles Lock Eastlake (1793-1866), President of the Royal Academy, and at the time of his death Director of the National Gallery. His first great work was a painting of Buonaparte at the gangway of the *Bellerophon* in Plymouth Sound, now in the possession of Lord Clinton.

The joint history of the triple community of Plymouth, Devonport, and Stonehouse, has some curious features. In name Stonehouse, the smallest of the 'three towns' is the oldest. Devonport is the youngest, but under its earliest designation of Stoke was by far the most important member of the triad, as it first appears in history in the pages of 'Domesday.' It was then the property of Robert of Albemarle, whose name is still preserved in the title of the parish—Stoke Damerel—and had a population of twenty-five against the seven of Sutton and the one villein who occupied Stanehvs under Robert the Bastard. While hamlets were developing into the ville of Sutton, and that into the burgh of Plymouth, and while the building of 'stane and lime' which named the ancient manor of Stonehouse was growing into a walled town, Stoke Damerel continued a mere village. It passed from Damerells to Courtenays, Kemiells, Branscombes, and

Britts, until it came to the Wises, and Sir Thomas Wise signalized his ownership by building a stately mansion on the craggy headland opposite the domain of the Edgcumbes, and calling it, with that imitation which is the sincerest flattery, 'Mount Wise.' All but the name has long passed into oblivion, and cannon frown and soldiers dwell where the manor-house once stood. In 1667 Stoke was bought by Sir William Morice, Secretary of State to Charles II., and some time member for Plymouth; and early in the last century passed to its present owners, the St. Aubyns, by the marriage of Sir John St. Aubyn to Catherine, coheiress of the Morice family. As the whole town and parish, with a few unimportant exceptions, belongs to the St. Aubyns, it is now by far the most valuable manor in the West of England.

Devonport, as a town, dates only from the reign of William III. Though Plymouth had so long been a naval port of resort of the first rank, it had few Government establishments and no dockyard. Woolwich, Deptford, and Portsmouth yards go back to the reign of Henry VIII.; and Chatham was founded under Elizabeth. Charles II. established Sheerness, and is credited with the intention of creating a dockyard at Devonport, the advantages of the harbour there having been recognised among others by Ralegh. Until 1690, however, the royal ships at Plymouth were wholly dependent upon the accommodation of private yards. William of Orange saw the need of remedying this state of things soon after he came to the throne, for plans for a 'dock in the Hamoaze' were prepared in 1689; and in the following year a little creek was utilized in the construction of the first basin and dock. This was the germ from which has grown the great naval arsenal of the West, the works of which now all but monopolize, in one form or another, the water-side for miles along the eastern shores of the Tamar estuary.

Plymouth Dock was the original name of the new town; and at first officers and artisans alike were accustomed to live in Plymouth and go to and fro their work daily. The first dockyard was completed in 1693; but it was not until 1700 that the first private house of the new town was erected, a rough wooden structure at the landing-place at North Corner, which became the principal centre whence the houses spread. There are still in this locality a few of the original dwellings left—buildings curiously compounded to all appearance of the cottage and the cabin, the self-instructed architects being at times singularly successful in transferring to the shore some of the leading characteristics of the stern quarters of the old Dutch-built men-of-war.

As war followed war, so the dockyard extended; and as the dockyard extended, so the town grew; until, about the middle of the last century, 'the Dock' was enclosed by ditch and rampart, long since improved out of existence in favour of more massive works, in their turn so outgrown as to be practically useless. The earliest return of the population is for the year 1733, when it was 3,361, about half that of Plymouth. Fifty years later it was equal to that of the elder town; and by the beginning of the century was largely in advance, having a population of 23,747 to the 16,040 of Plymouth and the 3,407 of Stonehouse. While war lasted Devonport grew more rapidly than Plymouth, the natural trade of which was almost wholly destroyed or given up for privateering. But at length commerce asserted its superiority; and the census of 1841 showed Plymouth once more in advance, with a preponderance which it has since increasingly maintained, active as the development of the Government works has from time to time been.

Devonport was one of the large centres of population enfranchised by the Reform Bill of 1832, when it and Stonehouse were thrown together to make one constituency. It was incorporated as a municipality in 1837, having been previously governed by a body of Commissioners operating under a local Act. The name was changed from Plymouth Dock to Devonport in 1824.

Devonport now consists of the old town 'within the lines;' of the ancient village of Stoke, which has developed into a very handsome residential suburb—the tower of the mother church being the one antiquity the place can boast; and of the great and growing annexe of Morice Town or New Passage, which has enormously developed since the commencement of the Keyham Steamyard in 1844. Keyham was the original 'manor-place' of the Wises and their predecessors. Beyond the Keyham Yard are now Seamen's Barracks; and farther up the river towards Saltash the Bull Point and Kinterbury Powder Works and Magazines. The villages of Millbrook and Torpoint, and to a certain extent the town of Saltash also, on the Cornish side of the Tamar, are so far suburbs of Devonport that they are partially inhabited by men employed in the Government establishments.

Of the few notable points in the local history, the blowing up in 1796 of the *Amphion* in harbour, when 200 lives were lost, is one of the most memorable; and in 1840 occurred the great fire in the dockyard, when the *Talavera* and *Minden* were burnt, and large quantities of valuable stores and naval antiquities.

Stonehouse has a history, though never yet thoroughly worked out. The township in legal documents is called East Stonehouse, by way of distinction from a hamlet on the opposite side of Hamoaze at Mount Edgcumbe, named West Stonehouse, said to have been burnt by the French in one of their raids. Carew, writing at the end of the sixteenth century, notes that 'certaine old ruines, yet remaining, confirme the neighbours' report.' It stood near the edge of the water at what is now called Cremyll.

There is no evidence to show whether West Stonehouse was included in the manor of Stonehouse held by Robert the Bastard at the date of the compilation of 'Domesday.' Probably it was not, and East Stonehouse was really the elder town; but Devon then, and until recently, included Mount Edgcumbe and adjacent lands west of the Tamar. After the Bastards the manor came to a family named thence of Stonehouse, and from them it passed by marriage to the Durnfords, whose heiress in turn carried it to its present possessors, the Edgcumbes. Apart from the building whose solid character gave the manor its name, there is little evidence, until Stonehouse came into the hands of the Durnfords, that it consisted of more than the castellated mansion of its lords, with some buildings of a monastic character, doubtfully connected with the great Priory of Plympton. The Durnfords, however, did their best to foster their infant town; and James Durnford, as noted, brought down upon him the Abbot of Buckland, as lord of the hundred of Roborough, by setting up a pillory and tumbrel at 'Estonhouse' and holding courts there, wherefore, 26th Henry VI., it was ordered that the pillory and tumbrel should be 'deposed, destroyed, and removed,' that no courts should be held by Durnford which interfered with the abbot's view of frankpledge, and no hindrance put to the execution of the abbot's precepts or the action of his bailiffs, etc., in the manor. At this time, and long afterwards, Stonehouse to some extent came under the jurisdiction of Plymouth. It formed part of the very extensive ancient parish of St. Andrew (to which it is yet appendant by patronage), and there are records of inquests being held there by a Plymouth coroner, though it never fell within the municipal boundary.

Stonehouse was little more than a fishing village from the time of the Durnfords until the reign of Henry VIII., when it grew more rapidly; so that early in the seventeenth century, Sir William Pole describes it as a 'convenient big town, well inhabited.' The first trace of any corporate authority known to exist is in a deed of the 36th of Elizabeth, which refers to the government of the town being in the hands of the lord, Peter Edgcumbe, Esquire, under rules and directions made with 'the consent & ffrancke agremt of xij. discrete & able psons of & w^t^hin the said Towne and liberties.' This would be something in the nature of a select vestry; and the government of the township continued strictly parochial until the establishment of a Local Board of Health, although it has a population of some 15,000.

The ecclesiastical connection of Stonehouse with Plymouth probably originated with the extensive rights exercised by the Plympton Priory, which was not only liberally endowed by the Valletorts, but received from 'John de Stanhurst' a grant of free fishery 'per totam terram meam.' Though this deed is not dated, it cannot be later than Henry I.; for in the latter part of the twelfth century the fishery is mentioned in a Valletort grant as an ancient right. A Joel of Stonehouse was living there in the reign of Henry III.

The present parish church, dedicated to St. George, replaced in the last century an ancient chapel dedicated to St. Lawrence, the existence of which it is said can be followed back to 1472. St. George, however, appears to have a good claim to the dedication; for a deed, dated 12th Henry VII., mentions John Melett and Laurence Serle as 'custod capell sci georgii martii de Est Stonehouse;' and there is no trace of more than one ancient chapel in the town. Stonehouse became the settlement of a body of Huguenot refugees after the Revocation of the Edict of Nantes; and for several years the chapel was used jointly by the French and English inhabitants. Eventually the former obtained a meeting-place of their own, and continued to meet there until 1810, when they became finally absorbed, as the Huguenots of Plymouth had been three years earlier, in the native population. One of the refugees—Duval—has left his name to the headland of *Devil's* Point.

There is good proof that Stonehouse was a place of some importance in the closing years of the sixteenth century, from the fact that an Act of Parliament was obtained to bring into the town a supply of fresh water, the needs of the shipping being alleged as a leading cause. A leat, or water-course, was accordingly made, though it did not answer the end designed. There appears then to have been some falling off. Stonehouse had a Royalist lord in Colonel Edgcumbe, and a tolerably numerous Roundhead population. Its interest was therefore very equally divided; and it took no active part in the great struggle. On one side lay Plymouth, garrisoned for the Parliament—its exterior lines of defence, indeed, included Stonehouse; on the other was Mount Edgcumbe, held for the King. Stonehouse must have had walls of some kind, for it had barrier-gates until 1770; but it was not a place of any strength, and held wisely neutral. Hence, doubtless, its choice in 1643 as the place of meeting of the negociants of the fruitless treaty of peace between Devon and Cornwall.

Like Devonport, Stonehouse has been to a large extent absorbed by the action of the Government, which in one form or another occupies the larger proportion of its water-side. Here the Naval Hospital, fronting the Military Hospital at Devonport on the other side of a creek; there the Royal William Victualling Office, the finest pile of buildings devoted to victualling purposes in the country; and there again forts and barracks, the latter the headquarters of a division of Royal Marines. What shipping-trade continues is carried on in Stonehouse Pool, on the western shores of which Devonport is attempting to utilize for commercial purposes the only available piece of foreshore that the Government establishments have left free.

CHAPTER XXV.

PLYMPTON.

PLYMPTON has all the marks of a very ancient settlement. When it was founded the waters of what is now known as the Laira stretched up the valley to its site, and immediately above the farthest tidal reach were reared the earthworks which now bear the ruins of the fortress of the Redverses, but which were certainly held by the Kelt, possibly adopted by the Roman, and in turn extended and strengthened by the Saxon, ere the Norman made it the centre of his power in the wide district around. Traces of this history may yet be read in the castle and its surroundings.

In all probability Plympton takes name from its ancient position at the head of the estuary of what is now known as the Plym, or, as these estuarine creeks are commonly called in the locality, lake—*pen lin* in the Western Keltic tongue, contracted, as in other instances in Cornwall, into *plin*, the form which the first syllable takes in its earliest occurrence in 'Domesday'—Plintona. Plymouth, at the lower end of the estuary, did not assume that appellation until the original meaning of the word had long been lost; and the consequence appears to have been a curious transference of names. The modern Plym is made up of two rivers, the Mew or Meavy, and what in later days has been called the Cad, but through the Middle Ages was known as the Plym. The old form of Meavy is Mewi, and this in the Kornu-Keltic would mean 'greater water.' There is no reasonable doubt that Laira—formerly Lary—the name *now* applied to the estuary, which means the 'lesser water'—is the original name of the second tributary, and that the estuary and the river—the Plym and the Lary—have somehow exchanged titles. There is a bridge over the Plym called Cadover, a corruption of *coed weorthig*—the 'farm-place in the wood,' and the second change of name from Plym to Cad arose from the 'over' being held to imply that the bridge crossed the Cad. The Plym is now commonly understood of the *rivers* between their junction and the estuary.

Failing such an explanation, many are the hypotheses that have been advanced to account for the fact that the 'ton' of the Plym is not, and never was, upon the river now known by that name, and is, indeed, nearly two miles distant, though quite as great a distance from the estuary. It is, however, well within historic times that the tide flowed up to the walls of the castle, and that Plympton stood literally, as well as nominally, at the 'head of the lake.' Moreover, throughout the Middle Ages the chief traffic between Plymouth and the great Priory of Plympton was by boat. This was the route adopted by the Black Prince at his visits to the West, when the Priory afforded him entertainment. A record of acts done by him as Duke of Cornwall at Plymouth and Plympton, in 1362, is still in the possession of the Earl of Mount Edgcumbe; and the house seems to have become somewhat impoverished by the many claims on its hospitality caused by its contiguity to the port of Plymouth.

At the compilation of 'Domesday' Plintona was the chief centre of population for many miles. There is, therefore, much show of reason for the appearance here also of the ubiquitous couplet:

> 'Plympton was a borough town
> When Plymouth was a furzy down.'

William held it in succession to the Confessor, and had an enumerated population of twenty-three within his demesne; while there were twelve villeins in the portion held by the canons. Though all was included in one entry, the germs of the division thus already existed which in later years made the territory of the Priory the parish of Plympton St. Mary, and the lands of the secular lord the Borough of Plympton Erle (from its owners), or Plympton St. Maurice, from the early patron saint of its church, in later years assigned to St. Thomas of Canterbury.

The remains of Plympton Castle consist of a mound surmounted by the ruins of a shell keep, which rises at the eastern end of a rectangular enclosure or base court. The earthworks are in excellent preservation, and there are traces of exterior defences. The Norman masonry is simple, and with no special features of interest save the occurrence of the cavities in the walls, which show the original places of the beams inserted to strengthen and support the stonework upon the doubtful foundation of the mound. It is probable that the Norman castle was, in great part, if not wholly, built by Richard de Redvers, Earl of Devon, to whom Henry I. granted the honour and castle. It was practically demolished in the ensuing reign under his son, Baldwin, who had espoused the cause of Matilda against Stephen, but whose garrison at Plympton surrendered without striking a blow. This was the only occasion on which Plympton Castle has figured in history, and from that day to this as a fortalice it has been a mere ruin; though Plympton was a station of the Cavaliers at the siege of Plymouth. The honour of Plympton—of which were held 120 knights' fees—followed the fortunes of the great house to which it belonged. It passed from the Redverses to the Courtenays, and continued in the latter, with the exception of the intervals when that powerful family lay under royal displeasure, until the death of Lord Edward Courtenay, in 1566. The property was then scattered among various families, but was subsequently to a large extent brought together again by purchase by the Earls of Morley; and in them the lordship of the castle and manor is now vested.

The Parkers, originally of North Molton, acquired by their marriage with the heiress of Mayhew, temp. Elizabeth, the manor of Boringdon, and thenceforward made it their chief residence, until in 1712 they purchased Saltram, once the seat and residence of Sir James Bagge, the creature of Buckingham, and the 'bottomless bagge' of the patriot Eliot. The Parkers were raised to the peerage in 1774, as Barons Boringdon; and in 1815 advanced to be Viscounts Boringdon and Earls of Morley. Saltram House was rebuilt by them early in the last century, and was long reported the largest mansion in the county.

Plympton Priory was one of the most ancient and notable religious houses in Devon. The canons who held two hides of the Plintona manor under William, were the successors of men who had been seated there in all probability for a longer period than any other religious in Devon outside Exeter. There is yet extant a copy of a Saxon document of reasonable authenticity, dated 904, which records a grant by Eadweard the Elder to Asser, Bishop of Sherborne, and the convent there, of twelve manors, by way of exchange for the monastery which in the Saxon tongue is called 'Plymentun.' The college consisted of a dean and four canons; and when they refused to give up their wives, or, as Leland said, 'wold not leve their concubines,' it was suppressed by Bishop Warelwast, nephew of the Conqueror, in 1121. In its stead he founded what afterwards became the great Augustinian Priory of St. Peter and St. Paul, which was so enriched with liberal gifts by the Redverses and

Valletorts and other benefactors, that at the Dissolution it was the wealthiest house in the West, with revenues valued at £912 12s. 8d. The magnificent Priory Church, where Warelwast and some of the Courtenays were buried, adjoined the parish church of St. Mary; and a few traces yet remain. Of the domestic buildings all that is left is the refectory, converted into a dwelling which has a Norman crypt.

The priors, as already stated, were lords of a portion of Plymouth in its infancy, and their part of the ancient manor of Sutton was then called Sutton Prior. Before that town could be incorporated, their consent had to be obtained; and the terms were finally settled at an inquisition held in the nave of the Priory Church in 1441, a fee farm rent of £41 being then deemed an adequate compensation. The Priory had two appendant cells—one, Marisco, near Exeter; and the other at St. Anthony in Roseland, Cornwall. The site has been in the Champernownes, Strodes, and Fowneses.

Plympton Erle was chartered by its feudal lords. Baldwin de Redvers made it a borough town, and granted the burgesses its market and fairs in March, 1241. These were confirmed in 1284. Municipal functions were retained until 1859, when, in consequence of the charter conferring no exclusive jurisdiction as against the county, it was allowed to lapse. As a Parliamentary borough Plympton dated from 23rd Edward I., and it was continuously represented until the fatal 1832. Few towns in Devon have had more distinguished representatives. Serjeant Hele sat for the borough under Elizabeth. Many of the Strode family, whose ancestral seat of Newnham is close by, were returned at various times; and among them that William Strode who was one of the famous 'five members.' Strange that a town of such marked Puritan proclivities should also have chosen such a staunch Royalist as Sir Nicholas Slanning. Sir George

Treby, the judge, and Sir John Maynard, were other notable members; and, most notable of all, in 1685, Sir Christopher Wren became a 'burgess' of Plympton. In later days, the most prominent representative was Lord Castlereagh. When he sat, however, Plympton had long been a purely nomination borough; one half of the representation belonging to the Trebys, and the other half to the Edgcumbes.

Quaint as many of the surroundings of Plympton Erle still are, chief interest centres in the comparatively modern and modernized Grammar School. Founded from the bequest of the great educational benefactor of Devon, Elize, or Elizeus, Hele, and erected in 1644, here was born, July 16, 1723, while his father, the Rev. Samuel Reynolds, was head-master, the greatest English portrait-painter, Sir Joshua Reynolds, P.R.A. The old dwelling has given place to a modern edifice; but the school and its quaint cloister still remain—the school in which not only Reynolds, but Northcote was educated, which was the first school, moreover, of another President of the Royal Academy, Sir C. L. Eastlake, and of which Benjamin Robert Haydon was 'head-boy' in 1801. No school in England holds such a relation to Art, therefore, as the ancient Grammar School of Plympton. Sir Joshua never forgot his native town, and to the last kept up kindly relations. Nor was he by any means without honour in his own country. His townsmen were proud of him, and did him what respect lay in their power, electing him in 1773 their mayor! On this occasion he gave the town his portrait, painted by himself; and it hung in the Guildhall until 1832, when the thrifty Corporation, to their lasting disgrace, sold it to the Earl of Egremont for £150.

Of the families connected with Plympton and its neighbourhood, the Parkers have already been noted. The Strodes of Newnham, lately extinct in the male line, were seated at Strode, in Ermington, as early as the reign of Henry III. Newnham was acquired by marriage with a coheiress of the Newnhams, temp. Henry IV. Richard and William Strode, the two most notable members of the family, have been already mentioned. Dr. William Strode, poet and divine, died in 1644.

The Woollcombes, who have been seated at Hemerdon for several generations, in the reign of Elizabeth lived on the adjoining estate of Challonsleigh. Chaddlewood was long in the extinct family of Snelling (now in Soltau Symons), and Beechwood is the seat of Lord Seaton.

The adjacent parish of Brixton is associated with such old family names as Brixton, Calmady, Coplestone, Fortescue, Maynard, Drake, Pollexfen, and Hele; but its chief claim to notice here is as the residence of that most worthy member of the wide-spreading family of Hele—Elize Hele, of Wollaton, who bequeathed in 1635 the manor of Brixton Reigny and all his estates to charitable uses, and thus became the great school founder of his native county.

It is a question whether the Heles really sprung from Hele near Bradninch, or Hele in Cornwood, where they can certainly be traced to the reign of Richard II.; but the latter is probably a younger branch. Cornwood, noted in 'Domesday' as possessing three wild horses—ancestors, no doubt, of the native breed of Dartmoor ponies—is connected with several distinguished families. Chief among these was that of Ralegh, which obtained Fardell by marriage with the heiress of Newton. At this ancient mansion, now a farm-house, Wymond Ralegh, grandfather of Sir Walter Ralegh, lived; and here no doubt Walter, the father, was born. There is a baseless tradition that it was also the birthplace of the great Sir Walter himself. That, however, was at East Hayes.

Slade, with its fine hall, once the seat of the family of that name, has long been the residence of the Spurrells, and their descendants, the Podes. Blachford is the seat of Lord Blachford, whose ancestors were sometime leading merchants in Plymouth, and for many years filled chief places in the Corporation. Their original settlement in Cornwood was Wisdome, of which place John Rogers was created baronet in 1698. The present is the first Lord Blachford, and was the eighth baronet.

Plymstock Manor was part of the possessions of the Abbey of Tavistock under the Confessor, though not a portion of the original endowment, and a tradition attaches to its connection with that house which falls into place more appropriately in the section on Dartmoor. In Plymstock parish are the great limestone quarries of Oreston, out of which the material for the Plymouth breakwater was hewn, and in which were found the first bone-caves that formed the subject of scientific investigation and marked a new departure in geological discovery. There was much fighting here from time to time in connection with the siege of Plymouth, and traces of earthworks are yet visible. Here, too, was the site of the ancient Keltic settlement at Staddon referred to under Plymouth. Staddiscombe was the birthplace (1717) of the learned Nathaniel Foster, translator of Plato. It is also the reputed birthplace of Walter Britte, an able and active disciple of Wiclif.

Wembury has already been mentioned as the probable site of the battle of Wicganbeorge. Its name has been interpreted to mean the 'Viking's bury' or fort; while a kindred origin has been sought for the name of the adjoining parish of Revelstoke, the 'revel' representing *reafere*, a 'rover, robber,' and *reafful*=rapacious. Moreover the situation of the respective churches close to the water's edge seems to have in it something of a commemorative character. Wembury Church is dedicated to St. Werburga, and thus falls into place as one of the proofs of Mercian influence in Devon, advanced by Mr. T. Kerslake. Wembury, which belonged to Plympton Priory, does not appear in 'Domesday,' though some of its manors do. The manor of Wembury was acquired in 1592 by Sir John Hele, the well-known serjeant-at-law, who erected what was regarded as the most magnificent mansion in the county. It was held for awhile by the Pollexfens; and early in the present century the house was pulled down by the then owner, Mr. Lockyer. Langdon was for several generations till recently the seat of the Calmadys.

Radford, in Plymstock, has been a seat of the Harris family for nearly 500 years. Here Ralegh is said to have been kept in ward on his return in 1618, and here at times Drake stored much of his treasure.

The last parish to be noted in connection with this group is Yealmpton. Risdon records a tradition that Æðelwold had a palace here, and that here also his 'lieutenant,' Lipsius, was interred; and with Risdon the statement begins and ends. Under the name of Yealmpton the manor does not appear in 'Domesday'; but it can hardly be other than the Elintone entered among the royal manors next to Plintona, ranking next to it also in importance, and having one hide held by the clergy of the ville—described in the Exon book as of St. Mary of Alentona—in alms. The use of E or A for Y in 'Domesday' is usual; and there are many reasons which combine to make this identification all but certain.

In the churchyard at Yealmpton stands one of the ancient inscribed stones already noted under Tavistock, bearing one word only, but that variously read. The common rendering is TOREVS, and that is the reading current in the neighbourhood, where it is looked upon with some little interest, and traditionally regarded as commemorating some ancient chieftain or king. The other reading is GOREVS, but the point can hardly be regarded as definitely settled, and it may not be amiss to note that the ancient village of Tor is within a mile, and that the name, as it stands, is closely allied to that of the little river Torry at Plympton some five miles north, which, moreover, appears in 'Domesday' as Torix.

Kitley is now the chief seat of the ancient family of Bastard, which claim descent from the Robert Bastard who appears in 'Domesday' as the holder of nine manors. They obtained Kitley by marriage with the heiress of the Pollexfens, Edmund Pollexfen, the last male of the family, dying in 1710. Since then they have acquired several adjoining estates, including Bowdon, once the seat of a family of that name, Coffleet, and Lyneham.

Lyneham, for nearly four centuries, was the seat of the great Devonshire family of Crocker, referred to in the already-quoted rhyme, who are now represented by the Bulteels. In Yealmpton Church is one of the finest brasses in the county, to Sir John Crocker of Lyneham, cupbearer to Edward IV.

Windsor here was the seat of Richard Fortescue, from whom, according to Sir W. Pole, are descended the Fortescues of the east of England. Pitton was the residence of the North Devon Woollcombes before their removal to Ashbury.

CHAPTER XXVI.

MODBURY.

MODBURY is one of the oldest market-towns in the county, and returned representatives to Parliament in the reign of Edward I. We know nothing of it until 'Domesday,' when one Richard was the tenant under the Earl of Moreton, who held it 'unjustly.' The parish comprises several ancient manors. Orcherton, at the time of the Survey, was held from the Earl by Reginald de Valletort. The Valletorts soon became the dominant race, and from them Modbury came to the Champernownes, who held it as the seat of the family from the reign of Edward II. until 1700. There were several distinguished members of this race, and one of them, Arthur Champernowne, was knighted in 1599 for his eminent services under the Earl of Essex in Ireland. There is a curious story that Queen Elizabeth was so exasperated by the refusal of the Champernowne of her time to lend her a fine band of musicians, that she found occasion to compel him to part with nineteen manors.

A Priory was founded at Modbury, in the reign of Stephen, by an ancestor of the Champernownes, as a cell to the Abbey of St. Peter sur Dive, Normandy. When the alien houses were suppressed, this passed at first to Tavistock Abbey, but afterwards to Eton College.

Wimpston, as noted heretofore, is the ancestral home

of the wide-branching Fortescues, who ceased to reside therein, however, in the reign of Elizabeth.

Brownston was granted by Adam de Morville to the Abbey of Buckfastleigh.

Among other families connected with Modbury are the Prideauxes and Heles of Orcherton; the Saverys of Shilston; the Edmerstons and Rouses of Edmerston; the Challons of Leigh; and the Traynes and Swetes of Trayne. It was a Savery of Shilston, Thomas, who about 1697 invented the first practical steam-pumping apparatus.

Old Port, a very remarkable fortification of unknown antiquity, on the Erme, gave name to the De la Ports, and is suggested by Mr. R. J. King as of older date than Saxon times. 'It may have been the work of the Romans before their withdrawal .... or it may have been raised by some British King of Damnonia, working and building under Roman traditions, for defence against the Saxon host.'

Modbury was the scene of the opening passage in the great drama of the Civil War, so far as Devonshire is concerned. All the chief towns had declared on the side of the Parliament, when, in 1642, Sir Ralph Hopton persuaded Sir Edmund Fortescue, of Fallapit, then High Sheriff, to call out the *posse comitatus*. Hopton and Slanning with a force of between two and three thousand captured Tavistock, and then Plympton, whence they marched to Modbury, which had been appointed for the rendezvous with Fortescue. Here some thousand trained soldiers and volunteers speedily collected; and an attack in force upon Plymouth would not long have been delayed, had not Colonel Ruthen, in command there, taken the initiative. Very early in the morning he despatched about 500 horse and dragoons, as if an attack on Tavistock were intended. Speedily wheeling southward, however, they came round through Ivybridge, and fell upon Modbury quite unexpectedly, about nine in the morning, after a five hours' march. The day was won at once. The trained bands, crying out 'The troopers are come!' ran away, leaving their arms behind them; the unarmed *posse*, who were mostly at Modbury sorely against their will, were no whit slow in following the example. Resistance there was none, save on the part of Sir Edmund Fortescue and his friends, who garrisoned the castellated house of Mr. Champernowne, and made a stout defence until it was fired and further resistance was hopeless. With the loss of one man the Roundheads thus not only dispersed an embryo army, but took a number of important prisoners —the High Sheriff; John Fortescue, his predecessor in that office; Sir Edward Seymour; Edward Seymour, M.P., his eldest son; Colonel Henry Champernowne; Arthur Basset; Thomas Shipcote, the Clerk of the Peace—altogether about a score of prominent Royalists, who were straightway shipped from Dartmouth to London.

Modbury is probably the last place in the West of England where the old adage, ' Good wine needs no bush,' had an association in custom. The great fair at Modbury —known as St. George's Fair, and held for nine days—is still proclaimed by the manor portreeve and borough jury in ancient form upon the spot where once stood the market cross, and within the last fifty years it was the custom in the town to hang out a holly bush from private houses where drink was being sold during fair-time, as an indication of the fact. The bush did duty for an Excise license in the old days, and the custom appears to have lingered on at Modbury long after it had ceased to be legal. The fair was one of the most important in the district. Within living memory it afforded the only opportunity for the purchase of cloth in the town; and travelling braziers were accustomed to ply their avocation only on these occasions.

Ermington was a market-town under a grant made in 1294. The manor and hundred had been given by

Henry I. to Matilda Peverell. Strachleigh was the seat of a family of that name for ten descents from the reign of Henry III. The last of the name died in 1583; and the Strachleigh brass is one of the features of the church. Another is the fact that the altar continued from the Reformation to be set tablewise, and enclosed by a balustrade. The church belonged to the Priory of Montacute. Strode has already been mentioned as the original seat of the Strodes. Ivybridge in like manner gave name to its owners, thence passing to the Bonviles. Woodland is noteworthy for the fact that the last male of that ilk, Sir Walter de Woodland, was a follower and attendant of the Black Prince. The tradition is yet current in the parish, of the fall, near Strachleigh, in 1623, of a meteoric stone weighing 23 lb.

Harford has a place in history as the native parish of John Prideaux, Bishop of Worcester (1578-1650), whose success in life, singularly enough, dated from a disappointment that at the time cut him to the heart—his rejection for the post of parish clerk of the adjoining parish of Ugborough. By the kindly help of the mother of Sir Edmund Fowel (a family long settled at Fowelscombe), he found his way to Oxford, and rose from the kitchen of Exeter College in the short space of sixteen years to its rectorship; thence passing in 1641 to the see of Worcester. Ejected when the Puritan party obtained the upper hand —a fate that was certain to so decided and ardent a politician and theologian—he bore his reverses with unruffled equanimity, and died cheerfully in pious poverty; a singular contrast to his miserable depression when he failed in his clerkship candidature. He had learnt better what failure really was. 'If I had been chosen clerk of Ugborough-I had never been Bishop of Worcester.' In Harford Church is a monument erected by Prideaux to his father and mother, and one to Thomas Williams, Speaker of the House of Commons in 1602.

Ugborough was one of the manors of the Briweres, and passed to the Mohuns. Fowelscombe, in this parish, was the original seat of the Fowel family, created baronets in 1661. At Widcombe here was born, in 1620, Admiral Sir John Kempthorne, who first showed his mettle by engaging in the frigate *Mary Rose* a squadron of seven Turkish men-of-war, and sinking or capturing the whole. He was made Admiral for his distinguished services in 1665, under the Duke of York, and took part in several engagements with the Dutch, as well as that at Solebay. Subsequently one of the Commissioners of the Navy, he died at Portsmouth in 1679.

Holbeton tithes were appropriated to the Priory of Polsloe, and the manor of Battisborough belonged to the Abbey of Buckfastleigh. The manor of Holbeton passed, with that of Ermington, to Matilda Peverell. Flete, the most important estate in the parish, continued in the Damerells from the Conquest till the reign of Edward III. It was the chief seat of the Heles, and came to the Bulteel family by entail. The house has been recently rebuilt by its present owner, Mr. Mildmay, a connection of the Bulteel family; and Membland, long the residence of the Hillersdons, whom the Bulteels represent, now belongs to Mr. Baring, another connection, and one of the old Devonshire Baring stock. Pamflete is now the seat of the representative of the Bulteels, Mr. John Crocker Bulteel.

Kingston, which was included in the Peverell grant, was afterwards in the Martyns, Audleys, Bourchiers, and Wreys. Wonwell gave name to a family long extinct.

Bigbury was held by lords of that name as early as the reign of John; and after nine descents was brought by a coheiress to one of the Champernownes of Beer Ferrers, from whom it descended through the Willoughbys to the Paulets. There is a fifteenth-century Bigbury brass in the church.

CHAPTER XXVII.

KINGSBRIDGE AND SALCOMBE.

THE well-built and thriving little town of Kingsbridge, though left out in the cold by abortive railway schemes, and dependent for communication upon coaches after the olden fashion, has long distanced Modbury in the race for the honour and profit of being the chief town of the South Hams. This, of course, is largely due to its position at the head of the long many-branched estuarine creek which divides the great southern promontory of Devon, with its bold headlands—the Bolt Head and Tail, Prawle Point, and the Start—into two nearly equal portions. Of this district it forms not only the natural, but the topographical centre; and the wonder perhaps rather is that it has not developed still more important results.

The manors of Kingsbridge and Churchstow were, in the thirteenth century, the property of the Abbey of Buckfast. Originally Kingsbridge had been a part of Churchstow; but the growth of a little centre of population at the head of the 'Kingsbridge River' made special provision for its spiritual wants necessary. A chapel was accordingly erected, and dedicated to St. Edmund, king and martyr. This served its purpose for the time, but burials had still to be performed at Churchstow; and as the daughter village grew, this burden became too heavy to be borne. In 1414 (Aug. 26), therefore, probably at the instance of Abbot Slade, Bishop Stafford consecrated the Chapel of St. Edmund a parish church, and blessed its cemetery. The further growth of the community is shown by the fact that some half-century later the Abbey obtained a grant for their town of Kingsbridge of a weekly market, and a three-days' fair, though the market, at least, was of far older date.

The earliest allusion to Kingsbridge as a borough occurs in the Hundred Rolls. When the Abbot of Buckfast was summoned, in 1276, to answer for the rights claimed by him in the manor of Churchstow, the jury found that within that manor there was a new borough, which answered for itself by six jurors, and had a market on Friday, with a separate assize of bread and ale. This, then, was Kingsbridge, though it is about fifty years later that the word is first found. As in the case of Bridgewater, the bridge in the name is a corruption, and the true title Kingsburg, though what the King had to do with it is by no means clear.

Up to the time of the Dissolution, Churchstow and Kingsbridge remained appendant to the Abbey of Buckfast. They were then granted to Sir William Petre, and in his descendants they remained until 1793, when they were purchased by the Scobells. Kingsbridge Manor is now the property of Mr. Hurrell.

Though the distinction is commonly sunken, Kingsbridge really consists of two little towns—long since one in fact, though not *de jure*—Kingsbridge and Dodbrooke. Of these the latter is by far the older member of the twin community. Probably named from a Saxon owner, Dodda the thegn, at 'Domesday' we find it one of the few Devonshire manors in female hands, its lady being Godeva, widow of Brictric the Sheriff. That it early assumed some importance is proven by the grant of a weekly market and annual fair, in 1256. For a long period the manor was in the Champernownes, the most interesting point in its personal history. A large woollen trade was carried on here well on into the present century.

The southern district of Devon, which is known in the county as the South Hams, produces a beverage of archæological interest—'white ale,' chiefly brewed now in the neighbourhood of Kingsbridge, where it was tithable from time immemorial, and commonly held to be of purely local origin. It is made of malt wort, wheaten flour, and eggs, and is fermented with a material called 'grout,' the preparation of which is kept a secret. Not many years ago this 'white ale' was the common drink of the district; but its use is rapidly dying out with its old friends. Mr. P. Karkeek, who has made the beverage a study, has come to the interesting conclusion that it is really the old English ale, described by all contemporary authorities as a thicker drink than beer, which is distinguished from ale by the addition of hops—in short, that 'the white ale of the South Hams is a survival in some form of the ale once drunk by our forefathers all over England.'

Kingsbridge Church contains a monument to George Hughes, the leader in the middle of the seventeenth century of the Puritan clergy of Devonshire, who, when ejected from Plymouth, retired to this little place to end his days. The inscription is by his son-in-law, John Howe.

The town has its full share of worthies. Thomas Crispin, in 1670, was the founder of the Grammar School, further endowed with exhibitions by William Duncombe, who, under his will, in 1698, established a lectureship. Here also lived at Knowle for many years, and here died in 1815, the celebrated ornithologist, Colonel Montagu. The most worthy native was William Cookworthy, chemist and potter, the discoverer of china clay and china stone in Cornwall, and the founder of the Plymouth

China Works, where the first true porcelain made in England was produced, and the productions of which are now most highly valued. Born at Kingsbridge in 1705, and left when quite a lad by the death of his father, who was a weaver, in very poor circumstances, he walked to London to enter on his duties as an apprentice with a firm of chemists, named Bevan. By their aid, he subsequently established a drug business in Plymouth, and lived in that town until his death, in 1780. He made his great discovery of the existence of the materials for the production of porcelain between the years 1745-50; and, after long experimenting, reached such perfection in their use, that he obtained a patent in 1768, and manufactured large quantities of china at Plymouth in the next few years, after which the factory was removed to Bristol. Cookworthy was a singular mixture of Quaker and Swedenborgian, and a firm believer in the divining-rod.

A more widely known, though personally a far inferior, worthy was the notorious Dr. Wolcot, whose writings are familiar under the name of 'Peter Pindar.' He was born at Dodbrooke (1738-1819), and was the most powerful master of forceful satire of a rough-and-ready type in the English tongue—our greatest caricaturist in rhyme. Most unpleasant in character, he claims praise less for his abilities than for his sturdy independence, and for the manner in which he discovered and encouraged the genius of John Opie, R.A.

Fallapit, in East Allington, or Alvington, was until recently the seat for several centuries of one of the branches of the Fortescues, coming to them by marriage with the heiress of the Fallapits. Garston, in West Alvington, is an ancient seat of the Bastards, whence they removed to Kitley. Almost the whole of the Kingsbridge promontory is celebrated for the mildness of its climate; and at Garston, as at Combe Royal and at

Salcombe, orange and lemon trees flourish in the open
air to an extent unknown elsewhere in England. As
Malborough, South Milton, and South Huish are daughter
churches to West Alvington, this happy mildness may
be regarded as the peculiar prerogative of that parish.
Bowringsleigh, here, was the property and residence of
the ancient family of Bowring.

Thurlestone, which lies near the mouth of the Avon,
takes its name from a remarkable natural arch on the
coast, known as Thurlestone Rock=the stone that is
pierced or 'thirled.' The arch is of red Triassic con-
glomerate, resting uncomfortably upon Devonian clay
slate. The parish figures in 'Domesday' as Torlestan, held
in demesne by Judhel of Totnes, with a soldier as under
tenant, and the large enumerated population of thirty-
five.

Ilton, in Malborough, once belonged to the Bozuns,
then to the Chiverstons, and finally came to the Courtenays.
Sir John Chiverston built the fortified mansion, afterwards
known as Ilton Castle, in 1335. In right of their estates
in Malborough the Courtenays exercise important rights
of wreckage along the coast ; and used to hold Courts of
Admiralty at the various maritime villages within the
manors of their royalty. Such courts were usually con-
vened by the manor steward on the occasion of any
wreck, and stringent codes of laws were enforced.

A small district near the Bolt Head, known as the
'Sewers' from the frequent occurrence of that name in
East, West, Middle, and Lower Sewers, has been suggested
as marking the site of an early Saxon settlement—reading
sewer as *sæ-ware*=' sea-dwellers.'

Salcombe, in the parish of Malborough, is the chief
port of the Kingsbridge district, lying on the western side
of the estuary near its mouth, and has of late risen into
some favour as a seaside and invalid resort. For this it
is excellently adapted by the beauty and grandeur of the

scenery in the neighbourhood, and by the mildness of its climate. On the opposite side of the water is Portlemouth, which seems to derive its name from its position, and which appears in some of the records of the early Middle Ages as the name of the harbour generally.

Salcombe Castle was the last place in Devon which adhered to the cause of Charles I. The ruins still stand on a semi-insular rock in the Salcombe estuary, a position of great strength and of considerable importance. The Castle dates from the reign of Henry VIII., and was one of the numerous little strengths built by him on the Western coasts to defend the principal ports from sudden forays. When the war between Charles and his Parliament broke out it had long fallen into decay, and was commonly known as the 'Old Bullworke.' Sir Edmund Fortescue of Fallapit, the Royalist High Sheriff of Devon in 1642, and for many months a prisoner at Winchester House and Windsor Castle, on his release undertook to refortify and man the ancient walls. Prince Maurice gave him a commission for this purpose in December, 1643, while he was engaged in the siege of Plymouth; and Fortescue evidently carried out his work thoroughly.

Little is known of the history of Fort Charles, as Fortescue named the Castle, except in its last stage. On January 16, 1646, Fairfax captured Dartmouth, and immediately set forces to watch Fort Charles, under Colonel Inglesby. It was then garrisoned by sixty-six men, Sir Edmund being Governor; and there were plenty of provisions and munitions of war. As it was impregnable to ordinary attack, a regular siege had to be made. This was conducted by Colonel Weldon, Parliamentary Governor at Plymouth, the blockade of which had been raised by Fairfax. Weldon brought a train of siege artillery with him from Plymouth, and the battery commenced on the last week in January. Very little damage was done by the firing on either side; and if a memorandum left by

Sir Edmund is to be accepted as a complete return, only one of the garrison was killed and two wounded, while, on the other hand, only one of the besiegers is recorded to have been slain.

The siege lasted nearly four months, and the surrender was probably due to the hopelessness of continuing the struggle. The Royalist cause was utterly lost, and nothing was to be gained by holding out. Moreover the blockade was strictly kept; and provisions no doubt were beginning to run short, when, on the 7th of May, the articles of surrender were agreed upon. They were most honourable to the defenders. The garrison marched to Fallapit, with drums beating, colours flying, muskets and bandaliers; nor did they deliver up their guns until they had fired three volleys. All the officers kept their arms, all the officers and men their private property; and all had leave to depart to their houses, and three months in which to make their peace with Parliament or leave the kingdom. As to the fort itself, it was provided that it was never to be known by any other name than that of Fort Charles, and that neither it nor any coat of arms belonging to it was to be defaced. The key of the Castle is still in the possession of Sir Edmund's representative.

There is a curious local tradition attaching to a little corner of land—some acre in extent—at Splatt Cove, in Salcombe Harbour. It belongs to the Bastard family, and the legend is that their Norman ancestor had command of one of the vessels of the Conqueror's fleet, which was driven by a gale into Salcombe, and that it was upon this very spot the leader and his men landed. The retention of the land by the Bastards is ascribed by the country folk to this historical connection. Mr. Karkeek, however, has shown not only that the legend has no pedigree, but that it is inconsistent with known facts. The name of Robert the Bastard does not occur in the Battle Abbey Roll, and though he is mentioned in

'Domesday,' neither of his Devonshire manors can be connected with Splatt Cove.

Hope Cove has its connection with the great Armada drama. The *St. Peter the Great*, one of the Spanish hospital ships, had escaped with the remnant of the fleet, rounded Scotland, and was on her way homeward, when by stress of weather she was driven upon the rocks on this inhospitable coast, much to the advantage of the country folk, who made liberal spoil. Out of 190 persons on board, about 150 were saved. An effort was made to recover the stores, and special inquiry had to that end by Anthony Ashley, but it was not very productive.

Portlemouth, already noted, contains the manor of West Prawle, one of the estates with which Blundell endowed his school at Tiverton. Scobbahull, in the adjacent parish of South Pool, gave name to the family of Scobell.

Stokenham is connected with several families of note. Given by John to Matthew Fitzherbert, it continued for several generations in his descendants, and the last of the family, Matthew Fitzjohn, was summoned to Parliament by Edward I. as a baron. Dying without an heir, the manor passed to the King, and Edward gave it to Ralph de Monthermer to be held of the Crown. As it had been held under the Courtenays of the honour of Plympton, the Earl of Devon petitioned Parliament for the redress of this grievance, which he obtained. The manor descended through the Montacutes and Pooles to Hastings, Earl of Huntingdon, and was by him sold to the Amerediths. Stokenham Church once belonged to the Priory of Bisham, in Somerset. The church of the adjoining parish of Sherford is a daughter to Stokenham, but Sherford Manor was part of the estates of St. Nicholas Priory, Exeter. Kennedon, in this parish, in the fifteenth century became a seat of the family of Hals. Here lived John Hals, Justice of the Common Pleas in 1423, and here was born his son, of the same name, who, in 1450, was made Bishop of Lichfield and Coventry.

Slapton has several claims to notice. It belonged to the ancient family of De Brian as early as the reign of Henry II., and descended to the Percy Earls of Northumberland, as the representative of Sir Guy de Brian the younger, through the sole heiress. The St. Maurs claimed it ineffectually by descent from Guy's sister. The Percys sold the manor to the Arundells of Wardour. Guy de Brian, one of the first Knights of the Garter, founded a collegiate chantry at Slapton in 1373, and the remains of his house are known as Poole Priory. Here lived for several years, on his return from captivity in Spain, Sir Richard Hawkins, son of Sir John, from whom the Hawkinses of Kingsbridge were descended. Slapton Lea is a long lake stocked with fresh-water fish in profusion, separated from the sea simply by a bar of sand and gravel. Stockleigh, a seat of the Newman family, whose principal residence is at Mamhead, is close by; and not far distant is the quaint fishing village of Torcross. These, however, are in Stokenham. The Courtenays held Slapton of the Bishops of Exeter by stewartry of the Installation Feasts, as detailed under Crediton.

The Barton of Hach Arundell, in Loddiswell parish, has a double family name, having at one time belonged to the Haches, and at another to the Arundells. License was granted, about 1463, to Thomas Gyll, junr., to castellate his mansion at Hach Arundell, and enclose a park. As *Heche* was the holder of the manor T.R.E., after which it passed to Judhel of Totnes, it seems no way improbable that Hach may in the first place have been named from him. The Avon is a good salmon river now, and Judhel's fishery at Loddiswell returned **thirty salmon** yearly.

CHAPTER XXVIII.

TOTNES.

TOTNES is the first link in the legendary history of England. Brutus, the Trojan, according to early Welsh and Breton tradition, landed 'on the coast of Totnes;' and in the pages of Geoffrey of Monmouth one may read the full-blown myth, ending in the destruction of the last of the aboriginal giants—Goemagot—by Corinæus, afterwards Duke of Cornwall. There was a time when all this was deemed purely historical. Totnes, claiming to be the landing-place of Brutus, has yet a traditional 'Brutus Stone,' on which the Trojan hero is said to have stepped when he landed—a boulder of no great dimensions, well up the main street. Plymouth cherished the belief that the combat between Corinæus and Goemagot took place upon her Hoe; and so far back as the fifteenth century there were graven in the sward of that eminence two huge figures, popularly supposed to represent the combatants, renewed as need was, and of unknown antiquity. It is quite possible, indeed, that both the 'Brutus Stone' of Totnes and the 'Gogmagog' of Plymouth originated (with the Gog and Magog of London City) in the popularity of Geoffrey's story. Historically they cannot be carried back so far.

A careful examination of the passages in the older

Chronicles wherein Totnes is noticed shows, however, that this was not the modern town. Geoffrey of Monmouth speaks of the 'coast' of Totnes, and the 'shore' of Totnes, and the 'port' of Totnes, and always with some such qualification. The inference, therefore, is that the name was used by ancient writers as that of a district. It was evidently so employed by Higden in his 'Polychronicon,' in quoting the length of Britain as 800 miles, a 'Totonesio litore,' rendered by Trevisa 'from the clyf of Totonesse,' which is really only another name for the Land's End. Totnes thus seems to be in truth the ancient name for the south-western promontory of England, perhaps a name for Britain itself, in which case we can understand somewhat of the motive that led early etymologists to derive Britain from Brute, or Brutus. The myth may be so far true that an elder name was supplanted, and that it lingered longest in the western promontory. Whether the modern Totnes is nominally the successor of the ancient title, the narrow area into which this vestige of far antiquity has shrunk, may be doubtful, for the word is as capable of a Teutonic derivation as of a Keltic. The last syllable may be the Northern *ness*, but it may as well be the Keltic *enys*= 'island.' And so while *Tot* may be an 'enclosure,' it may equally be the *Dod* which still exists on the west coast in the name of the Dodman headland — the 'prominent rock' (man=*maen*, a stone). Totnes, therefore, can be read 'the projecting or prominent island.' The speculation may be pardoned in dealing with a point of such singular interest. In any case, it seems probable that this story of Brutus the Trojan is not absolute fable, but the traditionary record of the earliest invasion of the land by an historic people.

The most amusing derivation for the name of the town is that quoted by Westcote and Risdon—*Tout al' aise*= 'all at ease'! presumed to represent the feelings of Brutus when he stepped on shore, and exclaimed in the words of a traditional couplet :

> ' Here I stand, and here I rest,
> And this place shall be called Totnes.'

But the 'authorities' on this head are very sceptical here concerning the extent of the French education which Brutus had received when—

> 'The Frenche of Parys was to *alle* unknowne.'

This same line of argument disposes also of the idea that Vespasian landed at Totnes town instead of simply on the 'Totnes shore,' which again has led to Exeter being mistakenly identified as Caer Pensauelcoit, as in Geoffrey's gloss, 'quæ Exonia vocatur.' Mr. T. Kerslake has pointed out that in all probability the oldest name for the place at which Vespasian landed is Talnas, as given in the 'Brut Tysilio.' This, he argues, would resolve itself into '*t-Aln-as*, and suggests that the landing really took place in Ptolemy's estuary of the Alaunas, or Christchurch Haven; and that Pensauelcoit is to be found at Penselwood, in the Somerset, Dorset, and Wilts border-land, in which, indeed, the old name is still visibly extant.

Totnes has been claimed as a Roman station, but without adequate authority. An ancient paved way leading towards Berry Pomeroy *may* mark the line of a Roman road, but all that can definitely be said is that the town does stand on the line of one of the ancient British trackways. The idea that it was connected with the Fosseway is corrected elsewhere.

Totnes was an Anglo-Saxon mint, and continued to issue coins for some time after the Conquest; but only twenty-six varieties of pennies are known to have been struck here, and the probability is that the number was considerably greater. The extant series commences with Æðelred II., who began his reign in 979, and continues under Cnut. Then, however, there is a gap, and nothing more is known of Totnes mintage, save a penny of Rufus. Probably further research by numismatologists in this direction would be rewarded. It can very well be understood that the mint would cease its operations when the Norman lord of the town fell under the displeasure of Rufus, but intermission of the nature suggested is not so easily accounted for.

The definite history of Totnes prior to the Conquest is scanty; but its position at the time of the compilation of 'Domesday' shows not only that it was then a town of considerable importance, but that it must have been of great antiquity to have attained such a position. One of the four burghs of Devon, it had a larger population than either of its rivals, save Exeter, having ninety-five burgesses within the burgh and fifteen without tilling the land. This would give the community a total population of 500 or 600, while Exeter in all probability had some 2,500 to 3,000.

Before the Conquest Totnes formed part of the demesne of the Confessor. William gave it with 107 manors in Devon to his follower, Judhel or Joel, who made Totnes his chief residence, and was thereafter named Judhel of Totnes. An active and liberal man, Judhel found time, before he was banished by Rufus, to leave his mark upon the head of his barony. Totnes Castle is doubtfully said to have been built by him. The keep, which remains in fine preservation, seems of later date; and probably replaced the 'strength' which he undoubtedly reared upon the mound that still marks the site of the ancient British tortalice. The walls of the town are far later than his time; and the most important of the two gates which continue is not earlier than the sixteenth century. The present circumvallation dates in all probability from 1265, when Henry III. gave the burgesses liberty to enclose the town with a wall, and to collect 'murage' for that object.

But Judhel undoubtedly founded the Priory of St. Mary,

portions of which are now used as the Guildhall, prisons, and sexton's house; he also granted the Church of St. Mary of Totnes to the great Benedictine monastery of Sts. Sergius and Bacchus at Angers.

When Judhel was banished the barony was given to Roger de Novant. Under John it was divided, Henry de Novant holding one moiety and William de Bruce, a grandson of Judhel, the other. The Novant half passed to the Valletorts, and then to the Cantelupes, who also acquired the remaining portion. The heiress of Cantelupe brought the barony to Lord Zouch, and in that family it remained until, on the attainder of John Lord Zouch in 1486 for siding with Richard III., Henry VII. gave the castle and lordship to Sir Richard Edgcumbe of Cotehele. Sir Piers Edgcumbe, in 1559, sold the manor to the Corporation; and the barony was bought by Lord Edward Seymour of Berry. It subsequently went out of the Seymour family, but was again acquired by them, and has descended to the Duke of Somerset.

The earliest known charter of the borough was granted in 1215 by John, who authorized the foundation of a Guild Merchant; and extant documents relating to this Guild date back very nearly to this period. Thus there is still preserved on the back of an old roll of the members a memorandum of an agreement between the burgesses of Totnes and the Abbot and Convent of Buckfast in 1236, that the abbot and monks had been received into the Guild to buy, but not to sell. Two years later, when William de Cantelupe, as lord of the manor, exempted the Abbot and Convent of Torre from payment of tolls, the Guild were able to exact from the fraternity an annual acknowledgment of two shillings for this concession, so that independent municipal rights certainly existed. A curious feature of the rolls of the Guildry, which continue down to 1377, is that on the admission of each new member, his or her seat, in order of precedence, is carefully defined. A still more interesting point is the well-marked development of the Guild Merchant into the Municipal Corporation. This is clearly shown: the rolls continue the proceedings of the Common Court of the Guild into the Court of the Borough of Totnes, which merges in the Court of the Mayor. The first record of the election of a mayor is in 1377, and from that date to the present day, the list of mayors of Totnes is complete and uninterrupted.

The town first sent members of Parliament in 1295, and survived the fatal 1832, but acquired so evil a reputation that it was disfranchised in 1867.

The Priory was dissolved in 1542, and the site granted to Katherine Champernowne and others. During the reign of Edward VI. the appropriation of a portion for educational purposes originated the Grammar School, still held in the original building adjoining the Guildhall. The Guildhall itself, which also formed part of the Priory, was granted to the Corporation by Elizabeth.

Totnes men have played a conspicuous part in the national history; but the town itself—*pace* Brutus—has not been the scene of many notable events. Its annals are mainly those of a thrifty, energetic, prosperous manufacturing and trading community, concerned in its own affairs. Important so far back as the twelfth and thirteenth centuries, its woollen manufacture flourished for some five hundred years. Its commerce, too, was considerable, especially with France. But the Totnes folk were not oblivious of outside duties. A Totnes man, Sir Edmund Lye, ranks among the boldest seamen of Elizabethan days, and as one of the heroes who bore his part in the defeat of the Invincible Armada. Totnes contributed largely towards the fitting out of the *Crescent* and the *Hart*, two vessels sent from Dartmouth to join the Anti-Armada fleet.

It was under the Stuarts, however, that Totnes made

17—2

itself most conspicuous in national affairs. When in 1625 Charles I. passed through the town on his way to review his expedition at Plymouth, he had a most hearty and loyal reception, accompanied with a gift of £200 in 'a faire purse.' Perhaps he bore this in mind when, in the following year, he created George Carew, Elizabeth's Lord President of Munster, Earl of Totnes. It is certain that the Totnes folk set their loyalty on one side when ship-money was levied, for one of the foremost remonstrants against this impost was a Totnes man, the chosen representative of the borough, Sir Edward Giles of Bowden. Moreover, when the levy was made, many of the inhabitants refused to pay. They would be the less disposed to do so, no doubt, because they had been great sufferers by the ravages of the Turkish and Sallee pirates on the coast of Devon, which the royal ships were utterly unable to suppress. And the mind of the burgesses was abundantly evident when they sent to the Long Parliament men of such note as Oliver St. John, Hampden's counsel, and Serjeant Maynard.

It seems somewhat strange that, with this marked Parliamentary sympathy, Totnes was not the scene of any fighting, but was occupied without conflict by the soldiers of each side in turn. Naturally, however, it had its share of the burdens of war. Goring's soldiers were of very bad repute, and it was agreed that £150 should be given him 'for the preservation and more safetye' of the town. Prince Charles (afterwards Charles II.) had £100, and his officers demanded £10 more; while £42 13s. 4d. was required by the King's friends at Exeter; and £7 was actually paid to keep Goring's horse out of the town. When Goring left Totnes in January, 1646, Fairfax marched in. His troops were no way objectionable, but it cost the inhabitants over £170 to supply them with clothing. To the Roundheads succeeded a third visitor, the worst of the series. The plague, which in 1590 had carried off 258 persons, reappeared, and this time had 276 victims. The place was almost deserted, and the grass grew in the streets.

Like nearly all the boroughs of the West, Totnes manifested the national reaction of feeling at the Restoration, and indeed in rather exaggerated form. The King was reminded that the burgesses had joined in the demand for a free Parliament; the present made him when Goring's men were bribed to behave themselves was called to his mind; and then was left to him the settlement of all matters in Church and State. One of the members chosen to Charles's first Parliament was Thomas Clifford, the ' C ' of the Cabal. Charles was not ungrateful. His father's Earl of Totnes had held the title but three years; he gave a Totnes viscountcy in 1675 to his natural son, Charles FitzCharles, Baron Dartmouth and Earl of Plymouth; and this lasted five years. What was more to the purpose, however, was his grant of a charter, in 1684, under which a wool-market was established.

By the time James succeeded, Totnes had very nearly returned to its old Puritan mind. Some, at least, of the inhabitants were among the followers of Monmouth; and it was with reason, therefore, that Jeffries selected the town for the display of the mangled remains of some of his unfortunate victims. The spirit of the Corporation was more clearly manifested when, in 1687, they were called upon to admit Sir John Southcote, a Roman Catholic, without the administration of the oaths, to the place of Recorder, from which Sir Edward Seymour, the well-known leader of the country party, had been removed. They refused, and their charter was taken away; to be restored, however, in the following October, when the movements of the Prince of Orange were understood. When the old charter was seized, the old corporation were displaced, and among the new corporation Southcote of course found room.

Under the Revolution regime Totnes became loyal once more; and its loyalty was shown most conspicuously when, in 1725, it was proposed to levy a land-tax of four shillings in the pound for warlike purposes. The Corporation petitioned in favour of the tax, and expressed themselves willing to pay the other sixteen shillings rather than submit to a foreign yoke!

Totnes, on the score of its ancient 'rows,' often termed piazzas, has been appropriately called 'the Chester of Devon.' Portions of these piazzas are extremely ancient. There is an arch of the twelfth century, and several pillars of the fifteenth, carrying one back to the palmy days of the old town, when it was one of the chief clothing marts of the kingdom—as the phrase 'the hose of fine Totnes,' celebrated throughout the land, plainly indicates. There are still also a few perfect Elizabethan façades of considerable interest, and some rich ceilings of the time of Charles II. Yet more noteworthy is the fine Renaissance carving in a room of the time of Henry VIII., which forms the upper chamber of the East Gate; and which bears testimony, not only to the taste, but to the loyalty of the authorities in the earlier half of the sixteenth century, since the central features of the composition are heads of Henry and of Anne Boleyn.

Totnes has distinguished itself in connection with literature and art. Setting aside the fact that John Prince, the author of the well-known 'Worthies of Devon,' was vicar of Totnes before he became vicar of Berry Pomeroy adjoining, and wrote his delightful work, it is something for one little community to be able to claim such men as Edward Lye (1694-1767), the learned Anglo-Saxon scholar and the author of the 'Dictionarium Saxonico et Gothico-Latinum,' great-grandson of Sir Edmund Lye; as Benjamin Kennicott (1718-1783), the distinguished Hebraist, son of the parish clerk of Totnes—himself master of its charity school ere he went to college and acquired that learning which resulted in the production (1776-80) of his great work on the text of the Hebrew Scriptures; and as William Brockedon, painter, writer, and inventor (1787-1854). Some of his works may be seen in the Assize Court at Exeter, Totnes Guildhall, and the Churches of St. Saviour, Dartmouth, Dartington, and Cornworthy. He was a watchmaker by trade, like his father; and one of his inventions was the method of compressing plumbago used in the manufacture of black-lead pencils.

Charles Babbage (1792-1871), astronomer and mathematician, is erroneously regarded as a Totnes man. However, he was Devonian by descent; and eventually became Mathematical Professor at his College at Cambridge—Trinity. He is best known to the general public by his marvellous calculating machine, or 'Difference Engine,' which enabled him to construct his tables of the logarithms of the natural numbers from 1 to 108,000. As a writer, his best known work is the ninth 'Bridgewater Treatise.'

On the other side of the Dart, but forming part of the borough of Totnes, is Bridgetown, in the parish of Berry Pomeroy, the property of the Duke of Somerset.

The Castle of Berry Pomeroy, shrouded in dense woods on a bold bluff above a feeder of the little river Hems, is the finest ruin left in Devon. The Berry naturally indicates the presence of some defensive works in early times; and perhaps Alric, its last Saxon owner, had his chief 'strength' here, seeing that Ralph de Pomeroy, to whom it was given with fifty-eight other lordships by the Conqueror, built a castle at Berry, and made it the seat of his barony. A great family, and of wide-reaching influence, did the Pomeroys become; and for nearly five centuries they continued in the front rank of Devonshire landowners, though they ceased to be summoned to Parliament in the closing years of the reign of Henry III. A few vicissitudes they had, but still they retained their estates, and no badge in Devon was held in greater honour than the Pomeroy lion, until the fatal day when Sir Thomas Pomeroy, the last Pomeroy lord of Berry, placed himself at the head of the Western Rebellion in the reign of Edward VI.; and with the failure of the movement lost all his estates, though he saved his life. Berry then passed to the Seymours, in whom it still remains, probably by purchase.

Of the fortalice of the Pomeroys there are sundry important fragments, including the gateway and its towers. Lord Edward Seymour, son of the Protector Duke of Somerset, was the first of this name who lived at Berry. His son, Sir Edward, built within the walls of the ancient castle a stately home, which was destroyed, it is said, by fire about a century later, and has never been rebuilt: thus the ruins at Berry are of two very distinct periods and characters. The last Seymour who occupied the mansion was the haughty Sir Edward, who replied to the question of William III., 'I believe you are of the family of the Duke of Somerset?'—'Pardon me, Sir; the Duke of Somerset is of my family.'

Dartington, under the name of Derentun, is the first known Saxon settlement in Devon; since the register of Shaftesbury Abbey records, under date 833, that a Dorsetshire lady, named Beornwyn, had relinquished her share of a patrimonial estate near Almer, in Dorset, to take up her abode on another hereditary property at 'Derentun homm in Domnonia.' She may well have been the ancestress of Alwin, who, at the Conquest, had to yield it with other manors to William of Falaise, some of whose most important possessions lay in this immediate district. It is a noteworthy fact that among the 'Domesday' under-tenants in Dene and Rattery, Englishmen are mentioned. Dartington was the seat of the barony of William of Falaise, and passed in succession to the Martyns and the Audleys. Richard II. gave it to his half-brother John Holland, Duke of Exeter; and he erected the great hall and its associated quadrangle, if, indeed, a portion of the latter is not somewhat earlier. The part of the mansion now inhabited was rebuilt in the time of Elizabeth. Margaret, Countess of Richmond, had a grant of the manor in 1487 for life. It came to the Champernownes in the sixteenth century; according to Pole by an exchange for the site of the Abbey of Polsloe. The first Champernowne of Dartington was Sir Arthur; and when the male line failed in 1774, it passed to the female side in the Haringtons, who took the ancient name. From a mistaken idea that the Templars had to do with this manor, it is occasionally called Dartington Temple.

Harberton, adjoining, now chiefly entitled to notice from the screen of its church, was the seat of the barony of the Valletorts, but the manor of Englebourne belonged to Buckfastleigh. It seems remarkable that the seats of four baronies like those of Totnes, Berry, Dartington, and Harberton, should have been planted so closely together, within a radius of less than three miles.

Dean Prior takes its name as part of the endowments of the wealthy Priory of Plympton, to which it was given by William Fitz Stephen in the reign of Henry II. It was purchased at the Dissolution from Henry VIII. by William Giles of Bowden, near Totnes, and in the mansion which the Gileses built there long resided Sir Edward Giles, born at Totnes about 1580, one of Prince's 'Worthies,' and a prominent Devonian throughout a long career. A soldier in the Low Countries, under Elizabeth; a courtier, knighted by James I. at his coronation; constantly chosen one of the representatives of Totnes during the reigns of James and Charles—he proved himself not only a statesman, but a patriot, by remonstrating against ship-money in 1634. Five of the remonstrants were sent for to Court, including Sir Edward, who excused himself on the score of ill-health, and died in 1637. His sister Christian married George Yarde, whose heiress, in 1789, married Frances Buller, and the family is now represented by Lord Churston.

The epitaph on Sir Edward Giles and his wife, placed beneath their handsome monument in Dean Prior Church, was written by Robert Herrick, who was for many years Vicar of Dean. Ejected under the Commonwealth, he recovered his living at the Restoration, and there he died, in advanced age, in 1674. Dean does not seem to have been to his taste, if we may judge from sundry passages in his poems, by the style in which he speaks of its 'warty incivility,' and the dislike he expresses for 'this dull Devonshire.' Yet he continued to enjoy life in his way; nor could his 'Hesperides' have flourished as they did in a soil really uncongenial to his spirit. He is remembered by a handsome modern brass.

Rattery is only noteworthy for two things—that it was given by Robert Fitzmartin, temp. Henry I., to the Abbey of St. Dogmaels, in Pembrokeshire; and that it contains Marley House, one of the seats of the Devonshire Carews.

In Ashprington is the domain of Sharpham, which is one of the few places in the West where a heronry is to be found. The rookery is reputedly the largest in the kingdom, but that is a point on which it would hardly be wise to express an opinion.

Cornworthy, adjoining, contained a house of Austin nuns, which was founded in all probability by the Norman lords of Totnes. The manor belonged to Judhel, and was both populous and flourishing; for it had a recorded inhabitancy of 33, a mill, and a fishery rendering 30 salmon a year. The Dart even then enjoyed a reputation which it has never lost, for it remains the best salmon river in the county. There is only a gate left of the Priory, which was one of the smaller houses.

CHAPTER XXIX.

DARTMOUTH.

ALTHOUGH of considerable antiquity, Dartmouth yields precedence to Totnes, to which it was formerly subservient. Towns at the mouths of rivers are almost invariably less ancient than ports higher up their course. The reason is obvious. The borough of old had commonly a castle for its nucleus, and gathered under the protection of the owner of the stronghold. The feudal lord reared his 'strength' as a rule conveniently central to his territories; and if a site near the coast was chosen, some inaccessible fastness was commonly selected, where no town could rise. And when trade sprang up, and trading communities increased in wealth and importance, similar causes continued at work. Defective roads made the employment of water-carriage a necessity wherever possible. The unsettled state of the times rendered it essential that infant commerce should be conducted in places which were not exposed to surprise, and could offer sustained defence against attack. But trade progressed, and traffic grew; and by-and-by the advantages of ready access from the highway of nations counterbalanced the disadvantages. Then were founded such places as Dartmouth, guarded by castles and chains in a manner that in an earlier age would have been impossible.

Dartmouth is not a large place now, but in its infant

days three villages occupied its site, and their memory is preserved in the official name of the borough—'Clifton-Dartmouth-Hardness.' The origins of the Clifton and the Dartmouth are clear enough. Hardness seems to indicate a Scandinavian origin—'By the headland,' or 'The headland landing-place.' There are several instances of the 'ness' on the south coast of Devon. The earliest historical reference to Dartmouth deals rather with the harbour than the town; its mention as the place where Swegen, son of Godwin, slew his cousin Beorn.

However this may be, it is certain Dartmouth was the port whence Rufus sailed to Normandy in the last year of the eleventh century; and that eight hundred years ago at least the national importance of its magnificent land-locked deep-water harbour had been recognised. In 1190 Dartmouth was selected as the rendezvous for the fleet, or a portion of the Crusading fleet, of Richard the lion-hearted. But whether ten ships sailed from Dartmouth on this occasion, or 164, the numbers cited by rival authorities, it is idle to attempt to decide.

There is the usual obscurity in the early stages of the corporate history of the town. John paid it two visits, one in June, 1205, when he came from and returned to Dorchester; the other in October, 1214, when he came by sea from Rochelle and went on to Dorchester; and while, according to Leland, he 'gave privilege of Mairaltie' to Dartmouth, at an inquisition in 1319 the burgesses claimed to have been a free borough in the reign of Henry I. Both these points are questionable.

For example, there is no doubt that Totnes is the older town and long held superiority over Dartmouth; yet Totnes goes no farther than John for its earliest known charter; and Dartmouth was not freed from the control of the lord of Totnes until William la Zouch, owner of the barony, granted his rights therein to Nicholas of Tewkesbury. There may have been some confusion between the town of Dartmouth and the port of Dartmouth, which with its water-rights became a royal appanage, and has continued to the present day a member of the Duchy of Cornwall. Yet La Zouche granted to Tewkesbury not only the usual manorial rights, but the toll and custom of the port and of the river up to Blakston next Cornworthy, reserving free passage from Totnes to the sea, without any malicious impediment.

But there must have been a charter of some kind before the reign of Henry III., for by him it was confirmed; and the fact that the oldest extant seal of the borough (temp. Edward I.) represents a king in a ship, with John's badges of the crescent and star, certainly indicates an ancient claim to some connection with that monarch, whatever its precise character may have been. There was a market as early as 1226.

During the thirteenth and fourteenth centuries Dartmouth rivalled the Cinque Ports in importance and fame, and was for awhile the foremost seaport in the provinces. It was frequently made the rendezvous at which vessels from other ports assembled before departing upon some great expedition. Perhaps the importance it assumed in the reign of Edward III. had something to do with the fact that in 1327 Nicholas of Tewkesbury transferred his rights to the King, who, ten years later, granted the town another charter. That ancient landmark in maritime history, the siege of Calais, ranks Dartmouth the third port in the kingdom. Fowey found 47 ships and 770 men; Yarmouth 43 ships and 1,905 men; Dartmouth 31 ships and 757 men, and Plymouth 26 ships and 603 men. Yet in 1310 Dartmouth had pleaded its inability to maintain one ship for the King's service without exterior aid, which was supplied by Totnes, Brixham, Portlemouth, and Kingsbridge. Edward III. provided in his charter that two should be found. Probably the prosperity of the little town was greatly stimulated by the privilege of piracy given to it by this monarch, who is described in 'The Libel of English Policy' as selecting

> 'Dartmouth, Plymouth, the third it is Fowey,
> And gave them help and notable puissance
> Upon pety Bretayne for to werre.'

But the sailors of the Cinque Ports were little better, and fought and plundered among themselves; and Fowey was so deeply imbued with this spirit that when Edward IV. made peace with France its seamen continued war in his despite on their own account, and had to be set in order by the aid of the Dartmouth men, who took away the chain of the harbour, its chief defence. The fame of Dartmouth at this time is further attested by the fact that Chaucer chose it as the probable residence of his 'shippeman.'

> 'For ought I woot he was of Dertemouthe.'

A man of experience and trust—

> 'Ther was non swiche from Hull to Cartage.
> Hardy he was, and wys to undertake;
> With many a tempest had his berd been schake,
> He knew wel alle the havenes, as they were
> From Gootland to the Cape of Fynystere,
> And every cryke in Bretayne and in Spayne.'

Dartmouth must have had many such men; and of this stamp must have been its chief worthy, John Hawley, whose effigies in armour, between those of his two wives, are to be seen on the Hawley brass in St. Saviour Church. Chaucer no doubt had visited Dartmouth and heard of Hawley, the seven-times mayor, the great merchant who had so many vessels and traded to so many parts, that the old rhyme is still remembered:

> 'Blow the wind high, blow the wind low,
> It bloweth fair to Hawley's Hoe.'

And there is good evidence that Hawley was something more than a 'mere merchant,' and perchance fairly answered to that part of the shipman's character, wherein it is said :

> 'Of nyce conscience took he no keep.
> If that he faughte and hadde the higher hand,
> By water he sente hem home to every land.'

On one occasion Hawley attacked and took thirty-two wine vessels; but whenever he felt aggrieved, whether with his own countrymen or with foreigners, he always kept the law, because he made it himself to suit the occasion. There was no maxim, indeed, of the truth of which the Dartmouth folk of the Middle Ages were more thoroughly convinced, than that 'Heaven helped those who helped themselves.' Hence not only their incessant warfare with the French, but their repeated disputes with other ports. A memorable instance of agreement is, however, the fact recorded by Walsingham, that when, in 1385, the English Admiral was afraid to attack the French fleet because of the jealousies within his own, the Portsmouth and Dartmouth men, on their own account, made great havoc among the French vessels in the Seine.

Of course so very busy and aggravating a port had to take as well as give. How frequently Dartmouth was assailed in its turn, it is hard to tell. It is said to have been burnt in 1377; and an attack was certainly made in 1404. According to the French Chronicles, Du Chastel, the Breton, was the leader, and the attack was repulsed by a force of 6,000 men, and with heavy loss. Du Chastel was killed, but a month later his brethren avenged his death by making an unexpected attack and consigning the town to the flames. So far the French historians. The English chroniclers do not mention any second descent; of which, indeed, there is no trace to be found—and aver that Du Chastel and his men were beaten by the plain country people, ' at which time the women (like Amazons), by hurling flints and pebbles and such-like artillery, did greatly advance their husbands' and kinsfolks' victory.' Patriotism and gallantry alike, therefore, compel us to accept this version of the affair, especially as the names of several of the captured Breton knights are preserved.

An important fact in the status of Dartmouth at this period was its appointment in 1390 the sole port for the exportation of tin. To this time particularly date back the ancient fortifications of the town, now, for the most part, either fallen into ruin or modernised: the two castles at the harbour-mouth, Dartmouth and Kingswear, between which of yore a strong chain was hauled up each night, and in special time of peril; and the inner guard of Bearscove and Gomerock; while the wealth and liberality and taste of the age are seen in the noble church of St. Saviour, with its magnificent oak screen—the chancel of which is the work of Hawley.

Special need of defence is shown in the license granted to John Corp to embattle his house at the entrance of the harbour; and it is a point worth noting that in the adjoining church of Stoke Fleming, the oldest brasses in the county are to John Corp (1361), and to Elyenore, presumably a Corp also (1381).

It was inevitable that Dartmouth should take a prominent position in Elizabethan times, though it had been distanced in the race by Plymouth. Two great names at least of the Elizabethan galaxy of Devonian worthies belong to Dartmouth. One, 'lovable John Davis,' born at Sandridge in the adjoining parish of Stoke Gabriel, who commenced the career of Arctic voyaging which led to the discovery of Davis's Straits in 1585; and who made several voyages to the South Seas and East Indies, meeting his death in 1605 at the hands of pirates in the Malaccas.

Near Dartmouth is Greenway, the seat of the famous Gilberts. The family was settled here in the reign of Edward II.; and here were born—their father being Otho Gilbert and their mother Katherine Champernowne—

Humphry and Adrian Gilbert, the famous half-brothers of the still more famous Sir Walter Ralegh.

It was in consequence of its connection with the Gilberts that Dartmouth obtained the honour of being the first port in Devon to send out an American colonizing expedition. Having written a discourse to prove a passage by the North-West to Cathay and the East Indies, Humphry obtained a patent from Elizabeth, empowering him to discover and settle in North America any savage lands. His first voyage in 1579 was unsuccessful. In his second, in 1583, he took possession of Newfoundland, which had long been a fishing station for various nations; but was drowned on his return voyage before he could turn this formality to any practical account. Few are unfamiliar with the brave way in which he met his death:

> ' He sat upon the deck,
> The book was in his hand ;
> " Do not fear, Heaven is as near
> By water as by land." '

It was in all probability this same earnest-minded devout man who boldly proposed to Elizabeth to strike once for all a blow at the maritime power of her adversaries, by destroying without warning the foreign fishing fleets at Newfoundland; offering himself to the work, even if repudiated directly it was done, in the confident belief that it would be to the glory of God and for the safety of the kingdom. After Humphry's death, Adrian, a man of advanced scientific knowledge for the times, solicited a patent for the search and discovery of the North-West passage. Though the Gilberts did not succeed in their aim, they yet secured for Dartmouth a very liberal—indeed, at first a preponderant—share of the Newfoundland trade, which the ports of Devon so long enjoyed.

Dartmouth had its part in the victory over the Armada. Two ships, the *Crescent* and the *Hart*, were fitted out by the town and neighbourhood, manned by 100 men, to join the fleet which assembled in Plymouth Sound. Beside these were five volunteers: Sir Walter Ralegh's *Roebuck*, Sir John Gilbert's *Gabriel*, Sir Adrian Gilbert's *Elizabeth*, Gawen Champernowne's *Phœnix*, and the *Samaritan*—the latter surely one of the oddest of odd names for a man-of-war.

Dartmouth is associated, too, with a melancholy incident in the life of Ralegh. Hither was taken the great carrack, the *Madre de Dios*; and hither was brought Ralegh in disgrace, the 'Queen's poor prisoner,' to see to the safety of her stores and treasure, a work in which, as Cecil reported, he 'toiled terribly.' Cecil himself was disgusted with Devon. 'Fouler ways, desperate weather, nor more obstinate people, did I never meet with.' No one will agree with Cecil now, and Dartmouth itself remains the most quaint and picturesque old town in the West.

The Corporation of Dartmouth must have been tolerably wealthy in the early part of the seventeenth century; for in 1642 they authorized the advance, by the hands of their representatives in the Long Parliament, of £2,668 7s. 6d., to help in reducing the Irish rebels, the same to be recouped out of their lands. The money appears to have been paid, and the Corporation were so fortunate as to secure a map of their property; but somehow or other matters stopped there. It is hardly necessary to indicate the proclivities of Dartmouth at this period. It fell, nevertheless, into the hands of Prince Maurice after a siege of one month and four days, and remained a Cavalier stronghold until the end of the war, the most zealous Roundheads of the town having joined the garrison at Plymouth. It was taken by assault by Fairfax in January, 1646. Dartmouth was stormed at three points by Colonels Pride, Hammond, and Fortescue; Kingswear Fort, on the other side of the river, which was held by Sir Henry Cary, then came to terms; finally, the Governor, Sir Hugh Pollard, who had taken refuge in the castle, surrendered. Thus, with comparatively little loss, the last town in the district that held out for Charles was taken, and with it 1,000 troops, 120 guns, and 2 ships.

This is the last event which connects the town with the general history of the country; but its most important personal association has yet to be named. Somewhere about the year 1670, there was born in Dartmouth a man who did more to lay the foundations of the present manufacturing greatness of the kingdom, and to advance the progress of industrial operations throughout the world, than any other who can be named. This was Thomas Newcomin, the inventor of the first practical working steam-engine, upon which, after it had been many years in useful operation, the work of James Watt was based. Newcomin, with whom was associated another Dartmouth man, named Cawley, perfected his engine in 1705. Hardly anything is known of him except that he was a locksmith and ironmonger, and that he died in 1729. The date of his birth is quite uncertain, but no doubt has ever been thrown upon his being a Dartmouth worthy. The house in which he lived was pulled down a few years since, and the ·materials worked into a house called 'Newcomin Cottage.' West-Countrymen are proud of the fact that to Newcomin the world owes the stationary steam-engine, and to Trevithick, of Hayle, in Cornwall, the locomotive. Newcomin's engine was a perfectly new machine, though it had to a certain extent a predecessor in the ingenious device of Savery of Shilston; and Trevithick's engine was the first that proved the practicability of steam locomotion on railroads.

Dartmouth first sent members to Parliament 26th Edward I., but the returns are not continuous from that date. In 1832 it lost one member, and in 1867 it was disfranchised. It had long attained, like its neighbour Totnes, an unpleasant reputation, and on one occasion, it is said, £400 was given to a voter to induce him to abstain from voting. For a long time the members of the Holdsworth family had considerable sway in the Corporation. They held the post of Governor of Dartmouth Castle in something like hereditary succession, the office gradually dropping into a sinecure, and at last becoming a mere title, and disappearing with the death of the last 'Governor Holdsworth,' who was one of the representatives of the borough before the Reform Bill of 1832.

Dartmouth has a prominent link with the elder Nonconformity. Its Independent congregation was founded by the celebrated Puritan preacher and divine, Flavel, who was ejected in 1662 from St. Saviour, and died in 1691, at the age of sixty-one. It is rather a remarkable fact that a brass was erected to his memory at the time of his decease in St. Saviour, but removed by order of the Corporation in 1709. It now occupies a prominent place in the Independent Chapel, and concludes with the words:

> 'Covld Grace or Learning from the Grave set free,
> FLAVELL, Thov had'st not seen Mortality;
> Thovgh here Thy dusty part Death's Victim lies,
> Thov by thy WORKS thyself dost Eternize,
> Which Death nor Rust of Time shall Overthrow;
> While Thov dost Reign above, These Live Below.'

A number of French gold coins found on the beach at Blackpool Sands, about half-way between Dartmouth and Slapton, have been, with good reason, treated as relics of the landing of the Earl of Warwick at Dartmouth, on the 13th of September, 1470. Ships, money, and men for this expedition were supplied by the French King. The coins included écus d'or of Louis XI. and Charles VII. of France, with other coins of Charles V. and Charles VI.; and gold nobles of Edward III. and V. and Henry V. are also stated to have been discovered at the same place. Most of the coins certainly found at Blackpool were, however, French, and their dates show that they were probably lost between 1465 and 1483.

CHAPTER XXX.

ASHBURTON AND BUCKFASTLEIGH.

IT has been commonly assumed that Ashburton is the 'Aisbertone' recorded in 'Domesday' as being held by Matilda in succession to Brictric, and under her by Judhel of Totnes; and that when he was banished it became the property of the Bishops of Exeter. 'Aisbertone,' however, possessed not only fisheries, but a saltwork, and was therefore adjacent to the sea; and the true Ashburton of 'Domesday' is the 'Essebretone' which the Bishops of Exeter held before the Conquest, and to which 'Domesday' gives a population of sixty. The little stream which at the time Ashburton was founded was named the Ashburn, has long been called the Yeo, which is simply the Saxon *ea*=water. Whether the Ashburn was so called by the early settlers from the ash-trees in its valley, or whether the 'ash' is merely the Keltic *uisg* (=water) which occurs in Devon as *exe*, *axe*, *ug*, and *ock*, it would hardly be safe to say. The northern termination 'burn' is, however, interesting as a trace of that peculiar system of district nomenclature almost confined in Devon to the Dartmoor area, and appearing to indicate the settlement of various river basins by isolated bands of Teutonic colonists of differing origin.

The Bishops of Exeter held Ashburton until it was assumed by the Crown under James I., and subsequently sold in moieties to Sir Robert Parkhurst and the Earl of Feversham. The first portion, passing through the families of Stawell and Tuckfield, came by the heiress of Roger Tuckfield to Samuel Rolle, descended to the Trefusis family, and is now the property of Lord Clinton. The other moiety has been in Duke, Palk, Mathieson, and others, and was at length purchased by Mr. Robert Jardine, who was the last member for the now disfranchised borough. The annual court-leet and court-baron of these lords is held alternately by their stewards in the chapel of St. Lawrence, in ancient form. At this court a portreeve and a bailiff are elected, and the various minor manorial officials, the bailiff being the summoning officer, while the portreeve of one year is almost always the bailiff of the preceding.

The most notable of the ecclesiastical lords of Ashburton in his connection with that town, was Bishop Stapledon, who held the See of Exeter from 1308 to 1327. He was partial to the little burgh on the verge of the Dartmoor highlands, and frequently resided in its manor-house. Two years after his accession he procured the grant of a market and fair; and four years later still founded the Guild or Fraternity of St. Lawrence, giving it a chapel which he had erected within the precincts of his court. The present edifice, therefore, very closely marks the site of the episcopal palace. The Guild had to find a priest to pray for his soul after death, and for the souls of the other holders of the see. Moreover, the priest was to keep a free school; and whatever overplus there might be on the endowment was to be spent in the 'reparacion and maintenance of ledes for the conduction of pure and holesome water to the town of Aysheperton, and upon the relief and sustentacion of such people as are infected when the plage is in the towne, that they being from all company may not infect the whole.' Though the charter of St. Lawrence was surrendered to the Crown, together with the chantry, in 1535, and though of the ancient fabric the tower only remains, Bishop Stapledon's foundation retains in effect its ancient educational uses. Up to the suppression of the Guild the free school was carried on as directed; and when the chantry fell into the hands of the King there were found burgesses of Ashburton far-seeing and liberal enough to buy the chapel and the ground round about. For a time the school was supported by voluntary contributions, but by-and-by endowments began to come in, and the free school developed into the Grammar School, which, with this record of five centuries and a half, continues to the present day.

The school has made its mark in the reputation achieved by three of its pupils—John Dunning, first Lord Ashburton; Dr. Ireland, Dean of Westminster, and William Gifford. Dunning (1731-1783), the son of an attorney practising in Ashburton, by dint of the most untiring perseverance, and after enduring many a hardship, rose to the first rank in his profession as a lawyer, acquired an immense fortune, was elevated to the peerage, and died at the early age of fifty-one. His title has been revived in the family of his wife, Elizabeth Baring. Devon has produced many eminent lawyers, but none more eminent than John Dunning. William Gifford (1776-1826), the distinguished critic and translator, born five years before the death of Dunning, had one of the hardest fights in his early days recorded of any Devonshire worthy. An orphan at thirteen, with no friend in the world, no relative save a younger brother, an apprentice to a hard master, slaking his thirst for learning by beating out pieces of leather smooth, and working algebraic problems upon them with a blunt awl—most forlorn was his lot until a surgeon of Ashburton, named Cookesley, obtained the cancelling of his indentures, and with the help of other friends had him sent to school. Two years only qualified Gifford to enter as Bible clerk at Exeter College, and thence his career was one of continued success. First editor of the *Quarterly*, he resigned that post only two years before his death; and the quondam shoemaker's apprentice found a grave in Westminster Abbey, of which his old schoolfellow, Ireland, became dean. Five years younger than Gifford (1782-1842), the son of a butcher, Ireland went from the Ashburton school to a Bible clerkship at Oriel, and speedily won preferment and fame. Like Gifford a ready and ripe scholar, Ireland was most munificent in his gifts for the promotion of learning. £10,000 was given by him to establish a professorship at Oxford for the exegesis of Scripture; and the Ireland scholarship, founded by him in 1825, has become the chief honour of its kind Oxford has to bestow.

Ashburton was first called upon to send representatives to Parliament in 1298; but does not appear to have exercised that duty again until 1407. From this date until 1640 it returned one member only, and then was required to send two, which has been held to indicate that the town leant to the popular side. This was unquestionably the case, but it is not quite clear that the fact could have helped it to greater weight in the legislature. In 1832 the borough was once more restricted to one member, and in 1867 was finally disfranchised after some exceedingly close contests, which did not altogether increase its reputation.

Ashburton has never been prominent in the national history; and one of the few facts noted is its occupation by Fairfax in January, 1646, apparently unopposed.

The church is remarkable for the discovery, during a restoration in 1840, of a number of long earthen jars built into the wall of the chancel, the purpose of which has been much controverted. They are commonly held to have been acoustic vases; but since, when found, their mouths were covered with pieces of slate, this explanation seems doubtful; and it is averred, on the other hand, that they had in them certain hard substances, thought to be 'dried hearts.' The church is supposed to have been founded about the year 1137 by Ethelward de Pomeroy, the wrongly reputed refounder of the Abbey of Buckfast; but the chancel would date some two centuries later. Again, the church has been regarded by some authorities as collegiate, by others as having been a dependency of Buckfast Abbey. There is no evidence for either supposition, but some connection between the Abbey and Ashburton may be presumed.

The Abbey of Buckfast, Buckfastleigh, or, as in 'Domesday,' Bucfestre, is a foundation of great age, one of the very few religious houses in Devon which had existence before the Conquest. The early history of Buckfast is lost in remote antiquity; but the monks claimed, in the reign of Edward I., to hold the manor of Zele Monachorum by the gift of Cnut; and 'Domesday' shows the Abbey a flourishing institution with considerable possessions. It has been said that this original house was dissolved by the Conqueror, its estates confiscated and given to the Pomeroys, and that it was refounded by Ethelward de Pomeroy, son of William. This rests, however, solely upon a single sentence of Leland, and the whole weight of evidence is in favour of the unbroken descent of the house from Saxon times. Ethelward de Pomeroy was no doubt a benefactor, and hence the tradition. 'Domesday' gives Bucfestre as the head of the Abbey, and notes the fact that it had a smith.

Originally, so far as can be ascertained, Benedictine, Buckfast became a daughter-house of Savigny, united to the Cistercian Order in 1148. There is no certain proof when Buckfast changed to the Cistercian rule, but this would in all probability be in the latter half of the twelfth century. The Abbey flourished under the care of the farmer monks, who in 1236 were admitted into the Guild Merchant of Totnes. In April, 1297, Edward I. visited the Abbey; and in 1340 Abbot Philip obtained a grant of a weekly market at Buckfastleigh, and of a yearly fair at Brent. Under his successor, Robert Simons, a case was decided in 1358 which has an important bearing on the constitutional and social history of the kingdom. One Richard Avery, of Trusham, complained that the abbot—*vi et armis*—had carried off property to the value of £100. The abbot's rejoinder was that, Avery being a villein of his manor of Trusham, he ought not to be called upon to answer. Avery declared that he was a free man and not a villein; but the jury decided that he was *nativus*, and the abbot had judgment. Hence, even in the latter half of the fourteenth century the villein had no rights, at least against the lord of the soil. His position is also indicated by another lawsuit later in the same abbacy (1384), when Simon charged Walter Rosere and William Buriman with carrying off his villeins, Christina Barry and John Barry, of Down St. Mary, whereby he was injured to the extent of £20. It would not be safe, however, to infer from this special instance the nominal value attached to villeins in those days, though they formed a distinct element in the appreciation of estates. Simon appears to have had a taste for litigation, and engaged in sundry actions of an important character concerning fishery rights.

None of the abbots was a man of mark, unless we except William Slade, a Devonshire man, who became head in 1413. 'He was not only a scholar and a theologian, but an artist,' and zealous in the discharge of his duties. He was a student and an author, and some of his works are mentioned in a list of the Abbey library given by Leland. The last abbot was Gabriel Doune or Downe, who was appointed in 1535, and surrendered in February, 1538. He was probably 'the author of the plan which resulted in the capture, imprisonment, and death of Tyndale;' and Mr. J. Brooking Rowe thinks that he was foisted upon the monks of Buckfast better to carry out the designs of the King. This at least is certain: he received a pension of £120, and was appointed rector of Stepney, prebendary of St. Paul's, and finally, upon Bonner's deprivation, was constituted by Cranmer residentiary.

The gross income of the Abbey at the Dissolution was £499 13s. 10¾d.

The Abbey and the adjacent lands were granted to Sir Thomas Dennis, and descended in his family. A century later they were the property of Sir Richard Baker, the historian. Eventually they were sold in parcels, and the remains of the Abbey, with the modern house built upon the site and in part with its materials, are now once more the home of monks of the Benedictine order, who are successfully engaged in its reconstruction upon the ancient lines.

A century since the old monastic buildings were of great extent. At present the manufacturing prosperity of Buckfastleigh is the brotherhood's chiefest monument. The great wool-traders of their age and district, the founders of the mills which in process of time became converted to the purposes of the woollen manufacture, the Cistercians of Buckfastleigh were in no very remote sense the originators of the trade of the locality. Buckfastleigh and Ashburton, by the steady adoption of new processes and improved machinery, have maintained their reputation for high-class woollen goods, and thus unite with North Tawton in proving that it was less through necessity than by bad management that this great staple industry of Devon was driven to the North.

Ashburton, as one of the original Stannary towns of the county, was associated with mining enterprise, historically at least, as far back as the twelfth century; and it continued that association, though more in name than in fact, until 'tin coinage' was abolished in 1838. Buckfastleigh, however, remains the centre of a mineral district, which has been from time to time worked for copper with more or less success.

An interesting relic of the past of Buckfastleigh is an ancient path across the neighbouring moor, still called the 'Abbot's Way.' This was the road used by the monks of Buckfast, Buckland Monachorum, and Tavistock, to communicate with each other, and it is the shortest path between these places across the moorland. Save in the enclosed country, the Abbot's Way is distinctly marked, and in parts is still well worn. At a place called Broad Rock the road from Buckfast forks, one portion leading to Tavistock, and the other to Buckland.

It is probably due to its association with Buckfast that Brent had a little cruciform Norman church, the central tower of which was found, in the course of recent restoration, to have been retained as the western tower of the later fabric.

Holne Chase is one of the finest examples of the ancient chase left in the kingdom, and the only chase in Devon retaining aught of its ancient aspect. The woods, with those of Buckland-in-the-Moor, known as the Buckland Drives, extend for many a mile along the valley of the Dart. The most picturesque part of the course of that river is known as the 'Lover's Leap,' from the customary legend 'made and provided,' where a precipitous rock affords it a *locus in quo.* Holne, under that name—so that it must even then have been noted for its hollies—was one of the 'Domesday' manors of Baldwin the Sheriff, and from the entry, 'formerly waste,' seems to have been recently taken out of the Dartmoor border-land. It was part of the barony of Barnstaple, and has passed with Tawstock to the Audleys, Bourchiers, and Wreys. Estates here were given to Buckfast by Valletort and Bauzon, and the church belonged to that Abbey. Here, while his father was serving the vicarage, Canon Kingsley (1819-75) was born. Buckland was once in a family of that name, subsequently in the Arcedeknes, and afterwards came to its present owners, the Bastards.

There are several 'camps' in the neighbourhood, the most important of the series being Hembury, near Buckfastleigh. To this a curious tradition attaches, firmly believed in the locality. A party of marauding Danes are said to have found their way up the Dart, and seized upon this stronghold; and to have carried thither the women of the district at their pleasure. Eventually 'a lot of women determined, as the men could not get rid of them, to allow themselves to be taken in a body by the Danes to the castle, and in the night each cut the throat of the man who lay by her.' The Saxon men made an attack at the same time, and the Northmen were annihilated.

Devon has been famous for cider for many a century. In fact, it claims to have had at Plympton the first orchard planted in England. Be that as it may, there is no part of the county more noted for cider now than the valley of the Dart, nor a parish which has a higher reputation than Staverton.

Widecombe Church is sometimes called the 'Cathedral of the Moor,' although, previous to a recent restoration, nothing could be more ludicrously appropriate than the text blazoned in the south porch of the edifice, without the least suspicion of a double application: 'How dreadful is this place!' The fabric gives historic interest to its rugged moorland parish. Dedicated to one of the most famous British saints—St. Pancras—its foundation would seem to be very remote; and the probability is that the romantic, bowl-shaped valley in which it stands—the 'wide combe' truly—is the seat of one of the oldest of the continuing moorland settlements.

'Domesday' shows by its references to the five manors which are included within the parish of Widecombe-in-the-Moor that it was fairly settled, considering the period and character of the country; but at a much later date, when the tin streams of the district came to be vigorously worked, it must have been really populous, as population went. The tradition runs that the magnificent western tower—which is of much later date than the body of the church, and which for sharpness and finish of detail is not only the glory of the Moor, but the finest among the granite towers of the West—was built by a body of neighbouring tinners, who cared not for cost. It has also been noted that the bosses of the nave roof appear to indicate a connection with alchemy, if not with ordinary metallurgy. One of the devices is that of Basil Valentine's 'Hunt of Venus'—three rabbits, each with a single ear, which join in the centre.

The 'Widecombe thunder-storm' has found a niche alike in history and folk-lore. On Sunday, 21st October, 1638, while the congregation were assembled, a terrible darkness overspread the face of day, and 'suddenly, in a fearful and lamentable manner, a weighty thundering was heard, the rattling whereof did answer much like unto the sound and report of many great cannons, and terrible strange lightening therewith, greatly amazing those that heard and saw it, the darkness increasing yet more, so that they could not see one another; the extraordinary lightening came into the church so flaming, that the whole church was presently filled with fire and smoke . . . which so affrighted the whole congregation, that the most part of them fell down into their seats, and some upon their knees, some on their faces, and some one upon another, with a great cry of burning and scalding, they all giving themselves up for dead, supposing the last judgment day was come, and that they had been in the very flames of hell.' They had good reason for their fright, if not for their conclusion. A fiery ball zigzagged through the church, cleaving the skull of one man into three pieces; dashing the head of another against the wall so violently that he died that night; firing the clothes and tearing the flesh of others of the congregation; overturning pews and shattering walls and windows. When the blast was over there was dead silence, until one Master Rowse exclaimed, 'Neighbours, in the name of God shall we venture out of the church?' Whereto Master George Lyde, the minister, evidently believing that it was indeed the end of the world, rejoined, 'It is best to make an end of prayers, for it were better to die here than in another place.'

Of course the storm was set down to the special malice and device of the devil, and there were not wanting after the event those who could tell how his satanic majesty had called at an inn on the road to Widecombe for a drink, which hissed down his throat as if it were poured on hot iron. The visitation is one of the stock legends of the country-side, and the supernatural element is by no means banished from the popular mind. The story goes that when a modern teacher asked a child in an adjoining parish, 'What do you know of your ghostly enemy?' she had the utterly unexpected answer, illustrating the fatal tendency of an evil reputation to grow, 'Please, ma'am, he lives to Widecombe.'

The parish still retains much of its old-world character, and is remarkable even on the Dartmoor border-land for the number of its old farmhouses, yet in the hands of the ancient yeomanry of the county, a race which has almost wholly disappeared in the lowlands. Such old farmsteads are for the most part associated with clumps of ashes—the old Scandinavian tree of life, round which clusters a notable portion of the local folk-lore. The clumps are no doubt survivals of the influence of the Norse faith.

Widecombe is associated with a few great names. The manor of Spitchwick was the property of Harold before the Conquest; and was once held by the Fitzwarines and the Hankfords, and for some time by John Dunning, the first Lord Ashburton, who acquired a leasehold interest. The manor of Widecombe was long in the Fitz Ralphs, or Shillingfords. Blackaton Manor, once probably held by Judhel of Totnes, took name of Blagdon Pipard from the Pipards, as early as King John. Deandon was for some centuries in the Malets, who acquired it by descent in the female line from the Deandons; but since 1600 has been owned by the Mallocks of Cockington. Notsworthy, presumably held by the Earls of Moreton, was, during the sixteenth and seventeenth centuries, in the Fords of Bagtor, the most distinguished of whom was Sir Henry Ford of Nutwell, Secretary of State for Ireland to Charles II., who died in 1684. Dunstone, for two centuries at least after the Conquest, was the property of the Pomeroys.

Ilsington has a claim to notice, little and upland parish though it is, in the fame of its one distinguished son, John Ford, the dramatist, born at Bagtor, then the seat of his family, in 1586. The lines are very familiar:

> 'Deep in a dump John Ford alone was got,
> With folded arms and melancholy hat.'

The greatest of the dramatists of Devon, he is all but forgotten now; nor has Gifford's masterly edition of his works rescued him from oblivion. He was but twenty when he first ventured into print with his 'Fame's Memoriall on the Erle of Devonshire.' His first play was produced in 1613, his last in 1639; but nothing is known of the date and place of his death. Sir Henry Ford, already named, is supposed to have been his grandson. Though much modernized, the old manor-house where Ford was born is still standing.

Tor Brian is linked with several names of note, the most famous of its early lords being one of the foremost of Devon's worthies. Sir Guy de Brian, standard-bearer to Edward III., did such service at Calais that he had a grant of 200 marks yearly out of the Exchequer. In 1354 he went to Rome with Henry, Duke of Lancaster, to procure a ratification of the league between England and France from the Pope. In 1370 he again served in France, and in the same year illustrated his many-sided character still further by becoming Admiral of the king's fleet. Edward showed his esteem for Sir Guy by choosing him one of the Knights of the Garter. De Brian served Richard II. with equal success in France and in Ireland, by land and by sea, in the camp and in the court. He founded and endowed a collegiate church in his manor of Slapton, already noted, and died at an advanced age in 1391, leaving two granddaughters only.

In later years Tor Brian became the cradle of the noble house of Petre. Tor Newton was the birthplace of the celebrated Sir William Petre, the most eminent of a distinguished band of brothers. First brought to Court by Cromwell, he speedily became a favourite with Henry VIII., and was one of the visitors of the religious houses. The wealth thus acquired he had wit enough to keep, obtaining under Mary, from Pope Paul IV., a confirmation of the grants of Church property made by Henry. One of the means used to this end was the promise to employ the money in a way the Church would approve; and one of the ways adopted by him was the foundation of eight fellowships at Exeter College. He must have been a man of wonderful tact; for he held the office of Secretary of State and enjoyed equal favour under Henry, Edward, Mary, and Elizabeth. Under Henry he 'observed his humour;' in Edward's time 'kept the law;' in Mary's 'intended wholly State affairs;' and in Elizabeth's was 'religious.'

Two parishes in the Ashburton district still keep up the

ancient dedication feast with much of the old-fashioned heartiness, and without any pretence of business. With them the 'revel' has never developed into the fair. At Ideford the sports last three days, and open house is commonly kept. The date is fixed by the Nativity of the Virgin—the 8th of September. The first day is spent in hare-hunting on Haldon; the next in coursing on more enclosed lands; the evenings being devoted to parties. The third day is generally appropriated to excursions.

The 'revel' at Holne on Old Midsummer Day is evidently of far higher antiquity. Its chief incident is the roasting of a lamb whole in the 'Play Park' by the church. The inhabitants claim the right of taking the first ram they find on entering the Moor; but in these prosaic days they think it best to make a purchase. When roasted, the lamb is carried in procession, preceded by a fiddler, to an inn, cut up and distributed; after which sports commence, and dancing winds up the day. 'Old people who have made it a point to get a slice every year,' Mr. Fabyan Amery says, 'assure me "that a slice of revel lamb beats every other sort of roast meat in flavour and richness."'

The most remarkable district fair was that at Denbury, which came to a close by operation of the rinderpest in 1866, after continuing from 1285, when it was granted to the Abbot of Tavistock. It was held on the 19th of September, and was attended by all classes. The carriages of the county families of the district were to be seen there; it became the fixed day for the payment of rents; and it was in many ways the pivot on which the business and pleasure of the twelve months turned. Strangely, however, Denbury Fair, under the old name, kept in the old way, yet thrives in Labrador, established there generations since by Devonshire settlers, and still dear to their descendants, though these are quite ignorant whether Denbury be the name of man, woman, place, or thing.

CHAPTER XXXI.

TORQUAY, PAIGNTON, AND BRIXHAM.

Torquay in name dates back some two hundred years; but in fact was barely more than a name—a little pier or quay, and half a dozen fishermen's huts—until the early part of the present century, when the need of accommodation for the families of the officers of the fleets which made Torbay their rendezvous was felt.

If, however, the name is set aside, and traces of ancient life alone considered, no place in the kingdom has more distinguished claims to antiquity; for at Torquay is Kent's Cavern, the exploration of which has carried back the history of man in this country not merely to Palæolithic days, but to interglacial, perchance to preglacial times; while across the bay at Brixham is the Windmill Hill Cave, the exploration of which finally settled, with scientific investigators, the contemporaneity of man and the extinct mammalia, and the high antiquity of the human race. Discoveries of flint and bone weapons and implements, pointing in the same direction, have also been made in the submerged forest beds of Torbay. Taking Torquay in its representative sense, we may fairly say, therefore, that while it is almost the youngest town in Devon, it is far and away the oldest settlement; and that its age is not to be measured by common standards of chronology, but by the expression in geological terms of the work done by natural forces since the appearance of the first traces of man. The latest expression of opinion by Mr. Pengelly, F.R.S.—*the* authority on this special subject—is the probability of the inference that the hyæna did not reach the South of England until its last continental period, and that the men who made the Palæolithic nodule-tools found in the oldest known deposit in Kent's Cavern arrived either during the previous great submergence, or what is more probable, unless they were navigators, during the first continental period.

We cannot pretend to fill the gap that yawns between us and the era of even the later Palæolithic men; but the shores of Torbay afford evidence of continued occupation from the dawn of the historic period. Not many years ago extensive earthworks could be traced on the uplands between Babbacombe and Anstis Coves, which have been deemed, upon slight grounds, to be of Roman character, but were probably Keltic, and the Apaunaris—continuing in name in the modern 'Hope's Nose'—of the Ravennat. We have the 'Apa' also in 'Babba,' no doubt of Norse origin. A large camp at Berry Head, the opposite horn of Torbay, was undoubtedly occupied by the Romans. Still the situation is not one they would have chosen in the first instance, and it resembles too closely the ancient cliff castles of Cornwall, the chief defence consisting of a rampart cutting off the extreme point of the promontory and protecting it against attack from the land side, not to suggest an earlier date than the Roman occupation. The character of Torbay is such as to invite the landing either of friends or foes, for commerce or for war; and it has indeed been suggested as the 'Totnes shore,' whither the fabled Brutus found his way.

The neighbourhood was popular with the Saxons. The place-names in the vicinity are almost exclusively of Teutonic character, and it affords two of the rare local instances of the proven existence of a church before the

Conquest. 'Sce Marie cerce' appears in 'Domesday' as belonging to the Earl of Moreton, and as having been held by Ordulf 'T.R.E.' The enumerated population being sixteen only, in all likelihood the manor was the ancient ecclesiastical centre of the district. The Saxon font is still in existence, preserved through the churchwarden period by being partially buried, reversed, in the floor. It is ornamented with rude and very quaint carvings of figures of men and animals. The most notable exception to the prevailing Saxon nomenclature is Cockington, the first syllable in which is the Keltic *coch* = red, referring, no doubt, to the red Triassic cliffs of that part of Torbay.

Next in importance to St. Mary Church, as a predecessor of Torquay, and the actual germ out of which the modern town has grown, is the manor of Torre, held by William Hostiarius at the time of the Great Survey in succession to Alric, and possessing in 1086 an enumerated population of thirty-two; while that of the adjacent manor of Ilsham, which had fallen into the hands of this same 'servant of the King,' is set down at half-a-dozen. Such are the first definite facts in the history of what is now proudly called (not without reason or rivalry) the 'Queen of Watering-places.'

The first real step in advance was taken when, in 1196, William de Briwere founded the great Abbey of Torre. De Briwere was a man of mark. There is a tradition that he was born on the shores of Torbay; there is another that he was found exposed on a heath, as an infant, and thence acquired his surname. Prince makes him out to be the descendant of Richard Bruer, a companion of the Conqueror. Whatever his origin, he won wealth and fame. In some way not clear he succeeded to the manor of Torre; and he held prominent positions in the Courts of Henry II., Richard I., John, and Henry III.—a statesman of ability and trust. His family influence was greatly extended by the marriage of Reginald de Mohun, given him in ward by Henry III., with his fifth daughter, Alicia. This marriage carried Torre to the Mohuns, and the manor of Torre Briwere became the manor of Torre Mohun, in modern parlance Tormoham. Although one of the most powerful nobles of the West, De Briwere in the conflict between John and his barons took the side of the King, and orders were sent by that monarch in 1216 to Robert de Courtenay, Viscount of Devon and Governor of Exeter, to admit De Briwere and his forces into the city, if the garrison was not sufficiently strong.

Torre Abbey was founded upon a pre-existing church, which, like that of the adjoining parish of Paignton, was seemingly of Norman origin. It was dedicated to the Holy Saviour, the Holy Trinity, and the Virgin; and was first settled by an abbot and six monks in 1196. Norbertine or Premonstratensian, it became at length the richest house of the Order in the kingdom. De Briwere had himself been liberal of his gifts; and eight years had not elapsed from its foundation before William Fitz Stephen gave it the church of Townstal, which brought Dartmouth within the abbatal jurisdiction. Among its other properties were the manor and church of Wolborough; the manors of Ilsham, Collaton, Kingswear; lands at Buckland and Woodbury; the tithes of St. Mary Church; and several good livings.

The monks, moreover, were business men, and became members of the Totnes Guild Merchant. An amusing though unpleasant episode occurred in the abbacy of William Norton, who was charged, in 1390, with having abused his powers as lord of the manor by cutting off the head of a canon named Hastings. The canon was produced in the flesh to satisfy Bishop Brantyngham that he was not dead; and the Bishop took him at his word. Other people, however, were not so easily satisfied; and therefore to this day the headless ghost of Simon Hastings makes hideous the dull November nights by galloping a spectral horse through Torre avenues. At the Dissolution in 1539, the annual revenues of the Abbey were set forth at £396 0s. 11d.

The Abbey lands changed hands very rapidly. John St. Leger, to whom the site was granted, sold it to Sir Hugh Pollard. Pollard's grandson conveyed it to Sir Edmund Seymour, and he sold it to Thomas Ridgway, ancestor of the Earls of Londonderry, the lord of the manor of Torre Mohun, which John Ridgway and John Petre had bought of Edward VI. By the Ridgways the whole property was held until 1653. Torre Abbey was then sold to John Stowell, from whom nine years later it was purchased by Sir George Cary, of Cockington. Torre Mohun passed by the marriage of Lucy Ridgway, in 1716, to the Earls of Donegal; and in 1768 was purchased by Sir Robert Palk. It now belongs to Lord Haldon, his descendant; and Torre Abbey to Sir George Cary's representative, Mr. R. S. S. Cary. The Carys claim special notice among the notable houses of Devonshire.

The 'Domesday' manor of Kari, in the parish of St. Giles-in-the-Heath, was the first recorded seat of the Cary family; and one branch continued to reside there so late as the reign of Elizabeth. As early, however, as the reign of Richard II. it ceased to be their principal home. Sir William Cary then settled at Clovelly, and his brother Sir John, Chief Baron of the Exchequer, acquired, with many other manors, that of Cockington, only to lose them all by deciding for Richard against the Commissioners. His attainder was reversed in favour of his son Robert, who gained the favour of Henry V. by vanquishing an Aragonese knight in Smithfield. Two generations later the family were again in difficulty. Sir William Cary, grandson of Robert, was an ardent

Lancastrian; and one of those who, after the fatal battle of Tewkesbury, took refuge in the Abbey Church. Two days later the refugees were treacherously beheaded. The usual forfeiture followed; but Sir William's eldest son, Robert, obtained restoration from Henry VII. He was the ancestor of the present stock of Devonshire Carys. From his half-brother spring the ennobled Carys, represented by Lord Falkland.

The most notable Cary of Cockington was Sir George, born about 1540, who took a leading part in the land arrangements for the defence of the country against the Spanish Armada. In conjunction with Sir John Gilbert of Compton, he had the charge of a large number of prisoners, taken in the *Capitana*, flag-ship of Don Pedro de Valdez, captured by Drake in the *Revenge*, after she had been well battered by Hawkins in the *Victory*, and Frobisher in the *Triumph*. Captain Whiddon brought the *Capitana* into the bay, and her crew were lodged for a while in the great barn at Torre Abbey, hence to this day called the ' Spanish Barn.' Cary's general services during this eventful period were zealous and great. His chief claim to rank as a worthy of Devon is based upon his official career in Ireland. Appointed by Elizabeth herself Treasurer of Ireland in March, 1599, he entered at once upon his duties. They had a mournful commencement; for in the September following, his only son George was killed, while serving under the Earl of Essex against O'Neill. A few days later, Essex left for England; and, in addition to his Treasurership, Cary became Lord Justice. In Ireland, with one brief interval, he continued to serve until the death of Elizabeth; and when James succeeded, to his other posts was added that of Lord-Deputy. In October, 1604, his repeated solicitations procured his relief from the cares of State, and Sir Arthur Chichester was appointed in his stead. On his death in 1617, his estates passed to his nephews. The

Carys were staunch Royalists, and lost Cockington through the Civil Wars, when it became the property of its present owners, the Mallocks; but Sir George Cary, great-nephew of the Lord-Deputy, purchased Torre Abbey in 1662, and the family are thus still settled in the locality where they attained their highest eminence.

Several curious traditions are connected with the 'Spanish Barn,' all originating, of course, in its use as a temporary prison. One is that large numbers of the prisoners were starved to death, grafted upon which is the further detail that a farmer, who secretly gave them food, was hung by the country-folk, whose hatred to the foreigners was most bitter. Then it is said that a body of Spaniards, who had landed with the intention of plundering the Abbey, were kept on shore by an English fleet; and, flying for refuge to the barn, perished from starvation. Another tradition, quite irreconcilable with its associates, is that the blood of the Spaniards ran like water down 'Cole's Lane,' which, as Mr. White suggests, may have a foundation in fact if the prisoners, on their road to Exeter, tried to escape. But all the legends agree in this—that the spirits of the Spaniards still haunt the spot where they spent their last days.

There is very little of the original structure of the Abbey itself left. Of the church there are a few fragments, including portions of the tower and chancel and the entrance to the chapter-house. The domestic buildings are in better preservation, and a fine gateway remains fairly intact, with the tower. During the progress of the latest restorations a very handsome crypt was opened out.

Another Torquay antiquity, and almost the only companion of the Abbey, since the ancient mansion of Torwood Grange was removed, is a building known as St. Michael's Chapel, on the hill above the Torre railway station. There is no account of its origin, but it probably dates from the twelfth century, and its religious character seems clear. Beyond this there is only the old Grange at Ilsham, once appendant, like Torwood, to the Abbey.

In the early part of the seventeenth century Torquay seems to have been a place of some little importance under the name of Fleete (the Saxon name of the brook that formerly fell into the bay of the present harbour), which survives now only in Fleet Street; and it is rather remarkable that so distinctive an appellation should have been lost. A lease, granted in May, 1678, gives capital evidence of the existence of a centenarian among the inhabitants. It was on the lives of John Goodman, Philippa his wife, and Mary his daughter, for ninety-nine years, and an endorsement testifies that Mary surrendered it in person in June, 1777. Torre Mohun has exceptional interest for students of tenures in its custom of free bench. The widow of a customary tenant had her free bench, save in case of incontinency, but that could be cured by the performance of the conditions set forth in Budgell's well-known *Spectator* article. 'The custom of the Manor of Torre' figures prominently in some of the caricatures directed against Queen Caroline.

The history of Torbay is chiefly associated with naval expeditions. In early times its villages were included under the port of Dartmouth, and contributed to enhance the maritime fame of that historic port. Then we find it the seat of a steadily growing independent fishing-trade with Newfoundland, developed from the local fisheries which gave prosperity and prominence to Brixham. The first great fleet that used these waters was that which brought over William of Orange. Two years later Torbay was occupied by the French fleet which harassed the coast for the restoration of James, and a party from which burnt Teignmouth, finding that at Torbay the whole strength of Devon was drawn up to oppose them. Next, in 1703, Sir Cloudesley Shovel made

Torbay the rendezvous of the combined English and Dutch squadron under his command, destined for the Mediterranean. From that time onward its many advantages appear to have been continuously recognised; and it was a chief station of the British fleet during the great French wars. Torre Abbey was a favourite residence of Earl St. Vincent; and it was only natural that not Torquay only, but Paignton and Brixham also, the other members of the Torbay town triad, should profit by the presence of the relatives of the officers, who were in the habit of visiting them, and who in many cases found it convenient to take up their residence in the houses that were speedily built for their accommodation. This was the real commencement of Torquay as a watering-place.

The importance of Torbay at this period, in a national sense, had its drawbacks as well as its advantages. In November, 1803, it was confidently anticipated that Napoleon had chosen it as the scene of his descent on England. One reads with amusement now of the arrangements made at a very 'respectable and numerous meeting' for the assembly of the infirm and children, who were unable to walk ten miles in one day, in three divisions, to be removed inland by horse and cart, while the able-bodied who were not employed on particular service were to meet the clergyman at the church to consider how they could render the greatest assistance to their neighbours and country. Twelve years later Napoleon did make his appearance at Torbay, but as a prisoner on board the *Bellerophon*. He remained in Torbay from the 24th July to the 11th August, 1815, with the exception of four days during which the *Bellerophon* proceeded to Plymouth; and on the 11th he sailed for St. Helena in the *Northumberland*. Both in Torbay and Plymouth Sound there was an immense concourse of people in boats to see the fallen monarch; and the Torquay folk still recall with pride Napoleon's testimony to the charms of their surroundings: 'What a beautiful country; how much it resembles the Porto Ferrajo in Elba!'

It used to be said of Torbay, in consequence of its unsheltered condition, and of the manner in which it was employed as a naval rendezvous, that it would one day be the grave of the British fleet. Happily, the prediction has not been realized, and the construction of the breakwater at Plymouth having caused Torbay to be abandoned as a naval station, the danger may be held to have disappeared. That such fears were not groundless was amply proved in January, 1866, when, of a large number of vessels which were lying in the bay windbound, fifty were wrecked and nearly 100 of their crews drowned. The actual loss was never accurately ascertained. Many vessels were stranded, and several sank at their anchors. This led to a proposal to construct a breakwater; but nothing was done until the late Lord Haldon, at his own expense, formed a new harbour at Torquay, which has largely developed its yachting interest.

The manor of Paignton belonged to the See of Exeter before the Conquest. With the single exception of Crediton, it was the most valuable possession of the See when the Survey was taken, the returns having been raised from thirteen pounds to fifty. It had 36 serfs, 52 villeins, and 40 bordars, with 5 swineherds, and a salt-work. Hence we are not surprised to find in the tower doorway of its church evidence that it once possessed an important Norman fane. Paignton became a market-town in 1294; and at a very early date was selected by the bishops as an occasional residence. They held the manor until Bishop Veysey, by the royal requisition, conveyed it to William Herbert, Earl of Pembroke. Blagdon was the ancient seat of the Kirkhams, whose richly decorated Late Perpendicular chantry is the most notable feature of the church interior.

Additional interest attaches to the ruins of the old palace from the fact that its last episcopal occupant was the famous Myles Coverdale, eminent as a prelate, but still more eminent for his translation of the Bible. Probably a Yorkshireman, little is certainly known about him until the appearance of his version of the Scriptures in 1535. His first visit to Devon was as a kind of army chaplain to Lord Russell, while engaged in quelling the Western Rebellion in 1549. Two years later he was appointed coadjutor Bishop of Exeter, and then it was he occupied the Paignton palace. As his Bible had at this time been in print some sixteen years, the baselessness of the local tradition, that it was translated at Paignton, is apparent. The accession of Mary led to his banishment, but it does not seem that on his return to England, when Elizabeth brought safer times, he again visited Devon.

A note in the MS. autobiography of Dr. James Yonge, *circa* 1670-80, says, probably on the authority of current report at that date, 'Paynton was anciently a Borrough town, and, as Is sayd, held her charter by a whitepot (whence Devonshire men are soe called), which was to be 7 yeares making, 7 baking, and 7 eating.'

In the adjoining parish of Marldon is the fine old fortified house known as Compton Castle. Once the seat of a family of that name, it came to the Gilberts of Greenway by marriage with a coheiress. Though long a farm-house the 'castle' is in very fair preservation. The gateway and chapel preserve their ancient character tolerably intact; and the whole pile has a remarkably picturesque appearance. The elaborate machicolation is the most distinctive feature.

Brixham, for centuries a fishing-port of note, has long been the chief fishing-town in Devon; and its fishing-boats are unsurpassed in excellence. It is the 'Briseham' which Judhel of Totnes held in succession to Ulf, with its neighbour Cercetone, now Churston Ferrers. Brixham has in 'Domesday' a population of 39; Churston of 25 only, including 3 cotars; but we have no other clue to their ancient history beyond that implied in the fact that the latter parish was a Saxon 'church town' on the south side of Torbay, precisely as St. Mary Church on the north. Brixham passed to the Novants and Valletorts, and was some time held by the Bonviles. It is now very curiously owned. A division of the manor into quarters was followed by the purchase of the portion which came to the Gilberts by a dozen fishermen; and their shares have again been divided and subdivided among fisher-folk, who are commonly known as the 'quay lords,' though there are some 'ladies.' Thus there are more 'lords and ladies of the manor' at Brixham, from the representatives of the Duke of Bolton downward, than in any other town in England.

Nethway at one time belonged to Sir John Hody, Chief Justice of the King's Bench 1440, and the family continued to live there until 1696. Sir William Hody was Lord Chief Baron in 1487. Lupton, once in the Peniles, Uptons, and Haynes, has been for nearly a century the seat of a branch of the Buller family of Crediton, descended from Sir Francis Buller (1746-1800), Justice of the King's Bench, and raised to the peerage by the title of Baron Churston in 1858. Churston was long held by the Yardes in succession to the family of Ferrers, and came to the Bullers by the marriage of the heiress of the Yardes with Sir Francis Buller, the judge. The Churston Bullers have since used Yarde as an additional surname.

But the historical relations of Brixham are far more than personal. The old village, commonly called Higher Brixham, is about a mile from Brixham town, or Lower Brixham, anciently known as Brixham Quay. At this quay it was that there landed, on the 5th of November, 1688,

William of Orange, on his way to the English throne. Upon the pier, though removed from the original site, is a simple memorial, the inscription whereon sets forth, 'On this stone and near this spot, William, Prince of Orange, first set foot.' The event has happily suggested the device for the seal of the Local Board, which represents the landing of the Prince, with the words of his motto, 'I will maintain.'

A very full and detailed contemporary account of the landing of the Prince and his followers is contained in a pamphlet published by a chaplain called Whittle, who was on board the fleet. When the people who crowded the cliffs to see the ships understood who had come, great, he says, was the shouting and delight. Great was the delight also at Torre Abbey, where *Te Deum* was sung under the impression that the vessels belonged to France! The local traditions of the circumstances of the landing are curious, and undoubtedly embody sundry facts. William is said to have approached the shore and asked if he was welcome. Having explained his purpose he was told that he was. 'If I am, then come and carry me on shore,' said he, and immediately a 'stuggy [thickset] little man' jumped into the water and did so. This seems to be fairly historical, for it has been a constant tradition in the Varwell family that one of their ancestors not only assisted the Prince to land in the manner described, it being low water at the time, but gave him his first night's lodging in his house in Middle Street. Whittle, indeed, states definitely that William made his palace of one of the fishermen's little houses; and his leading followers were quartered in the houses around, while the troops camped out.

The unhistorical part of the tradition comes in with an amusing rhymed address, which the inhabitants are said to have presented to their illustrious visitor:

> 'And please your Majesty King William,
> You be welcome to Brixham Quay,
> To eat buckhorn and drink bohea
> Along with we.
> And please your Majesty King William.'

No doubt need attach, however, to the fact of the preservation of the stone on which William first stepped on landing.

Among other local traditions are some stating that the country-folk took quantities of apples to Brixham and other points on the line of march to give to the troops. The Nonconformists of the district were especially hearty in their greeting; but, as a rule, men of position were slow to give in their adhesion. The first to do so was Mr. Nicholas Roope, a member of an ancient family living at Dartmouth. There is some reason, however, to believe that the Prince had a secret interview with Sir Edward Seymour of Berry (who openly joined him at Exeter) at a house since called Parliament House, between Berry and Brixham. It is probable also that other influential persons were present. The muniments of the Seymour family yield no information upon the point, for all the documents relating to those transactions appear to have been carefully destroyed.

CHAPTER XXXII.

NEWTON.

NEWTON lies at the junction of the two parishes of Highweek and Wolborough, and has been formed by the fusion of a couple of adjacent villages, which sprang up respectively under the patronage of lords of adjoining manors, the choice of site being clearly dictated by a position which was anciently at the head of the Teign estuary, but has long been separated therefrom, first by marshy, and afterwards by reclaimed land. Of these two towns or villages, one was called Newton Abbot, from the fact that Wolborough, in which it stood, formed part of De Briwere's endowment of Torre Abbey; the other was named Newton Bushell, from the Bushells, its possessors in the latter half of the thirteenth century. Both names still exist, but Newton Abbot has developed so rapidly under the influence mainly of the railway system, of which it forms an important local junction, that the name of Newton Bushell is rarely heard, and even Newton Abbot is giving place to the simpler Newton.

We can hardly venture to identify positively either of the 'Wiches' of 'Domesday' with the modern Highweek. Wolborough is probably the Vlgeberge which Alured the Briton held in succession to Alwin; though the Vlveberie held by Ralph under Baldwin the Sheriff is almost as close. Highweek first appears, however, as part of the manor of Teignweek, given by Henry II. with Newton and Bradley to John, son of Lucas, his butler. As the name Bradley finds place more than once in 'Domesday,' it is possible that Newton Bushell may be one of its Niwetons, and thus have the respectable antiquity of some nine centuries. The manor of Teignweek has always carried with it a moiety of the hundred of Teignbridge; and the occurrence of that name in 'Domesday' proves the existence of a bridge there in Saxon times. Teignbridge is on the line of an old British trackway, and when the present structure was built in 1815, four previous bridges were found represented on the site; it is suggested that in the oldest of these we have Roman workmanship. Teignweek was given in 1246 to Theobald de Englishville, and by him to his foster-child and kinsman, Robert Bushell. The Bushells continued until Richard II., when their heiress brought it to the Yardes. In the Yardes it remained until 1751, when it was sold to Thomas Veale, and from him came to the Lanes. Bradley has long been the seat of the lords of Newton Bushell, and although much mutilated, still remains an interesting example in many of its details of a fortified mansion of the fourteenth century.

Newton Bushell became a market-town by grant in 1246 to De Englishville, but the market was allowed to lapse in favour of that of Newton Abbot, which was in existence in the reign of Edward I., if not earlier, and was acquired by the Yardes in the reign of Philip and Mary, and descended, with the estates, to the Lanes. The respective rights of the lord of the manor, and of the burgesses, are said to have been settled by deed in the reign of Edward II.

Wolborough continued part of the possessions of Torre Abbey until the Dissolution. In the reign of James I. it was bought by Sir Richard Reynell, the younger son of a family which had been settled in the adjacent parishes of the Ogwells as early as the fourteenth century. His heiress married Sir William Waller, the Parliamentary general; and Waller's daughter, in turn, Sir William Courtenay; from him it has descended to its present owner, the Earl of Devon, by whom the growth of the new town between the old town and the railway station has been judiciously guided and liberally developed.

Manorial jurisdiction still continued in full sway at Newton until the present generation, and forty years since the portreeves elected for each moiety of the ancient 'Newton' both had seals of office. It is now governed by a Local Board whose seal is a curious compound. The central device is the tower which represents the old chapel of ease of St. Leonard, and stands at the 'four ways;' then there are a mitre and pastoral staves to recall the Abbots of Torre, and a fleece to typify the ancient woollen trade.

At Ford House Charles I. was twice entertained at his first visit to Devon, in September, 1625. Ford was then the seat of its builder, Sir Richard Reynell, and it was in partial recognition of the liberal hospitality shown that Charles knighted Reynell's two nephews—Richard Reynell of Ogwell, and his brother Thomas, who was the King's server. Charles was on his way to Plymouth to inspect the expedition designed for Cadiz, and on his return again made a halt at Ford, attending service at Wolborough Church, and touching a child for the evil. The bills of fare for the two entertainments have been carefully preserved, so that we know that the first cost £28 13s. 5d., and the second £55 5s. Waller lived for a while at Ford during the Protectorate; and it was the first house of note that received William of Orange.

On what was once the pedestal of the ancient market-cross of Newton is a modern inscription, setting forth, ' The first declaration of William III., Prince of Orange, the glorious defender of the liberties of England, was read on this pedestal by the Rev. John Reynell, rector of this parish, 5th November, 1688.' It is very doubtful how far this may be regarded as an authority for anything more than the statement that the declaration was read from the spot. The date given is that of the landing, and the army did not reach Newton until the 7th. William appears to have reached Ford House on the 8th, leaving on the 9th; and it was while he was there, according to Whittle, the army chaplain, that the declaration was read by 'a certain divine' who 'went before the army,' and not by the 'minister of the parish.' If not Whittle himself, it is probable that the reader of the declaration was Dr. (afterwards Bishop) Burnet.

A hospital house was founded here by Lucy, Lady Reynell, in 1638, for the widows of clergymen. She set forth her idea of their need in the couplet:

'Is 't strange a prophet's widowe poore should be?
Yf strange, then is the Scripture strange to thee.'

Wolborough was the burial—probably the birth—place of a Devonian worthy—John Lethbridge, whose death is thus recorded in the parish register, 'Dec. 11, 1759. Buried Mr. John Lethbridge, inventor of a most famous diving-engine, by which he recovered from the bottom of the sea, in different parts of the globe, almost £100,000 for the English and Dutch merchants, which had been lost by shipwreck.' Lethbridge appears to have been the first who succeeded in turning diving-apparatus to any practical account; and there is still extant a silver tankard, on which is engraven a map of Porto Santo, where some of his chief exploits were done, and an illustration of the diving-apparatus at work. He dived on at least sixteen wrecks, some with good success.

Newton has long developed an important trade in potting-clays, which are found largely in the immediate neighbourhood, and worked by pits. Most of the clay raised is sent to Staffordshire; but of late there has been a rapidly increasing development of local potteries, and the town is now the centre of a group of works, dotted at intervals from Bovey Tracey—where a pottery has existed considerably over a century—to Torquay, which produces the finest English terra-cotta. This local industry now includes the utilization alike of the most refractory and the finest clays of the district, and has developed to its present proportions within the past twenty years. In connection with clay-pits at Zitherixon, there was found, about 1866, a singular wooden image, which appears to have been associated with an ancient phallic cult, practised in the district centuries before the Christian era. In 1881, a canoe was found in the clay-beds of the same Bovey basin, which Mr. Pengelly regards as at least of glacial age.

Haccombe is the most interesting parish in the vicinity of Newton, and one of the most singular in Devon. Of old time it was an extra-parochial chapelry; and as it was made an arch-presbytery by Sir John L'Ercedekne about the year 1341, so the rector of Haccombe is 'arch-priest' still. The college originally consisted of the arch-priest and five associates, who lived in community; but only the head now remains. As the seat of an arch-priest, Haccombe naturally used to claim exemption from the authority of an archdeacon; and Haccombe itself was regarded as beyond the jurisdiction of any officers, civil or military, and as being free, by royal grant, from any taxes. Probably fewer changes as to population have taken place here than in any other manor in Devon which has developed into a parish. When Stephen held it under Baldwin the Sheriff, it had a recorded population of 15. It now contains simply the manor-house, rectory, and farm; and the population is largely dependent upon the residence of the family at the time of the census. Normally, it is below 20; and at one enumeration it was but 13. Stephen took name from his manor, and the heiress of his family brought it to the Ercedeknes. By marriage it then came through the Courtenays to its present owners, the Carews. The church dates from the thirteenth century, and contains some fine effigies of the Haccombes, with brasses of the Carews, and a high tomb which probably commemorates the Courtenay owners—Hugh and Philippa, his wife. On the door of the church were formerly four horse-shoes, relics, according to the legend, of a wager made between a Carew and a Champernowne, as to who would swim on horseback the farthest to sea. Carew won the wager, and with it a manor, and nailed the shoes of his horse to the church door in 'everlasting remembrance.'

Kings and Abbots Kerswill are so named from the former being originally in the Crown, while the latter was part of the estates of the Abbey of Torre. Coffinswell adjoining, though named from the family of Coffin, was also in part the property of the Abbey. Daccombe, here, was the inheritance of a family of that name, and was given by Jordan de Daccombe to the same house. At Kingsteignton are the principal clay-pits of the neighbourhood. Like Teignweek, this manor carried with it a moiety of the hundred of Teignbridge. Early in the sixteenth century it came to the ancestors of the present owner, Lord Clifford. Two sons of vicars of this parish have gained some note—Theophilus Gale, a Nonconformist divine, born in 1628; and De Beeke, Dean of Bristol, whose father held the vicarage for sixty-one years. De Beeke was the discoverer of the Beekites in the local Trias, thence named. Teigngrace takes name from the Grace or Graas family, who succeeded the Briweres, after whom it had been previously named Teign Briwere. Stover is the Devonshire seat of the Dukes of Somerset. Teigngrace Canal was made by the Templars, former lords of the manor, for carriage of pipe-clay and granite.

CHAPTER XXXIII.

TEIGNMOUTH AND DAWLISH.

TEIGNMOUTH was evidently a place of resort in Saxon times; and the older annalists claim it as the scene of the first landing of the Danes. But that took place near Weymouth in the year 787; and it is many a long year after this date ere any mention can be found of Teignmouth. The first distinct reference to the locality appears to be the statement that in 1001 the Danes 'burned Tegntun and also many other good hams, . . . and peace was afterwards made there with them.' This Tegntun was not Teignmouth but Kingsteignton; still there is fair presumptive evidence that the germs, or something more than the germs, of this pleasant little seaport then existed. Thus much at least is clear, from a grant made by Eadweard the Confessor of certain lands which included what is now East Teignmouth, that in the year 1044 there stood at Teignmouth a church dedicated to St. Michael, while on the bank of the estuary there were certain sheds used for the manufacture of salt, called 'salterns.' St. Michael stood in what was commonly recognised as the older part of Teignmouth in the time of Leland. The old fabric was destroyed in 1821. Its very peculiar architectural arrangement, especially the singularly defensive character and venerable appearance of its towers, favour the idea that part at least of the ancient structure had remained from Saxon times; and that the fortress was quite as prominent in the minds of its constructors as the church.

There have long been two Teignmouths in the one town—East and West—and both for many centuries belonged, the one to the See of Exeter and the other to the Dean and Chapter. West Teignmonth was alienated in 1549 by Bishop Veysey, and was for a time in the Cecils, but has long been the property of the Cliffords. East Teignmouth was sold early in the present century by the Dean and Chapter, and is now the property of the Earl of Devon, whose ancestors are said to have acquired the manor of Teignmouth Courtenay temp. Edward III.

Teignmouth—speaking of the twin portions jointly—was anciently regarded as a borough, and sent representatives to a shipping council under Edward I. The market grant dates from 1253. The silver staff of the portreeve has engraven thereon for arms, azure a saltire gules between four fleur-de-lis converging. The Local Board use a seal with the same device, and the legend: 'SIGILL BURGHI TEIGNEMUTHIENSIS, 1002;' possibly the date refers to the descent of the Danes.

Teignmouth was one of the sufferers from the forays of the French during the Middle Ages. Stowe declares that it was 'burnt up' by them in 1340; but it is not quite clear how that can have been, when we find it in 1347 sending seven ships and 120 sailors to the expedition against Calais. For some centuries thereafter Teignmouth appears to have had an uneventful but a prosperous career; depending largely, indeed mainly, upon fishing. The salt with which the fish were cured continued to be manufactured upon the spot so late as the year 1692, operations having in all likelihood been carried on without a break from Saxon times.

It was in 1690 that the most memorable event in the history of Teignmouth happened. The French fleet were lying in Torbay, where the forces of the county were

drawn up to oppose their landing. Taking advantage of
this, certain of the galleys battered Teignmouth, following up a bombardment of 'near two hundred great shot'
by landing 1,700 men. The inhabitants, with that dis-
cretion which is so very much the better part of valour,
fled when the attack began, so that the invaders had an
easy victory. For three hours the town was ransacked
and plundered, and then fired, 116 houses being burnt, with
eleven vessels lying in the harbour. 'Moreover,' says a
MS. record of the disaster, written by Mr. Jordan, 'to
add sacrilege to their robbery and violence, they in a
barbarous manner entered the two churches in the said
town, and in a most unchristian manner tore the Bibles
and Common Prayer Books in pieces, scattering the leaves
thereof about the streets, broke down the pulpits, over-
threw the communion-tables, together also with many
other marks of a barbarous and enraged cruelty; and
such goods and merchandise as they could not or dare
not stay to carry away for fear of our forces, which were
marching to oppose them, they spoiled and destroyed,
killing very many cattle and hogs, which they left dead
behind them in the streets.' Something like a third of
the town was destroyed in this last invasion of Devonshire, and the loss sustained was computed at £11,030
6s. 10d. A brief for the collection of this sum was read
in all the churches throughout the country, and the money
raised. The event is commemorated by the name French
Street, given to a part of the town destroyed and rebuilt.

However, recovery was speedy. In 1744 the inhabitants, by permission of Sir William Courtenay, built a
battery on the 'Den' at East Teignmouth; and the port
is then said to have had a population of 4,000, and to fit
out twenty vessels for the Newfoundland trade. This
Den (= dune) is now a public lawn adjoining the beach.

Shaldon, a transfluvial suburb of Teignmouth, is partly
in Stokeinteignhead, and partly in Ringmore or St.

Nicholas; but has no separate history of importance. At Stokeinteignhead Church is one of the oldest brasses in the county—to a priest, *circa* 1375.

At Radway, in Bishopsteignton, are the ruins of the palace and chapel of the Bishops of Exeter, with whom the 'Bishop's-town-on-Teign' was for ages a favourite retreat. This 'fair house' was built by Bishop Grandisson in the early part of the fourteenth century. There is little left now to indicate the character of what the bishop himself, in a letter to Pope John XXII., called a beautiful structure, and described in his will as convenient and costly buildings. The few remains form part of a farmhouse. Comparing Bishops with Kingsteignton — the 'King's-town-on-the-Teign'— it has been wittily observed that the preference shown by the prelates for the more beautiful spot of the two, shows how superior the older bishops were in discernment. However, Bishop Veysey had to alienate it, like West Teignmouth, in favour of Sir Andrew Dudley, so that royalty got the upper hand after all.

The history of Dawlish begins in the reign of Eadweard the Confessor, with the grant in 1044 by that King of seven manses of land to his 'worthy chaplain' Leofric, afterwards the first Bishop of Exeter. The grant was at 'Doflisc,' which Mr. J. B. Davidson, to whom we are indebted for the full identification of the localities, read as 'devil water;' and it comprised not only Dawlish but what is now the present parish of East Teignmouth in addition, with almost absolute exactness. Two years later Leofric succeeded Lyfing as Bishop of Crediton, and four years later still removed to Exeter. After the Conquest Leofric gave these lands to St. Peter's Minster as part of the endowments of his See. Becoming the property of the Dean and Chapter, Dawlish was sold by them, like East Teignmouth, early in the present century.

Hardly any town in Devon has so uneventful a history as Dawlish. A village it remained all through the centuries, with a fitful fishing and smuggling life, until something like a hundred years ago its advantages as a bathing-place gave a new direction to energies which, after all, only needed to be encouraged. The one event in the history of Dawlish is connected with this development. A number of houses had been built by the side of the Dawlish Water, which flows down the centre of the pleasant combe to the sea, and several 'improvements' had been made, when, on the night of November 9th, 1810, a sudden torrent descending the valley from Haldon washed everything away. This is '*the* Flood' at Dawlish. Since then Dawlish has enjoyed steady and substantial progress, and has been made one of the most charming spots on the coast. Luscombe, the seat of a branch of the Hoares of Stourhead, a lovely domain, has a private chapel of great richness and beauty, erected from the designs of Sir Gilbert Scott.

Two chapels formerly existed in this parish, ruins of which remain and to which certain traditions attach. That at Cofton was in existence as early as 1376. Lidwell, or Lithwyll, was dedicated to St. Mary.

In the adjoining parish of Mamhead is the seat of Sir R. Newman. The manor passed through the Pomeroys, Peverells, and Carews, to the Balles. Sir Peter Balle, Recorder of Exeter and Attorney-General to Henrietta Maria, rebuilt the house, and planted many trees. The last member of that family erected an obelisk on Mamhead Point in 1742, and added greatly to the beauty of the place by his plantations. Mamhead is famed for its trees; and here, it is said, the ilex oak was first grown in England from acorns. Sir Peter Balle garrisoned his house for the King, and, as his epitaph states, 'suffered the usual fate of loyalty.' The present house was in great part rebuilt by Wilmot, Earl of Lisburne.

CHAPTER XXXIV.

CHUDLEIGH AND BOVEY TRACEY.

PROBABLY Chudleigh is one of the numerous Leges of 'Domesday,' and therefore not to be certainly identified, though it may be one of the two Chiderlies of the Count of Moreton. We first find it an appendage to the See of Exeter, saddled with the duty of providing twelve woodcocks, or in lieu thereof twelve pence, for the bishop's election dinner; and Bishop Stapledon in 1309 obtained the grant of a market. There was an episcopal palace, of which a few fragments yet exist, and here it was that Bishop Lacy died in 1455. The church had been dedicated by Bronescombe in 1259. The manor was alienated by Veysey in 1550, and came to its owners, the Cliffords, then of their present seat of Ugbrooke, in 1695.

Ugbrooke is said to have been attached to the precentorship of Exeter Cathedral until, in the sixteenth century, it passed to Sir Peter Courtenay, by whose daughter and coheiress, Anne, it was brought to her husband, Anthony Clifford of Borscombe, Wilts, a younger branch of the famous Cliffords of Cumberland. He was the ancestor of the Ugbrooke house, the first distinguished member of which was the celebrated Lord Treasurer, Clifford of the Cabal (1630-1673), whom Charles in 1672 created Baron Clifford of Chudleigh.

Chudleigh supplied quarters to Fairfax in January,

1646; and the only incidents of local note in its history have been its fires. The most disastrous of these occurred May 22, 1807, when 166 houses, nearly half the total number, were destroyed, and damage done to the extent of £60,000. An Act of Parliament was passed in the following year for the more easy rebuilding of the town and determining differences, and £21,000 was subscribed for the relief of the poorer inhabitants.

The scenery of Ugbrooke has been justly characterized as an epitome of that of the county; and not far from Chudleigh is a bold crag of limestone, called Chudleigh Rock, in which are a couple of caverns. One of these is associated with the folk-lore of the district as the Pixie's Hole, and with science by having yielded remains of the (locally) extinct cave mammalia.

Ashton was for over four centuries the residence of the Chudleigh family, who lived at Place. The manor was given by the Conqueror to Hervey de Helion, and held at 'Domesday' by his wife. It came to the Chudleighs about 1320. Sir George Chudleigh, the first baronet, sided with the Parliament when the Civil War broke out, and took part in the battle of Stratton. Not long after he changed sides, and had his house garrisoned in the Royalist interest. It was taken by a party of Fairfax's army in December, 1645; and Colonel James Chudleigh, Sir George's eldest son, was killed at the storming of Dartmouth in the following month, when Place was a garrison for the Parliament. The Chudleigh baronetcy ended in 1745, when Sir James Chudleigh was killed at the siege of Ostend.

Another notable Cavalier garrison in this locality was Canonteign, or Christow; and it, too, was stormed and taken by Fairfax's troops in December, 1645. The Roundhead Governor was Colonel Okey, executed at the Restoration as a regicide. Christow belonged to the Abbey of Bec. On the seizure of the property of the alien priories it passed to the Abbey of Tavistock; and at the Dissolution came, with other possessions of that house, to Lord Russell. Canonteign belonged to another alien house—that of De la Valle; but was granted by the fraternity, *circa* 1268, to Merton, Surrey. At the Dissolution this also came to Lord Russell. Another estate in the parish—Pope House—belonged to the Priory of Cowick. The manors of Christow and Canonteign, after passing through various hands, came to the Helyars; and were purchased, in 1812, by Sir Edward Pellew, afterwards created Viscount Exmouth.

Hennock Church was given to the Abbey of Torre in the reign of Richard I. by Philip de Salmonville. Bottor Rock, on 'the authority of the peasantry,' was a seat of 'Druidical worship.' With better grounds it is to be regarded as a genuine hill-fort of great age. At Lustleigh church-door is, however, an antiquity of much greater interest—a threshold-stone of Romano-British date, inscribed CATVIDOC CONRINO. The Prouzes, sometime lords of Lustleigh, are commemorated by a cross-legged effigy of Sir Wm. Prouz, temp. Edward II.; and there are a couple of figures ascribed to Sir John Dynham and his wife Emma.

Bovey Tracey has a history which, could it be fully worked out, would in all probability throw considerable light upon early village life in the county. The 'Domesday' entry is notable; for there can be no doubt that this is the 'Bovi' held by Geoffrey, Bishop of Coutances, in succession to Edric, with its 32 serfs, villeins, and bordars, its mill, and its added lands of 15 thanes, who retained between them two hides and half a virgate, paying therefore four pounds and thirty pence. The manor came to the Tracys, whence its distinctive name, as part of the barony of Barnstaple; and Henry Tracy obtained grant of market and fair in 1259. This was one of the Devonshire manors held by Margaret of Richmond, and has been in the Courtenays since 1747.

Bovey Heathfield is remarkable, geologically and economically, for its deposits of clay and lignite, or woodcoal. These are of Lower Miocene age, and fill the bed of an ancient lake. The association of clay and coal led to the establishment in 1772 of a pottery at Indiho (the house is traditionally said to be of monastic origin), which has been continued to the present time, though the lignite is no longer used for firing.

Bovey had a 'mayor,' and a customary mayor's show, though this officer was really the portreeve. At each annual manor court a bailiff and portreeve were elected, and the bailiff of one year was the portreeve of the next. The set day for the 'mayor's riding' was the Monday after the 3rd of May, called 'Roodmas Day;' and to properly discharge the duties of his office, the portreeve had the profits of a field called 'Portreeve's Park.'

One of the few incidents of note connected with Cromwell's visit in 1646 with Fairfax to the West of England, occurred at Bovey Tracey. He had marched from Tiverton through Crediton, and by the Teign valley towards Chudleigh, and suddenly fell upon one of Lord Wentworth's brigades at Bovey. The Royalists were all unaware of danger, and the officers were playing cards to pass the time, instead of keeping a sharp look-out; when suddenly, without warning, just as night had fallen in, Cromwell's troopers came upon the scene. The officers are credited with great presence of mind. Defence was out of the question; so they opened the windows, threw the stakes for which they were playing among the Roundheads, and, during the scramble for the silver, escaped by the back-door. Not so their men, some 80 of whom were captured, besides 400 horse and several colours. There was an end, thenceforward, of all hope of successful resistance in the field.

CHAPTER XXXV.

MORETONHAMPSTEAD AND CHAGFORD.

UNTIL Moretonhampstead was made a railway station, and Chagford had developed into a favourite moorland health-resort, no two country towns in Devon had a more thoroughly old-world character. It was within the memory, indeed, of the late Sir John Bowring that the only wheeled vehicle ever seen in Moretonhampstead was a wheelbarrow, and its communications with the outer world were either by foot, pack-horse, or pillion. The pillion lingered on much later, and seeing that the lady, riding behind the gentleman, had to clasp him closely for security at any rough part of the road, it is a wonder that with all its inconveniences it has not survived. The custom supplied a pleasant comment for an old Devonshire vicar, on the text of the man who had married a wife and could not attend the feast, ' A vain excuse, my friends —a vain excuse! he could have brought her behind him on a pillion!'

There is extant an amusing but utterly absurd tradition of the foundation of Moreton, as it is now commonly called for brevity, by a party of Flemings in three sections, consisting of the 'Moortown,' the 'ham,' and the 'stead.' It has just thus much of truth, that the place once possessed a considerable serge manufacture, in which probably Flemings had some interest. Moreton, however, is far older than the woollen trade, for it appears in 'Domesday' as a royal manor, which had belonged to Harold, to which pertained the third penny of the hundred of Teignbridge, and which had a population of twenty-eight. Under Edward I. the Earl of Ulster held it by the render of a sparrow-hawk, but for several centuries it has belonged to the Courtenays. Hugh de Courtenay obtained a market grant in 1335. According to the Lysonses, the manor of Daccombe, belonging to the Dean and Chapter of Canterbury, had the custom of free bench, and the lord was obliged to keep a cucking-stool for the use of scolding women. An ancient Baptist (Unitarian) Society here is traditionally said to have existed since the reign of Mary, and to have furnished members of the roll of martyrs. This would make it the oldest Nonconformist congregation in the county; but the oldest of which the origin is certainly known is the Baptist church at Tiverton, which dates from 1600. The woollen manufacture and the intercourse with the Low Countries consequent thereon, led easily to the introduction of Reformed views of religion into Devon.

A notable old poorhouse (1637) still remains at Moreton; and a field near the church is called the Sentry, *quasi*-Sanctuary.

Though the documentary evidence for the early history of Chagford is very slight, there are sufficient proofs in the rude-stone monuments of the locality to give it high antiquity; and in the traces of ancient mining to show that its selection as a stannary town had been preceded by long centuries of enterprise. Tin mining, indeed, was so prominent an occupation that the tinners were tithed, and each 'spallier,' or spade labourer, paid annually his 'shovell penny.' For many a long year Chagford seems to have steadily thriven, and to have developed a sturdy independence of character that its comparative isolation on the borders of Dartmoor greatly helped to maintain.

Within a very few years it was the quaintest of all the moorland centres; but its greater accessibility as a summer resort has hopelessly modernized its leading features. Nor is this to be wondered at. So delightful are its surroundings in the summer-time, and so proud are the natives of its attractions, common rumour avers that if a Chagford man is then asked where he lives, his sharp retort is, 'Chagford, and what do you think?' But in winter, so depressed is he by the change of conditions, the rejoinder will be 'Chaggyford, good Lord!' The joke is an old one, but an apt illustration of the sharply contrasted conditions of the moorland climate.

A scarce black-letter tract tells the 'True Relation of the Accident at Chagford in Devonshire.' The market-house fell in 'presently after dinner,' upon a 'tin court daie,' and Mr. Eveleigh, the steward, with nine others, died. This is the chief event in the purely local history, and Chagford has only one link of importance with matters of national concern. It lay too much out of the ordinary course of traffic to be greatly moved even when 'civil dudgeon' grew most high; and yet it was at a skirmish here, in 1642, that Sidney Godolphin fell.

Of the families connected with Chagford, the most important are the Prouzes and the Whyddons. The Coplestones at one time held the manor, and by Master Coplestone the markets were sold to the town in 1564. The Gorges, too, must have had an interest in the parish, from the frequent occurrence of their arms on the roof-bosses in the parish church, which was originally dedicated in 1261. Chagford was then held by Thomas de Chagford, and he, in 1299, sold it to Simon de Wibbery, whose descendants held it for nigh two centuries. Of the Whyddons the most notable was the eminent judge, Sir John, Serjeant-at-Law under Edward VI., and Judge of the Queen's Bench in the first year of Mary. He died January 27, 1575, and his monument forms one of the leading features of Chagford Church. Whyddon Park is a stretch of broken shaggy moorland hillside descending to the Teign.

That Gidleigh gave name to the family of Gidley is certain, but whether it came to them by a grant from 'one Martine Duke and Earl of Cornwall' to 'his nephew, Giles de Gidleigh,' as Westcote affirms, may be doubted, and certainly cannot now be proved. The family of Prouz, who were associated with the manor and built a castle here in early Edwardian times, of which the shell yet remains, are said to have acquired it by marriage with the heiress of Giles de Gidleigh; and, as one of the Prouzes is stated to have been steward to Richard, King of the Romans, it is not difficult to see how Westcote's story may have arisen. After the line of Prouz and their successors had long passed away, a Gidley, if not the Gidley family, came back again, and for awhile the manor was once more in the old name. Bartholomew Gidley (died 1686) was a local Royalist leader of note.

The district is one of the chief centres of the Druidical superstition of last-century antiquaries and their followers. Holy Street, in Gidleigh, giving title to the mill first painted by Creswick, and since his day by hundreds of artists, has been regarded as a Druidical *via sacra* purely on the score of its name, which in all probability indicates simply an ancient 'hollow' road. But this *via sacra* is very mild etymology when compared with the arguments used by Polwhele to prove Drewsteignton a Druidical 'capital,' by reading it 'Druid's-town-on-Teign.' Drewsteignton, as such, is not to be found in 'Domesday;' but from the extent of woodland is probably the Taintone held by Baldwin the Sheriff, in succession to Offers. The prefix unquestionably comes from Drogo or Drewe, who held the manor in the reigns of Henry II. and Richard I.

The place has, however, substantial claims to antiquarian celebrity. Here stands, on a farm called Shilstone, the only cromlech left in Devon, which once formed the central feature of a group of stone circles and avenues. It fell in January, 1862, and was 'restored' in the same year. Though the 'quoit' is two feet thick, fifteen in length, and ten in breadth, a builder and a carpenter of Chagford, by the aid of pulleys and a screw-jack, replaced it at a cost of £20; and thus very much reduced the vague wonder that commonly attaches to the erection of such structures. The village tradition is that the 'Spinster's Rock,' as it is called, was erected by three spinsters one morning before breakfast; and these have been suggested as the Valkyriur. Bradford Pool close by, with the cromlech, and with a logan stone in the bed of the Teign, at Whyddon Park, have all been 'prayed in aid' of the Druidical hypothesis: but the pool is only a collection of water in an old mining excavation, and the logan, like scores of others on the adjacent moors, is of purely natural origin. It is quite possible that Shilstone estate took name from the cromlech as 'Shelfstone;' and there was a Selvestan held by Osbern de Salceid in succession to Edric, which would suit the locality, and which is moreover remarkable for having adjacent a virgate of land that nobody—*nemo*—held T.R.E.

There is other evidence in the fine hill-forts of Cranbrook and Prestonbury, which command the gorge of the Teign at Fingle Bridge, that the neighbourhood was an important one in Keltic times.

Great Fulford, in the parish of Dunsford, has been the seat of the notable family of Fulford, literally from 'time immemorial;' and of no other house in Devon can it be suggested with so much probability that

"When the Conqueror came it was at home."

Direct history, at least, takes us back to the reign of Richard I.; and 'Domesday' shows a connection with the manor of Bovi, already cited as being held by Geoffrey, Bishop of Coutances, and as having attached thereto the lands of fifteen thanes. One of the estates held by these thanes is Filauefford; so that there is good evidence in 1086 that the Saxon owners of Great Fulford had not been dispossessed; while the parent stock of Fulfords were certainly there within a century. The other *Foleford* of 'Domesday,' held by Motbert under Baldwin the Sheriff, was a small manor, identifiable with Little Fulford in Shobrooke. Be all this as it may, among the most distinguished Crusaders of the West were Sir William, Sir Baldwin, and Sir Amias de Fulford. In the Wars of the Roses the Fulfords took the Lancastrian side; and Sir Baldwin, who fought at Towton, was beheaded at Hexham, in 1461. But the family remained true, and his son, Sir Thomas, was attainted for espousing the cause of the Earl of Richmond, in 1483. He also took part in the relief of Exeter, when it was besieged by Perkin Warbeck, in 1497. The forfeiture only lasted a couple of years.

In the Wars of the Commonwealth, as was to be expected, the Fulfords were staunch Royalists; and Colonel, subsequently Sir Francis, Fulford made Fulford a royal garrison. His son Thomas was killed in the service; and in December, 1645, the house was taken by Fairfax, and placed under the command of Colonel Okey. The mansion is, in the main, Elizabethan, and contains a royal recognition of the family loyalty in a portrait of Charles I.

Near the village of Manaton is a curious pile of rocks, called 'Bowerman's Nose,' the natural effect of weathering upon cubical-jointed granite. This has been deemed a rock idol, and held to have taken name from a certain Bowerman, who, according to a supposed 'Domesday' entry that no one has been able to find since it was fi st 'discovered' half a century since, held the manor. But Bowerman is only the Keltic *Veor* (*maur*) *maen* = the 'great rock,' as Manaton is *Maen y dun* = the 'rocky hill.'

CHAPTER XXXVI.

DARTMOOR.

THE great central waste of Devon, itself as large as many a county, has a history of its own. Its features are now so marked that we are apt to regard it as having always borne its distinctive character; and much error has arisen by reasoning from this false premise. Gaunt and bare the higher regions of Dartmoor were throughout the Stone and Bronze periods, and so are still; but its valleys and outskirts, in the days of its most ancient dwellers, were indistinguishable in natural characteristics from the county at large. Woods and heaths, broken only in their gloomy monotony by strips of water-made meadow skirting the wider river-courses, were the leading features, not of Dartmoor and its borders only, but of all Devonia; and the scanty population was scattered indifferently through its wilds. Dartmoor is simply the last refuge of the traces of these ancient days—a prehistoric island, girdled and wasted by the encroaching waves of an aggressive civilization. The very name is a proof of later differentiation. Dunmonia, Deuffnynt, the 'Land of Hills,' or the 'Land of Deep Valleys,' whichever may be accepted as the parent of the modern 'Devon,' are but two modes of expressing the same physical features, the ancient names of Dartmoor and the shire alike. Only when clearing and enclosure had given an artificial character to the lowlands did the upland country receive its distinctive name. The fact that the Saxons called the north of Devon the North Hams (*ham* = dwelling), and the south the South Hams, is a proof of the unpeopled character of Dartmoor in the Saxon period; and it is at least possible, indeed very probable, that the majority of the British settlements on Dartmoor, the traces of which still exist, were formed by the Kelts as they were pushed back by the encroachments of the Saxon colonists. Moreover, *Dart*moor is a name that must have been given by men who were more familiar with the Dart than with any other of the numerous rivers that descend from its plateau on all sides. The early history of Dartmoor is very far as yet from having been fully traced. Passed over in 'Domesday,' not afforested with certainty until the twelfth century, there appears good evidence that it is the remnant of an extended area of national or folk-land. A peculiar right of commonage continues known as Venville tenure—which is accompanied also by feudal service—enjoyed by residents in the parishes skirting the Moor. And this in all likelihood dates from Saxon times (*wang* = field in Saxon, and Wangefield is an early form of Venville), and represents the rights of common which the Saxon dwellers in the border district had enjoyed over the moorland waste, and which, maintained after the Conquest, have descended to the present day.

But we are here dealing with a comparatively modern period in the history of Dartmoor. This great waste has been pronounced by Mr. Lukis unrivalled in this country in the extent and character of its rude-stone monuments —its menhirs, lines, circles, huts, trackways, pounds. No doubt, like the barrows, with which these remains are in part contemporary, the construction of these primitive structures did continue even beyond the dawn of historic times; but they too, like the barrows, stretch back into a grey antiquity, the dimness of which we cannot penetrate.

The 'hut-rings' are small circular heaps of stones which formed the foundations of rude dwellings; the 'pounds' are much larger enclosures, which commonly surround or are associated with the rings. Both are found in considerable numbers in almost every part of the Moor. We have here dwellings and fortified or protected villages, but with little to date them by. Hovels as rude, and erected much upon the same plan, may be seen on the Moor now. These traces of ancient habitation are very frequent on the slopes overlooking the Dartmoor rivers, the beds of which have been 'streamed,' as it is called, for tin, and here represent the settlements of the ancient tinners, stretching in some cases with little interval for miles along the valleys. But if the hut-rings merge into the rude moorland dwellings of our own day in one direction, on the other they are linked with relics of which no tradition preserves the purpose—with 'menhirs' and 'lines,' or 'avenues,' with the so-called 'sacred circles,' and the 'cromlechs,' all or nearly all of which appear to be connected with, or to mark, interments.

One of the most notable groups of these remains is at Merrivale Bridge, where there are large numbers of hut and other rings, associated with stone avenues, or 'parallelitha,' and upright stones, or 'menhirs.' The series is commonly known by the name of the Plague Market, from a tradition that they were used as a market when Tavistock was attacked by the plague. The stones of these 'avenues' are small, and this is the case with most of the others, which are commonly associated with well-defined and accepted sepulchral monuments. Too much importance, however, has been attached to this special class of remains; there are ancient stone-faced hedges on Dartmoor, which, when the earth is removed, present 'avenues' precisely identical with those of Merrivale, and 'tracklines or boundary banks,' primitive fences, are common wherever there are traces of ancient habitation.

On Torhill, near the great central 'trackway'—the ancient Fosseway, traversing the Moor from east to west—are traces of an extensive settlement, possibly the Ravennat's Termonin.

The finest 'pound' on the Moor is the enclosed and fortified village of Grimspound, on the flank of Hamildon, which gives the structural relics of an ancient settlement in an almost perfect state. The only cromlech in the county is that at Drewsteignton, already described. The word 'cromlech,' by the way, has always been applied in the West of England to what is more generally known to archæologists as a 'dolmen.' Of the ordinary cromlechs, or 'circles' of detached stones, Dartmoor supplies several examples. The largest is the Grey Wethers, near Sittaford Tor. Commonly called sacred circles, and frequently classed with the rude-stone monuments generally as 'Druidical,' the fact yet remains that they are always either definitely associated with interments, or presumably so; while neither Devonshire nor the West of England, except in the active imaginations of the antiquaries of the last century and their followers, has ever yielded a scrap of evidence to connect them with the supposed Druidical priesthood, whose existence in Britain depends upon the hearsay report of Cæsar. The really historic Druids of the Kelts were simple 'medicine-men;' or, as Mr. W. C. Borlase defines them, 'magicians and white witches;' and neither history, tradition, nor folk-lore yields any trace of their existence in the West.

The commonest form of presumed Druidical memorial on Dartmoor is the 'rock basin.' The granite crests of the hills of the moorland, known as 'tors,' are dotted with hollows of various sizes, which were held to have been hewn out by the Druids, either to catch the blood of their victims sacrificed on imaginary altar stones, or to collect the pure waters from heaven for their religious or magical rites. Unluckily the geologist has decided that these basins—and some are of very remarkable dimensions—are of natural origin; and the Druids have never recovered from the shock. It is the same with the rocking or 'logan' stones. These are simply masses of weathered granite, nicely poised by the cunning hand of nature. Of many such upon Dartmoor, perhaps the best example is the 'Nutcrackers' at Lustleigh Cleave.

The geology of Dartmoor, indeed, has had a very marked influence upon its archæology. In the main it is a great granitic plateau, broken by numerous valleys, and dotted with the rocky peaks of the 'tors.' The granite is jointed, often with considerable regularity, and weathers into masses and piles irresistibly suggestive of Cyclopean masonry; while the hillsides are bestrewn for miles with huge boulders and blocks. These supplied the material of the ancient hut-circles and pounds, and they supply the material also of modern dwellings and boundaries, which have thence a rude and massive character. So with the moorland churches. Built almost wholly of granite—wall and mullion, tracery and pillar, crocket and arch—they have a style peculiarly their own, based upon the rugged and intractable stone of which they are reared.

Some of the most remarkable features in the history of Dartmoor are associated with its mining enterprise. Tin-mining in Devon and in Cornwall not only dates from a period of very remote antiquity, beyond the dawn of history, but the earliest records present it in the light of an organized industry carried on by men who formed a kind of corporation, bound to certain duties, and endowed with certain privileges. Originally the whole of the tin-miners of Devon and of Cornwall formed one body, and met for the regulation of their affairs upon Hingston Down. Later the two counties were divided, and the tinners of Devon had their own 'parliament'—as it was called—meeting in the open-air on Crockern Tor, which rises in the heart of the ancient mining district, immediately above Two Bridges. So far as history extends, the tin-mining areas of the West of England—the Stannaries—have always been an appanage of the Crown, passing to the Duchy of Cornwall upon its creation; but this gathering upon 'deserted Crockern' carries us back long before the Conquest, to the primitive assemblies at least of our Saxon forefathers. Toll of tin used to be paid to the Crown or to the Duchy, and for the collection of this toll it was enacted that all tin should be weighed and 'coined' at certain Stannary towns. The coinage consisted simply in striking off a corner (Fr. *coin*) of each block to ascertain its character, and in stamping it with the royal or Duchy arms in token that the quality was right and the dues paid. The earliest Stannary record dates in 1197, when some such system had evidently been long in operation. Chagford, Ashburton, and Tavistock, the oldest-named coinage towns, are mentioned as such two years later. John granted the tinners a charter in 1201; and in 1305 Edward I. recognised the separation of the tinners of Devon and Cornwall as two distinct bodies, and appointed Lydford as the Stannary prison for Devon. Not long after this Plympton became one of the coinage towns. The system of tin coinage continued in force with little variation until abolished by Act of Parliament in 1838. Under the old Stannary laws the tinners had very remarkable powers, extending so far in Devon as the right to dig for tin in any man's land, without tribute or satisfaction; and it is probable that the Crockern Tor Parliament was quite as much concerned in the assertion of these rights against the public as in regulating internal concerns. There was one rather serious provision against adulteration of tin, but with that exception the tinners had matters well-nigh their own way. The adulterator had a certain number of spoonfuls of the melted metal poured down his throat!

The Parliament which sat on Crockern Tor consisted of

twenty-four 'Stannators' from each of the four Stannaries of the county, elected in the court of that Stannary. It met when summoned by the Lord Warden, and was generally presided over by the Vice-Warden. Seats were wrought in the living granite (unhappily almost every vestige is now destroyed), and here under the open canopy of heaven the ancient court for centuries did its work. In later days luxury crept in, and it was held sufficient to open commission and swear-in the jurors upon the bleak hill-crest, and then adjournment was made to one of the Stannary towns. These Parliaments ceased to be held early in the last century, though the local Stannary courts survived. At that time—and probably there had been no deviation from the ancient practice—the election of the jurats was by universal Stannary suffrage, all tinners, tin-bounders, owners of tin and works, and adventurers in the same, and all spalyers or labourers, and other persons concerned in tin or tin works, being summoned to be personally present and take part in the election. The Stannary Court (reformed) is now held at Truro, dealing with mines generally within the old Stannary district, and not simply with those of tin. The judge is the Vice-Warden. We have here, then, an example of the continuance of an ancient local law court from times beyond record. It is quite possible that the court of the Stannaries is the oldest extant jurisdiction in the kingdom.

The forest of Dartmoor has always been appendant, from the earliest record, to the royal manor of Lydford; and long continued wholly within Lydford parish. There are records of the perambulations of the forest, and of the forest boundaries, as early as 1240. All lands in Devonshire, except Dartmoor and Exmoor, had been disafforested by John in 1203 or 1204; but Dartmoor was rigidly preserved, and there appears to be good incidental evidence of the rigorous manner in which the savage forest laws were enforced in the old saying anent 'Lydford law,' already noted. The term 'forest' must be understood strictly in the legal sense. Dartmoor at present contains one patch of ancient woodland—Wistman's Wood, near Two Bridges—a wild, weird grove of stunted oaks of vast antiquity springing among granite blocks; but though evidently once much more wooded than now, the greater part of the moorland area must always have been rocky and barren. Wistman's Wood has been read 'the Wood of Wisemen,' *i.e.*, Druids. There is little doubt it is the Keltic *uisg-maen-coed* = ' the rocky wood by the water.'

The most important step in the history of the Moor was taken when, early in the present century, Prince Town, the moorland capital, was founded, at the suggestion of Sir Thomas Tyrwhitt, Lord Warden, by the erection of a prison for the accommodation of the French prisoners of war, then crowding the hulks at Plymouth Dock. While the war lasted, Prince Town—named from the Prince Regent—throve and grew; when the war ceased, the prison and the houses which had sprung up around it were deserted, and the little town fell into ruin. At one time an attempt was made to utilize the prison for manufacturing purposes, by adapting it to the distillation of naphtha from the peat; but this did not prove commercially successful, and the place was again abandoned, until the present convict establishment was formed in 1855. The prison farm shows of what Dartmoor is really capable. Not far distant is a good example of what is called on the Moor a 'clapper bridge,' of unknown antiquity, slabs of granite on piled piers of granite blocks.

A cross upon a pedestal raised on a basement of three steps, which stood on the Moor near Fox Tor, popularly bore the name of Childe's Tomb; and was said to have been erected in memory of a luckless hunter of that name, who perished in a snow-storm at or near the spot. The structure was perfect seventy years since. The legend is a very curious one, and while it cannot be accepted as historic fact, does seem to embody some traces of Teutonic myth. Risdon mentions Childe's Tomb as one of the three wonders of the Moor (Crockern Tor and Wistman's Wood are the others); and the story, as commonly accepted, is that Childe lived at Plymstock; that being overtaken by a snow-storm, he killed and disembowelled his horse, and crept into the cavity for warmth; and finally wrote the following couplet in blood and died:

> 'The fyrste that fyndes and brings me to my grave,
> The lands of Plymstoke they shal have.' °

And then it is told how the monks of Tavistock and the people of Plymstock both heard of the sad event; how the monks obtained the body, and were bringing it to their Abbey, when they heard that the Plymstock men were lying in ambush to take it from them at a ford on the Tavy; and how they had a bridge built out of the usual track and so evaded their rivals, whence the bridge was called 'Guile Bridge.' And thus, it is said, the Abbey of Tavistock obtained the rich Manor of Plymstock. The baselessness of the whole ingenious fabric is proved by the fact that the Manor of Plymstock belonged to the Abbey of Tavistock before the Conquest, some centuries before the date assigned to Childe; but apart from this, the story as it stands is inconsistent and impossible. The delay that must have taken place in the removal to enable the Plymstock people to learn of the death in time to intercept the monks; the fact that Guile Bridge really replaced a ford to the Abbey, on the direct road to the Abbey Church; the inadequacy of the time at disposal for building such a structure, and its unnecessary character, seeing that the river could be forded—each of these points in itself is sufficient to show the unhistoric character of the legend. The 'Guile' is manifestly a corruption.

° Or: 'He that finds and brings me to my tomb,
The Land of Plemstock shall be his doom.'

CHAPTER XXXVII.

DIALECT AND FOLK-LORE.

WEST-COUNTRY English has a very peculiar interest in its historical relations. It was not merely in the spirit of enthusiasm that Charles Kingsley, himself by accident of birth a Devonshire man, exclaimed, 'Glorious West-Country! you must not despise their accent, for it is the remains of a nobler and purer dialect than our own.' Devonshire speech, in fact—as one of its greatest living masters, Mr. F. T. Elworthy, has shown—is 'the true classic English.' 'We all know that the English of Alfred's time, or, as it is called, the Anglo-Saxon, is the groundwork upon which our modern English has been built up. But Alfred's own variety was in his day the polite, the courtly, the only recognised literary—in fact, the standard form of speech; and Alfred was, as we all know, a West-Country man, speaking in West-Country, most likely Devonshire style.' Cædmon and Beda had long passed away, and until the year 1100 the language of Ælfred remained the only written English.

From about 1100 to the beginning of the fourteenth century Southern English still held a prominent position in the vernacular literature of the country, though several writers in the Midland dialect from time to time arose. In the fourteenth century, however, a change came. Wycliffe and Chaucer, writing in their own Midland dialect, not only reasserted 'the dignity of the despised language of the common people,' but made the form of English in which they wrote 'the recognised model of the English language.' There was no writer of Southern English to assert its claims to recognition at this critical period. The book language, which they modelled and partially created by the help of the printing press, quickly supplanted all the other forms. 'From that time forward the language of our great Saxon King was only represented by the spoken words of our West-Country forefathers. . . . Thus . . . the modern courtly dialect, now considered to be the correct English, is the descendant of what, in Alfred's time, was, by the then educated classes, held as much below the recognised standard, as our West-Country talk is now reckoned by dwellers in Park Lane and Belgravia.' Only once since those days has the good broad Saxon dialect of Devon been held in court favour: and that was in the reign of Queen Elizabeth, whose greatest heroes spake with the tongue of their fathers, and were not ashamed; and who made its rugged sounds dear to all who valued stoutness of heart and unquenchable courage of soul, and specially to the 'Great Eliza' herself. Even then, however, the dialect had its share of ridicule, as the vain efforts of Shakspere and his fellow-dramatists to reproduce it on the stage show. It is amusing to note how they thus— Shakspere and Jonson more especially—created a false rustic dialect which has continued to the present day upon the stage, but is known nowhere else.

There is a very interesting monument of the old Devonshire speech of the fourteenth century, in the English translation of 'Sir Ferumbras,' printed by the Early English Text Society in 1879. This poem was undoubtedly written by a Devonshire man in his own native tongue, though, in some way or other, he had become well acquainted with the use of Northern forms.

Throughout the work there are found the marks which still 'bewray the speech' of the true Devonian, whose language has not been reduced to the dull dead-level of the village school, with its artificial and unhistoric proprieties. Mr. Elworthy amusingly points out that 'Sir Ferumbras' shows it to have been as true five centuries ago as now, in popular proverbial parlance, that in Devon 'Everything is *he* except a Tom-cat, and that's a *she*.'

In a scientific point of view the chief feature of 'Sir Ferumbras' is, however, the manner in which it has enabled Dr. Murray to solve the vexed problem of the Devonshire 'min or mun = them,' which is one of the most notable peculiarities of the dialect, and which, while thoroughly familiar in Devon, is unknown, except in the mouth of Devonshire folk, beyond its borders. This 'min' is really derived from a word which appears in the poem as *hymen, hymyn, hemen,* a third person plural dative and accusative, specialized from the singular by an added 'en.' The need of this arose from the fact that while in the Northern and Midland dialects in the fourteenth century the dative and accusative singular was *hem*, as now, and the plural *hem* and *heom*, in the West *hem* stood for both numbers, and was pluralized by the 'en,' as in German added to *ihr* to form a plural accusative.

The true native dialect is most marked at the present day in the Dartmoor district, in the remoter localities of the North and West, and in the heart of the South Hams. The dialect of the East of the county is not so distinctive, from the more frequent admixture of Somerset and Dorset variations, though these counties generally share with Devon the possession of the old West Saxon speech. Along the line of the Tamar Cornish influence is manifest. This is most marked in Plymouth and Devonport, which are sometimes called the 'Cornishman's London,' and which have drawn large numbers, chiefly of the working classes, from that county. Here also the existence of an Irish quarter has had some effect. The popular speech of Exeter is almost purely Devonian, and there are many parishes in which the customary talk of the villagers would be nearly, if not quite, unintelligible to those who are only familiar with modern and polite, but are ignorant of ancient and historic, English.

The Keltic element is seen in the nomenclature of the county, but not in any special sense in common speech. It occurs chiefly in the names of the rivers, which supply indications also of the existence of different Keltic dialects. All the larger rivers have Keltic names; so have those of the middle class; and it is only when we come to the smaller streams that the Saxon can be traced. Minor affluents had no distinctive name in early Keltic times, nor would they receive any until the county was more thickly populated. The most remarkable river group is that which contains the Tamar, Tavy, Taw, Torridge, and Teign—all unquestionably related and all based upon one root-word for water, *ta* or *tau*, with varying suffixes for the purpose of definition. Thus Tamar is *Ta-maur*, the 'big water;' Tavy, *Ta-vean*, the 'little water.' In the Exe and the Axe we have the Gaelic *uisg*, again 'water'; and in Avon, *afon*, one of the commonest Kymric words for a river. Dart is the same name as Derwent, derivable from the old Kornu-Keltic *Dwr-gwyn*, the 'white river' or water. *Dwr* also appears in the Derle and the Deer, and probably in Otter, as *ydwr* = 'the water.' These are merely suggestive hints, for the subject is far too wide to be treated in detail here. A few Saxon names may, however, be mentioned. Lyn = *hlynn*, a 'stream.' In Lyd we have *hlyd* = 'loud.' Yeo is the Saxon *ea* = 'water.' A point of considerable importance as indicative of the varied character and origin of the Teutonic immigration, is the fact of the grouping of such common names for small streams, as brook, burn, beck, bourn, lake, water, and fleet. This is seen remarkably, as Mr. C. Spence

Bate has shown, in connection with the Dartmoor river basins, distinguishing those of adjoining streams from each other in a singularly definite and constant manner.

The folk-lore of Devon would take a volume to itself. With one exception it is thoroughly Teutonic. This exception is the Devonshire Pixy, who is not quite the northern Elf, but still less the southern Fairy. Cornish tradition is peculiar in its tales of giants, but these are unknown in Devon save through modern importation, while the Pixies are in large part common property. They are now said to be the souls of unbaptized children, but seem to represent the defeated Kelts, in some vague fashion. Similar stories are told of them as are current of the Brownie and the Elf; so that while the foundation is probably Keltic, the superstructure is Saxon—as with many of the local weather and other rhymes—and of the widest national type. One of the most prevalent phases of the 'Pixy cult' still extant is the practice of turning garments inside out as a remedy against being 'Pixy-led' after nightfall.

The 'Wish Hounds' of Dartmoor, and the 'Yeth Hounds' of North Devon, are the 'Gabriel Hounds' of Durham and Yorkshire; 'the 'Wild Hunt' of Germany; the 'Yule Host' of Iceland; the 'Hunt Macabe' in parts of France; while there is evidence of the later importation of this wild fancy into Cornwall in the form it assumes about Polperro, of the 'Devil and his Dandy Dogs.'

Whately's statement that 'the vulgar in most parts of Christendom are continually serving the gods of their heathen ancestors,' is literally true in the West. Living animals have been burnt alive in sacrifice within memory to avert the loss of other stock. The burial of three puppies 'brandise-wise' in a field is supposed to rid it of weeds. Throughout the rural districts of Devon witchcraft is an article of current faith, and the toad is thrown into the flames as an emissary of the evil one.

There are still to be found those who believe that the sun dances on Easter morning; those who, when they see the new moon, half in jest and half in earnest, wish and courtesy, and turn the money in their pockets; and those, too, who would not dare to insult the moon by pointing at her, for fear of some terrible revenge on the part of the offended luminary. The ship-carrying in honour of the crescent moon, adapted from paganism into Christian custom, which formed the central feature of the Corpus Christi pageant in mediæval Plymouth, has continued to the present day as a May-day 'garland.' A tradition that the mines on Dartmoor were worked when wolves and winged serpents dwelt in the valleys, may be connected with serpent worship, or may allude to the inroads of Norsemen in their 'sea-snakes.' To a Teutonic origin are to be traced a number of superstitions connected with the ash, the most vital of which is the passage of a ruptured child through a split ash sapling, the parts of which are then brought together again.

A very curious illustration of the growth of comparatively modern folk-lore is supplied by the remarkable set of legends which have been associated with the name of Sir Francis Drake. It is said that he brought the Plymouth Leat into that town by 'art magic,' compelling a Dartmoor spring to follow his horse's tail as he galloped ahead; that he made fire-ships for the destruction of the Armada by throwing chips of wood from Plymouth Hoe into Plymouth Sound; that he 'shot the gulf' which divided this upper world from the antipodes by a pistol; that he threw a boy overboard because cleverer than himself; that he fired a cannon ball through the earth to prevent his wife committing bigamy; that he rises to his revels if you beat his old drum; and that he offered to make Tavistock a magical seaport!

INDEX.

Abbot's Way, 284
Abbotsham, 150
Acland family, 46
Acland, Sir T. D., 46
Act of Uniformity, 33
Ædelstan's expulsion of the Britons, 9
Albemarle, Duke of, 160
Ælfryth, 181
Alvington, 248
Apaunaris, 292
Appledore, 148
Artavia, 116
Ashburton, 277; Guild of St. Lawrence, 278; discovery in church, 280
Ashburton, Lord, 279
Ashbury, 164
Ash-tree folk-lore, 287
Ashton, 317
Ashe, 65
Atherington, 113
Audley, Lord, 124
Axminster, 60; carpets, 63
Axmouth, 70
Ayshford, 100

Babbage, Charles, 263
Bagge, Sir James, 233
Baldwin, Archbishop, 40
Balle, Sir Peter, 315
Bampfylde family, 46
Bampton, 98
Bampton, John de, 99
Baring family, 43
Barlynch Abbey, 99
Barnstaple, 116; priory, 117; bridge, 117; guilds, 119; Huguenots, 121; pottery, 122
Barrows and barrow-builders, 2
Basset, Col. Arthur, 127
Bastard family, 239
Bath, Sir Henry, 170
Bath barton folk-lore, 171

Beeke, Dean, 310
Beer, 73; freestone, 73
Beer Alston, 199
Beer Ferrers, 198; mines, 199
Benson, Thomas, 140
Berry, Sir John, 99
Berry Narbor, 131
Berry Pomeroy Castle, 263
Bickleigh, 198
Bicton, 76
Bideford, 141; bridge, 145; witchcraft, 146
Bigbury, 244
Bishops Clyst, 53
Bishops Tawton, 123
Bishopsteignton, 314
Blachford, 237
Bloody Assize, 45, 62,69, 261
Bluett, Col. F., 100
Blundell, Peter, 94
Bodley family, 40
Bodley, Sir Thomas, 41
Boniface, St., 108
Bonvile family, 67
Bonvile, Lord, 67
Borough, Steven, 148
Borough English, 127
Bottor Rock, 318
Bourchier family, 126
Bovey Tracey, 318
Bovey basin, discoveries in, 309
Bovey lignite, 319
Bowerman's Nose, 325
Bowring, Sir John, 42
Bracton, Henry de, 164
Bradfield House, 88
Bradley, 306
Bradmere Pool, 324
Bradninch, 89
Brampford Speke, 44
Brannock, legend of St., 126
Branscombe, 77

Braunton, 126
Breakwater at Plymouth, 221
Brent, 284
Brent Tor, 191
Brian, Sir Guy de, 289
Bridestowe, 169
Britte, Walter, 237
Briwere, Wm. de, 293
Brixham, 301 ; lords and ladies, 302 ; landing of William of Orange, 302
Brixton, 236
Broad Clyst, 53
Broadhembury, 82
Brockedon, Wm., 263
Broke, de, 198
Bronze Period, 3
Browne, Wm., 189
Brutus the Trojan, 254
Brutus Stone, 254
Bryant, the mythologist, 222
Buckfastleigh, 283
Buckfastleigh Abbey, 281
Buckland-in-the-Moor, 284
Buckland, West, 104
Buckland Monachorum, 194
Buckland Abbey, 194
Budleigh, East, 51
Budleigh Salterton, 51
Budleigh pebbles, 51
Buller family, 302
Bulmer, Sir Bevis, 131
Bulteel family, 244
Burlescombe, 101

Cadbury Castle, 96
Cadover, 230
Canonleigh Nunnery, 100
Canonteign, 317
Carew family, 83
Carew, John, Lord Deputy, 83
Carew, Thomas, 83
Carew, Bampfylde Moore, 96
Cary family, 295
Cary, Chief Baron, 295
Cary, Sir George, 296
Carys of Clovelly, 151
Castle Hill, 103
Cavalier rising at South Molton, 25
Chagford, 321
Champernowne family, 240
Chichester family, 125
Childe the hunter, 333
Christow, 317
Chittlehampton, 113
Chudleigh, 316
Chudleigh family, 317
Chudleigh, Sir George, 317
Chulmleigh, 112 ; prebend myth, 112
Churchstow, 245
Cider, 285
Clayhanger, 99
Clifford family, 316
Clifford, Lord Treasurer, 316

Clovelly, 151
Clovelly Dikes, 150
Clyst Valley, 53
Clysthydon, 53
Clyst, St. George, 53
Cockington, 293
'Codex Exoniensis,' 31
Coffin family, 150
Coffin, Sir William, 150
Cogan, Sir Milo, 99
Colcombe, 68
Coleridge family, 85
Coleridge, Samuel Taylor, 85
Colyford, 70
Colyton, 68
Combe Martin, 131 ; silver lead-mines 131 ; curious custom, 132
Compton Castle, 301
Cookworthy, Wm., 247
Coplestone Oak, 200
Coplestone Cross, 110
Coplestone family, 111
Corinæus and Goemagot, 204
Cornwood, 236
Cornworthy Priory, 266
Corp brasses, 272
Cosway, Richard, 95
Countesbury, 133
Countess Weir, 37
Courtenay family, 56
Courtenay, Lord Edward, 57
Coverdale, Myles, 301
Cowick Priory, 44
Cowley, Hannah, 95
Cranch, John, 43
Cranmore Castle, 96
Crediton, 21, 105 ; bishopric of, 105 ; cathedral, 106
Crediton, barns of, 21
Crispin, Thomas, 247
Crocker family, 239
Crockern Tor, 330
Cross, John, 96
Crosse, Richard, 96
Croyde 'flint factory,' 127
Cruwys family, 111
Cullompton, 87
Culmstock, 88
Cutcliffe, John, 130
Cyneheard, 60
Cynewulf, conquest of Devon, 8

Dartington, 264
Dartmoor, 326 ; Venville tenure, 327; rude stone monuments, 327 ; trackways, 329 ; hut circles, 328 ; pounds, 329 ; rock basins, 329 ; geology, 330 ; mining, 330 ; forest laws, 332 ; traditions, 333
Dartmouth, 267 ; 'shippeman,' 270 ; invasion, 271 ; sieges, 274 ; worthies, 272, 275
Davey, Rev. Wm., 166

Index. 343

Davis, John, 272
Dawlish, 314; 'flood,' 315
Dean Prior, 265
Dedication feasts, 290
Denbury Fair, 290
Devonport, 224; dockyard, 224
Devonshire, 'Good Earl' of, 93
Dialect, 335; Keltic and Teutonic elements in place-names, 338
Dinant family, 152
Dodbrooke, 246
Doddridge, Sir John, 124
Dolbury Hill, 96
Domesday Hundreds, 11
Doones of Badgery, 134
Drakes of Ashe, 65
Drakes of Nutwell, 53
Drakes of Prattshide, 48
Drake, Sir Francis, 187
Drake myths, 340
Drewsteignton, 323
Drewsteignton cromlech, 324
'Druidical' monuments, 32; superstitions, 323-329
Duckworth, Sir T., 52
Dundonald, Lord, 80
Dunkeswell Abbey, 89
Dunmonii, 5
Duntze family 43
D'Urfey, Tom, 42
Durnford family, 227

Eadulph, first Saxon Bishop of Devon, 105
Early history, 1
Earthworks in East Devon, 59
East Budleigh, 57
Eastlake, Sir C. L., 223
Ecclesiastical history, 27
Ecgberht's conquest of Devon, 8
Eddystone lighthouses, 221
Edgcumbe family, 193
Edmonds, Sir Thomas, 222
Eggesford, 113
Elford family, 197
Elfrida, 181
Ercedekne, Sir John, 309
Erle, Sir Walter, 71
Ermington, 242
Exanmutha, 47
Exeter Assembly, 34
Exeter, 12; Roman, 13; Witenagemot; 13; Swegen at, 15; opposition to the Conqueror, 16; siege by Saxons, 17; Parliament, 18; siege by Stephen, 18; dukes of, 19; Lancastrian, 19; Richard III. at, 19; Perkin Warbeck, 20; siege by Western Rebels, 20; Cavaliers and Puritans, 24; William of Orange at, 25; Æđalstan's monastery, 27; Eadweard the Confessor, 27; foundation of see, 27; cathedral, 28; religious houses, 27, 30; bishops, 30; Puritan era, 33; mints, 35; guilds, 36, 38; merchant adventurers, 39; worthies, 40
Exminster, 54
Exmouth, 47
Exmouth Warren, 49
Exon Domesday, 31

Fardell, 236
Ferrers family, 198
Foliott, Gilbert, 200
Filleigh, 103
Fitz of Fitzford, 185
Flavel, John, 276
Flitton oak, 102
Floyer Hayes, 44
Ford Abbey, 64
Ford House, 307
Ford, John, 288
Ford, Sir Henry, 288
Ford, Thomas, 32
Folk-lore, 339
Follett, Sir W., 42
Fort Charles, 250
Fortescue family, 103
Fortescue, Sir John, 103
Fortescue, Sir Henry, 103
Fortescue, Sir Faithful, 104
Fortescue, Sir Edmund, 250
Fosseway, 5
Foster, Nathaniel, 237
Fremington, 125
Frithelstock Priory, 158
Fulford family, 324
Fulford, Great, 324

Gandy, James, 41
Gafulford, 8
Gale, Theophilus, 310
Garston, 248
Gates, Sir Thomas, 70
Gay, John, 124
Gereint, 7
Gibbs, Sir Vicary, 42
Gidleigh, 323
Gidley family, 323
Giffard family, 114
Gifford, Lord, 42
Gifford, William, 279
Gilbert family, 272
Gilbert, Sir Humphry,
Gilbert, Sir Adrian, 273
Giles, Sir Edward, 265
Gittisham, 81
Glanville family, 189
Glanville, Sir John, 189
Glanville, Serjeant, 189
Glanville, Joseph, 222
Godolphin, Sidney, 322
Gorges, Sir Ferdinando, 216
Great Fulford, 324
Greenway, 272
Greenway, John, 94

Grenville family, 141
Grenville, Sir Richard, 141
Grenville, Sir Bevil, 142
Grenville, Sir Richard, 186
Grimspound, 329
Gubbinses, the, 177

Haccombe, 309
Hach Arundell, 253
Halberton, 97
Hals family, 252
Haldon, 58
Haldon House, 55
Hamo's Port, 203
Hankford, Sir William, 158
Hannaditches, Roman villa at, 72
Harberton, 265
Harding, Thomas, 130
Harford, 243
Harris family, 238
Harris, Sir W. S., 222
Hart, S., 223
Hartland, 152; Abbey, 152
Hatherleigh, 162
Hawkins family, 208
Hawkins, Sir John, 208
Hawkins, Sir Richard, 208
Hawkins, William, 208
Hawley, John, 270
Haydon, B. R., 223
Hayman, Francis, 42
Heanton Punchardon, 127
Heanton Satchville, 165
Hearder, Jonathan, 223
Heavitree, 43
Hele, Elize, 236
Hele, Sir John, 238
Hemyock, 88
Hembury, tradition touching, 285
Hembury Fort, 82
Hennock, 318
Herle, Sir Wm., 130
Herrick, Robert, 266
Hieritha, St., 104, 113
Highweek, 305
Hilliard, Nicholas, 41
Hingston Down, 185
Hody, Sir John, 302
Hoker, John, 40
Holbeton, 244
Holcombe Rogus, 100
Holdsworth family, 276
Holne, 290
Holne Chase, 284
Holsworthy, 163
Holy Street mill, 323
Honeychurch, 164
Honiton, 79; corporate seal, 80; lace, 80
Hooker, Richard, 40
Hope Cove, Armada wreck in, 252
Horwood, 149
Howard, Lady, 186
Hubbastow, 147

Hudson, Thomas, 42
Hughes, George, 247
Huguenots at Exeter, 42
Huguenots at Barnstaple, 121
Huguenots at Plymouth and Stonehouse, 228
Humphry, Ozias, 81
Hunter's Lodge, folk-lore, 78

Iddesleigh, 164
Ideford, 290
Ilfracombe, 128; St. Nicholas Chapel, 128; attempted invasion, 129
Ilton, 249
Ilsington, 288
Inscribed Stones, 179, 238, 318
Instow, 148
Ireland, Dean, 279
Isabella de Fortibus, 37, 92
Isca Dunmoniorum, 13
Iscanus, Josephus, 40
Ivybridge, 243

Jackson, Wm., 42
Jacobstow, 165
Jewel, Bishop, 130
Joseph, Michael, 149
Judhel of Totnes, 257

Kelly, 193
Kempthorne, Sir John, 244
Kenn, 54
Kennaway family, 43
Kennicott, Benjamin, 262
Kent's Hole, 2, 291
Kerswill, Kings and Abbots, 310
Killerton, 46
King, Lord Chancellor, 42
Kingsbridge, 245; climate, 248
Kingsley, Canon, 285
Kingsteignton, 310
Kirton spinning, 107
Kitley, 239
Kitto, John, 222
Knowstone, 99

Landkey, 125
Landscore, 10
Lane, John, 88
Langton, Archbishop, 40
Leach, W. E., 222
Leofric, first Bishop of Exeter, 27
Lethbridge, John, 308
Lifton, 192
'Little Choky Bone,' 69
Littleham, 47
Lundy Island, 137; antiquities, 137; piracies, 138
Lustleigh, 318
Lydford, 172; mint, 174; law, 176; prison, 177
Lye, Sir E., 259
Lye, Edward, 262

Index. 345

Lyfing, Bishop, 182
Lyneham, 239
Lynmouth, 134
Lynton, 133

Malborough, 249
Mamhead, 315
Manaton, 325
Maristow, 200
Marwood, Thomas, 81
Marisco family, 137
Marlborough, Duke of, 66
Mayflower, the, 215
Maynard, Sir John, 190
Mayne, John, 163
Merton, 161
Meavy, 197
Merivale Bridge, 328
Merivale, J. H., 42
Mining antiquity of, 3
Modbury, 240 ; Priory, 240 ; fair, 242
Mohuns Ottery, 83
Molland Bottreaux, 102
Molton, North, 102
Molton, South, 101
Monkleigh, 158
Monk, General, 160
Monmouth, Duke of, 62, 69
Montagu, Col., 247
Morebath, 99
Moreman, Dr., 153
Moretonhampstead, 320
Morice, Sir Wm., 41
Moridunum, 71
Morthoe, 134
Morte Stone, 135

Netherton, 82
Newcomin, Thomas, 275
Newlands, 125
Newenham Abbey, 61
Newport Episcopi, 124
Newton, 305
Newton, clays, 308
Newton Poppleford, 52
Newton St. Cyres, 109
Norman Conquest, 17
Northam, 147
Northam Burrows, 148
Northcote family, 45
Northcote, Sir John, 45
Northcote, James, 223
North Devon, ancient roads in, 115
North Devon, Armada fleet, 143
North Lew, 162
North Molton, 102
North Tawton, 170
Nutwell, 53
Nymets, the, 114

Ockley, Simon, 42
Ogham inscriptions, 179
Okehampton, 167 ; castle, 168

Old Port, 241
Orange, landing of William of, 302
Ordulf, 181
Oreston caves, 237
Otterton Priory, 76
Otterton cartulary, 74
Ottery St. Mary, 84 ; college, 84 ; church, 85 ; school, 86
Oxenham family, 172
Oxenham, John, 172
Oxenham Omen, the, 171

Packhorses, 116
Page of Plymouth, 189
Paignton, 300
Palk family, 55
Palæolithic Man, 1, 60, 291
Pancrasweek, 165
Parkers, Earls of Morley, 233
Parliament House, 304
Parliaments, Tinners', 330
Peamore, 54
Peryam, Lord Chief Baron, 41
Peter Pindar, 248
Petre, Sir William, 289
Petrockstow, 165
Pilgrim Fathers, the, 215
Pilton Priory, 120
Pinhoe, curious tradition, 15
Pixies, 339
Plymouth, 201 ; prehistoric relics, 202 ; development out of the Suttons, 204 ; the Black Prince, 206 ; invasions, 206 ; Katherine of Aragon, 207 ; in the days of Elizabeth, 209 ; the Armada, 211 ; the colonization of New England, 213 ; siege of, 216 ; worthies of, 222
Plymouth Company, 213
Plymouth China Works, 247
Plymouth Dock, old name of Devonport, 225
Plympton, 230 ; Black Prince at, 231 ; Castle, 232 ; Priory, 233
Plymstock, 237
Plymtree screen, 90
Pole, Sir Wm., 68
Pollard family, 149
Poltimore, 46
Polsloe Priory, 44
Pomeroy family, 263
Pomeroy, Sir Thomas, 264
Poole Priory, 253
Portlemouth, 252
Potheridge, 160
Powderham Castle, 55
Pre-Roman civilization in Devon, 4
Prideaux family, 82
Prideaux, Bishop, 243
Prince Town, 333
Princess Henrietta Anne, 24
Prout, Samuel, 223
Prouz family, 318

Pullein, Cardinal, 40
Puritanism, 31
Pynes, 45

Quick, John, 222

Radford, murder of Nicholas, 67
Radford, 238
Ralegh family, 49
Ralegh, Sir Walter, 50
Ralegh, Bishop, 125
Rattenbury, Jack, 73
Rattery, 266
Red deer, 102
Redvers, Baldwin de, 167
Religious Houses, 27, 30, 44, 61, 64, 76, 83, 89, 99, 100, 117, 120, 152, 158, 179, 184, 205, 233, 240, 251, 253, 257, 266, 294
Revelstoke, 237
Reynell family, 306
Reynolds, John, 40
Reynolds, Sir Joshua, 235
Ring-in-the-Mire, 82
Risdon, the chorographer, 160
Rogers family, 237
Romansleigh, 103
Roman intercourse, 5
Rougemont, 17
Russell, Lord, 22

Salcombe, 249
Salter, William, 81
Saltram, 233
Sampford Courtenay, 21
Sampford Peverell, 97
Sampford Spiney, 197
Sativola, St., 27
Savery, Thomas, 241
Saxon colonization and conquest, 7
Saxon place-names, 10
Seaton, 72
Sewers, the, 249
Seymour, Sir Edward, 264
Shaldon, 313
Sharpham heronry, 266
Shaugh, 197
Shebbear, 165
Sheepstor, 197
Shillingford, 54
Shobrooke, 109
Shower, Sir B., 41
Shute, 67
Shute, John, 41
Sidbury, 78
Sidmouth, 74 ; residence of the Queen, 75
Sidwell, St., 27
Silverton, 90
Sir Ferumbras, 336
Sithric of Tavistock, 17
Slade, Abbot, 282
Slanning, Sir Nicholas, 198

Slapton, 253
Sokespitch family, 53
Southcott, Johanna, 81
South Molton, 101
South Molton, Cavalier rising, 101
South Tawton, 171
South Zeal, 171
Spanish Barn, the, 297
Spinster's Rock, 324
Speke family, 45
Splatt Cove, legend of, 251
St. Aubyn family, 224
St. Giles-in-the-Wood, 159
St. Leonards, 43
St. Mary Clyst, 53
St. Mary Clyst, battle at, 23
St. Mary's Church, 293
St. Mary de Marisco, 44
St. Thomas, 23, 44
Stadio Deventia, 202
Staddiscombe, 237
Stapledon, Bishop, 278
Starcross, 58
Stephens, E. B., 42
Stevenstone, 159
Stockleigh, English and Pomeroy, 109
Stoke Canon, 44
Stoke Damerel, 223
Stokenham, 252
Stoke St. Nectan, 153
Stonehouse, 226
Stone, Nicholas, 41
Stone Period, 3
Strachleigh, 243
Strodes of Newnham, 235
Strode, Richard, 177
Strode, William, 234
Stukely family, 153
Stukely, Thomas, 153
Stukely, Sir Lewis, 153
Sully, Sir John, 164
Sutton, old name for Plymouth, 204
Sydenham, 192
Swymbridge, 104

Tamarweorth, 200, 204
Tamerton Foliott, 199
Tavistock, 179 ; Abbey, 181 ; press, 183 ; mines, 185
Tawton, South, 171
Tawton, North, 170
Tawstock, 125
Teignbridge, 306]
Teignweek, 306
Teigngrace, 310
Teignmouth, 311 ; burnt by French, 312
Tenures, peculiar, 44, 49, 53, 76, 109, 165, 253
Termolus, 103
Teutonic mark, 10
Teutonic words, 338
Teutonic folk-lore, 340
Thorverton, 45

Index. 347

Thurleston, 249
Tindal, Matthew, 199
Tiverton, 91 ; fires, 95 ; school, 94
Topsham, 52
Torbay, 292
Torquay, 291
Tor Brian, 289
Torre, 293
Torre Abbey, 294
Torre Mohun free bench, 298
Torrington, 154 ; Margaret of Richmond at, 155 ; defeat of Hopton by Cromwell and Fairfax, 155 ; common rights, 157
Totnes, 254 ; legendary history, 254 ; mint, 256 ; Castle, 257 ; Priory, 257 ; guild merchant, 258 ; worthies, 259 ; 'rows', 262 ;
Totnes shore, 255
Tracy tomb at Morthoe, 135
Trelawny, Bishop, 30
Tremayne family, 192

Uffculme, 88
Ugborough, 244
Ugbrooke, 316
Umberleigh, 113
Underhill, Wm., 21
Upton Pyne, 45

Valley of Rocks, 133
Villenage in the 14th century, 282

Wadham, Nicholas and Dorothy, 77
Walchentone, 194
Walkhampton, 194
Walker's ' Sufferings of the Clergy,' 33
Walrond family, 88
Warelwast, Bishop, 28
Weare, 52

Wear Giffard, 159
Wembury, 237
Westcote, Thomas, 109
Western Rebellion, 21
Westward Ho, 148
Whitbourne, Richard, 48
Whitchurch, 193
White ale, 247
Whiddon, Sir John, 322
Widecombe, 285
Widecombe thunder storm, 286
Wiganbeorche, 204
Wiger, Sir John, 45
Williams, Thomas, 243
Winscott, 150
Winkleigh, 165
Wise family, 192
Wise, Sir Thomas, 224
Wistman's Wood, 333
Withycombe Ralegh, 49
Wolborough, 305
Wolcott, Dr., 248
Wonford, 43
Woodbury, 53
Woodland, 243
Woollcombe family, 236, 239
Woollen manufacture, 36
Worth, 96
Wrey, Sir Bourchier, practical engineering, 118
Wynfrid, 108

Yealmpton, 238
Yewe, 109
Yonge family, 69
Yonge, James, 222

Zeal Monachorum, 172
Zeal, South. 171